Cricket
in
Herefordshire
in the
20th century

Cricket
in
Herefordshire
in the
20th century

by

Ken Hook and Frank Bennett

Logaston Press

LOGASTON PRESS
Little Logaston, Logaston,
Woonton, Almeley, Herefordshire HR3 6QH

First published by Logaston Press 2007

ISBN : 978 1904396 82 6

Set in Times New Roman by Logaston Press
and printed in Great Britain by
Cromwell Press Ltd., Trowbridge, Wiltshire

To the Herefordshire cricket fraternity
with the hope that this book brings back
many happy memories

Enjoy the read.

Ken Howard

Frank Bennett

Contents

Memories of Herefordshire Cricket

I am delighted and honoured to have been asked to write a brief article for this book about Herefordshire Cricket. There have been one or two books written in the past on this subject but I think it's great that Ken Hook and Frank Bennett have set themselves the task of updating the story.

I have been involved with cricket from an early age and am still very much involved although I have not played now for over twenty years. I count myself very fortunate to have played in what I consider was a golden age of cricket which was from the mid nineteen-forties to the early eighties. It was a period when the cricket was played in a competitive but friendly spirit. It was a time when there was banter on the field but very rarely abuse and it was a time when you made lasting friendships not only with your team mates but often your opponents. This happened because at both club and professional levels the two teams tended to socialise after the game and talk through the day's play over a glass or two of beer. It may have been the breathalyser that largely ended all that!

I first played for Hereford City at the age of fifteen. To an impressionable schoolboy some of the leading Hereford players such as Jack Goodwin, Ted Strange and Sir Derek Bailey seemed larger than life characters. After National Service in the RAF I was lucky enough to be offered a contract by Worcestershire and thoroughly enjoyed my two years on the playing staff there. I was one of four Herefordshire-born players at Worcester at this time and was the only one of the four not to play for England! To be fair I hardly ever played for the county first team but it was great to be a colleague of fine players such as Reg Perks, Roly Jenkins, the Richardson brothers, Don Kenyon, Jack Flavell and many others. It was also a great thrill as a young pro to have the job of bowling to visiting batsmen such as Tom Graveney, Ted Dexter, and Colin Cowdrey in the nets before the start of play.

I left Worcestershire at the end of the 1956 season to go in to the family business and rejoined Hereford City. They were a very good team at that time and in the sixties and seventies were one of the strongest in this part of the country. In this period many fine players played regularly for Hereford such as Brian Smith, Keith Edwards, Eric Jenkins, Mike Rose, Ken Watson, Derek Stowe to name but a few. Tom Graveney in his foreword for this book well remembered playing against the Hereford side of this time.

Towards the end of my playing career I joined the committee of the Worcestershire County Cricket Club and had the great honour of being elected President in 2005. I was also involved in the formation of the Herefordshire Minor Counties Cricket Club and was its first President. One of the highlights of my cricketing life was being at Lords when Herefordshire won the Minor Counties Knock Out Cup in 2000. Another was watching the Village Final at Lords when in a thrilling game Kington beat Frocester. For a county with such a small population Herefordshire has regularly punched well above its weight.

John Chadd

Foreword

by Tom Graveney (Former England Test player)

I am delighted to have been asked to pen a few words for this long overdue book about Herefordshire Cricket. When I joined Worcestershire in 1961 I had to qualify by living in the County for a year, so I played for the Second X1 and Dudley in the Birmingham League. Worcester had a fine side and finished third whilst I was serving my 12 months before qualifying for Championship Cricket. I was amazed at the crowds at Worcester – even on a Monday morning during the early sixties there was a good gathering – I suspect quite a few of the spectators were from Hereford!! I only played once at Hereford, in a benefit match on the Racecourse. I remember we were in terrible trouble when we batted – 30 for 5 I believe!!

I remember saying that I hadn't expected to be in a test match!! However, John Chadd, who has done so much for both counties, eased our problems by putting on some rather more friendly bowlers. I haven't played in Herefordshire since!!! Anyway I hope this publication will be very successful and we will all be able to enjoy this wonderful game.

Sincerely

Tom Graveney

Acknowledgements

The authors wish to acknowledge the help and assistance that has been willingly provided from the following:

Hereford Record Office, Hereford Reference Library, Bromyard History Society, *Hereford Times*. Herefordshire Life, Simon Gwynne and staff at H.A.L.O. Leisure, Hereford.

Dr. Anthea Bryan, Francis Perkins, Ian Cameron, Ken Pole and Ernie Smith, who have sadly passed away before the book is published.

Derrick Jones, Maurice Joseph, Brian Savory, Tom James-Moore, John Worle, Stan Marston, Les Gibson, Len Sparrow, Trevor Watkins, Norman Rees, Colin Morris, Keith Bishop, Gordon Lamputt, Jeremy Finney, Malcolm Hughes, Simon Dent, Brian Goode, Richard Prime, Tim Ward, Derek Foxton, Derek Watkins, Tim Jones, Don Ambrose, Mike Williams, Vera Hadley, Trevor Owens. Mrs. J. Cornwall (Upton Bishop W.I.), David Bird, Brian Smith, Keith and Roberta Hodnett, Geoff Morris, Cliff Davies, Ted Johnson, Bryan Messam, Adrian Hope, Nigel Yarwood, Bill Masefield, Michael Scudamore, Dr. John Wood, Ray Chillington, Paul Notley, Chris Evans, Rex Roff, Terry & Pearl Teale, Alec Haines, Pat Downes, David Hodges, Alan Flaxman, Hedley Lawson, Ray Norton, Chris Graham, Stephen Bishop, Ken Vale, Alan Hartland, Mick Carroll, Margaret Noakes, George Warley, Danny Wright, Alan Roberts, Adrian Howard, Roger Pye, C.D. Forbes, Roy Wargen, Edward Simpson, Nigel Taylor, Allan Jones, James Roberts, Mike Peachey, Roy Jones, Kevin Gwynne, Clive Scott, Tony Baker, Ian Beaton, Andy Morris, Bill Jackson, Harold Gurney, John Gurney, Percy Yemm, David James, David Taylor, Ray & Sheila Hince, Richard Sparey, Mike Rose, Terry Court, Paul Selfe, Heather Hurley, Ernest Ridger, Brian Farley, Peter Sykes, Godfrey Davies, Dave Sharland, Neville Sandford, Peter Burgoyne, John Holland, Ivor Lloyd, Carol Roberts, Richard Fisher, Roy Joshua, Colin Wooley, John Eisel, Eddie Philips, Doc Lewis, Jim Clarke, Bill Morris, Norman Thomson, Richard Hope, Wyn Thompson, Jim Sandford, John Taylor, John Chadd, Bill Morgan, Nigel Davies, Windsor Jones, Bob Hall, Howard Tomlinson, Paul Everall, Clive Terry, Hugh Owen, George Follis, John Bunn, Ian Strangward, Kathleen Lawrence, Roger Smith, Gerald Marchant, Phil Bryn, Jeff Clarke, Harry Ellam, Hilda Griffiths, John Griffiths, Geordie Harbottle, Tony Hehir, Ivor Hunt, Randy Langford, Rosalind Lowe, Tim Lowe, Rob Powell, Norman Rees, Jim Roberts, Handley Scudamore, Nigel Shore, Tom Weale, Richie Watts, Eric Willliams, Norman Williams, Dr. Peter Wilson, Ian Pugh, Trevor Williams, Nick Osborne, Mike Tidmarsh, Nigel Heins, Peter Manders, Les James, Bob Gardiner, Bob Lovering, Brian Falkiner, John Hall, Colin Rogers, Trevor Jones, Des Brooke, Mike Evans, Frank Lane, Colin Gardiner, David Hill, Fred Jones, Mrs. Lewis, Joan Snell, Tim Peachey, Bill Alexander, Nick Nenadich, Gladys Edwards, Jonathan Cooke, Rodney Grinnell, John Murray, Mick Harman, Philip Stock, Bill Lucas, Adrian Berry, Tom Bailey, Tony Capon, Sue Wood, Bill Bishop, Peter Hall, Tony Hope, Brian Hehir, Chris Barker, John Morris, Arthur Howells, Dave Griffiths, Godfrey Brown, Raj Hoon, Ron Franklin, Mike Baldwin, Derek Brimmell, Laurie Teague, Michael Herbert, Robin Buchanan, Alan Lloyd, Jim Turner, Colleen Rogers, Ken Sharpe, Ruth Richardson, Jack Bannister.

And everyone else who has provided helpful advice and comments that the authors may have inadvertently omitted to mention.

The authors would also wish to acknowledge the help and assistance of Andy Johnson and Ron Shoesmith of Logaston Press in preparing this book for publication and Karen Stout for producing the index of names.

Introduction

The story of cricket in Herefordshire in the 20th century tells us a great deal about how life has changed in the last 100 years. Back in the early days of cricket in the county, teams revolved around the great houses where the lord of the manor would often gather together his friends and staff to take on other similar teams.

In those days, transport was not quite as easily obtainable as it is now and, while lengthy journeys were rare, with smaller teams from the north and south of the county rarely meeting on the field of play, nevertheless a certain amount of resourcefulness was required in getting the team from A to B. I know that my own club, Wormelow, in its pre-Second World War days, would often journey to away games in the back of the South Hereford Hunt lorry and there is no doubt that other teams would have been similarly imaginative, with horses and carts, bread vans and tractors and trailers all taking their part.

Cricket, ostensibly, passed for 'friendly' in those pre-league days and, although highly competitive on the field, left more room for socialising off it. As teams were generally travelling together by one form of transport or another, they were perhaps more inclined to stay for a pint, or several, than they are now in our breathalyser era. Bonds built up between clubs over a post-match drink and these were even strengthened in some cases by the transfer of equipment – even pavilions – from one to another.

Now, times have moved on, although, in many cases in teams throughout the county, a line can be traced back down the years through the family dynasties which have been established, with one generation playing alongside the next and so on through the decades.

This story of cricket in the 20th century is long overdue and, in years to come, I can imagine this volume sitting happily alongside Edwyn Anthony's *Herefordshire Cricket* which tells of the sport's beginnings in the county.

Ken Hook has laboured long and hard to collect all the information necessary but, as he will admit, he has had a lot of fun – and many extended discussions – with his 'informants' in putting it together. When Ken met Frank Bennett their enthusiasms and individual strengths worked favourably together. They have done cricket in the county a great service by putting together so much information which would otherwise have been lost and helped us all to rekindle many happy memories of the sound of willow on leather throughout our beautiful county.

I have been lucky enough to play cricket in Herefordshire for 35 years with, I hope, a few more to come. The pleasure of those years has been unquantifiable and the number of friends made countless. It is a delight and an honour to be associated with a book which provides so many reminders of those great times.

Richard Prime

CHAPTER I

International & First Class Cricketers

Whilst this book is primarily about Herefordshire Cricket Clubs and the thousands of people who have played cricket at club and county level in the County, mention must be made of those cricketers who have been talented enough to progress to international and first class cricket. Research has revealed the following: Jack Sharp; Henry Charles Preece; Charles Thornton; William Allan Smith-Masters; Sivell Lane; James Smith; Henry Foley; Christopher Foster; Matthew Crose Parry; Leslie R. Gardner; Reg Perks; Joseph and Henry Horton (the third Horton brother, Martin, was born in Worcester); Peter Richardson and his brother Dick, who were born in Hereford (but the third Richardson brother, Bryan, was born in Warwickshire and, unlike his brothers, did not play for Hereford prior to embarking on a first class career); John Chadd; Michael Rose; Stephen Watkins; and Justin Vaughan.

Hereford Cathedral School has had a great influence on Herefordshire born cricketers in the 20th century. Henry Horton, the Richardson brothers, Matthew Parry and John Chadd all attended there.

Jack Sharp, Lancashire and England

Jack Sharp had a sports shop in Liverpool

The most famous and gifted of all the Hereford born cricketers was **Jack Sharp**. Jack, whose correct Christian name was John, was born in Hereford on 15 February 1878. He was the son of Charles Sharp who had a butchers shop in Eign Gate and who was also the landlord of the Grapes public house in East Street. The Grapes was the headquarters of Hereford Thistle Football Club which Jack joined whilst still a teenager. He was a right-handed batsman and left-arm fast medium bowler and an outstanding fielder in the covers. In 1889 E. Baker at Clyde House School in Moorfields taught Jack and his brother Bert. Jack was clearly grateful for the coaching by Mr.

The Sharp brothers played football for Hereford Thistle in 1897

Baker. A scorecard of the match between Herefordshire Club and Ground and Hereford Early Closers in the *Hereford Times* for 18 June 1892, when Jack was just 14, listed both Jack and Bert Sharp playing for the Club and Ground.

There is a report in the *Hereford Times* for 23 July 1904 confirming that Jack Sharp had given a cricket bat to be awarded as a prize to the most promising cricketer in the school and that it had been won by M. Mason. The report noted that when Jack Sharp's name was mentioned at the prize giving at the school sports day a loud cheer went up. By coincidence, he had just scored 104 not out overnight for Lancashire against Sussex. In a 1909 issue of *Cricket Weekly Record* Jack described Mr. Baker as 'a compact little man with a considerable beard who was a fine cricketer, he was a jolly fine bat and I could never get him out'.

Jack was clearly a natural cricketer from a very young age, playing for Hereford Club and Ground from the age of 13 and when he was just 14 scoring 208 not out against Ledbury. In 1892 he played for the M.C.C. against Herefordshire. He joined Lancashire in 1899 and played professionally from then until 1914. He was the first cricketer from Hereford to play test match cricket for England, being picked for three tests against Australia in 1909 mainly as a bowler. He did little until the final match at the Oval when he scored 105 runs in 170 minutes on top of taking three first innings wickets. He played for Lancashire for 15 seasons as a professional and was in their unbeaten championship side of 1904.

He was awarded a benefit match in 1910 and chose the Roses match. As a result of his benefit he was richer by about £2,000 – a considerable sum of money at the end of the first decade of the 20th century. After the war he played for another seven seasons as an amateur and captained Lancashire from 1923 to 1925. He was also an England selector in 1924. He played, in total, 534 first class matches and 3 test matches. He scored over 20,000 runs including 38 centuries for Lancashire and he also took more than 400 wickets. He was made an honorary life member of Lancashire in 1936.

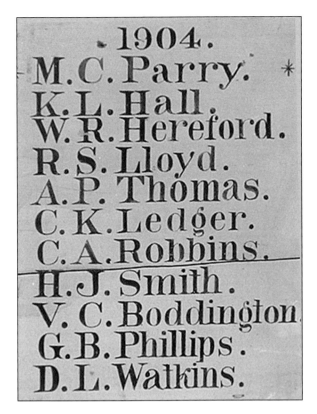

1904.
M. C. Parry. *
K. L. Hall.
W. R. Hereford.
R. S. Lloyd.
A. P. Thomas.
C. K. Ledger.
C. A. Robbins.
H. J. Smith.
V. C. Boddington.
G. B. Phillips.
D. L. Watkins.

M.C. Parry in the Cathedral School team, 1904

Charles Thornton

In addition to his skills as a cricketer Jack was also a first-class footballer, playing for Aston Villa, Everton and England. He played against Ireland in 1903 and Scotland in 1905. Whilst with Everton he won an F.A. Cup winners medal in 1906. After he retired, Jack became a director of Everton Football Club and also ran a sports shop in Liverpool. Jack Sharp died in Liverpool on the 27 January 1938 aged 59.

Bert Sharp, who was one of Jack's brothers, did not play first-class cricket but did play a lot of local cricket and football in Herefordshire. He, like his brother, played football for Hereford Thistle. He also played cricket for the Lancashire Second XI team in 1907 and was for some years professional at Prescot Cricket Club. Again, like his brother, he was a professional footballer playing at the top level.

William Allan Smith-Masters was born in Humber, Herefordshire, on 13 March 1850. He only played in one first-class match for Kent in 1875 and died in Camer, Kent, on 27 August 1937.

Charles Inglis Thornton was born at Llanwarne on 20 March 1850. He played for Cambridge University in 1870 and had a long career with Kent and Middlesex, stretching over 30 years, during which he played 216 first-class matches.

Henry Charles Preece was born in Weobley on 27 October 1867 and played two matches for Essex in 1895. He died in Highgate, Middlesex, on 17 September 1937.

Sivell Lane was born in Ledbury on 21 August 1881 and played three games for Gloucestershire in 1901. He emigrated to Canada where he died on the 10 February 1961.

Matthew Parry was born at Birley, Herefordshire, on 12 December 1885. He was educated at Hereford Cathedral School and Birmingham University. Matthew enjoyed success in local matches before he took up first-class cricket. In August 1908 he was playing for the Gentlemen of Herefordshire against the Gentlemen of Shropshire and took 9 wickets for 43 runs. He played two games for Warwickshire as an amateur between 1908 and 1910. In the match against Lancashire in 1908 he scored 10 runs whilst another Herefordian, Jack Sharp, was

Reg Perks coaching a Bringsty youngster

James Smith in 1913

scoring a century for the opposition, Lancashire. He played for his adopted country, Ireland, in 1925 when he was 40 years of age and scored 124 against Scotland in Dublin. Parry died in Carrigrohane, Co. Cork, on 5 February 1931.

James Smith was born in Ledbury on 26 September 1894. James was a left-hand batsman and a versatile slow, left-arm bowler who between 1923 and 1925 played 16 times for Worcestershire. When he was in his teens he played for Frome Valley, but the First World War interrupted his potential cricketing career. When his first-class career with Worcestershire finished he went back to Ledbury. In 1932 Worcestershire. presented him with a mounted ball to commemorate his taking 10 wickets for 27 runs for Ledbury against Worcester Cinderella. He died in Ledbury on 19 February 1980.

Christopher Knollys Foster was born on 27 February 1904 at Tarrington Farm. He only played in three first-class matches for Worcestershire in 1927. He died at Kingsthorne on 4 December 1971.

Henry Thomas Hamilton Foley was born at Stoke Edith Park on 25 April 1905. Whilst he played regularly in local cricket his first-class career was limited to one match for Worcestershire in 1925, when he scored 6 runs but did not bowl. Henry Foley died at Stoke Edith on 13 December 1959.

Reg Perks, whose full name was Reginald Thomas David Perks, was born in Hereford on 4 October 1911 and lived variously in Grandstand Road and Foley Street. Frank James, a Ledbury cricketer, coached Reg in the early days. He first came to the notice of Worcestershire by making up the eleven for the Gentlemen of that county who had arrived a man short for a game against Hereford Gentlemen. The match took place at Hereford Racecourse where his father was head groundsman. He was 15 and still at school. Reg had to serve a two-year qualification to play for Worcestershire and joined them in 1930 – his first wicket was none other than that of Jack Hobbs. He was a tall man who made full use of his height, bowling fast medium, right-hand, and could swing the ball both ways. He was not

Above: Reg Perks
Right: Hereford
Bulletin *1935*
Far right:
Insurance certifi-
cate 1954

B-r-r-r-r! Cricket? More like football. There's something to be said in altering the two seasons. About Christmas we shall be sweltering! Bowlers appear to relish this weather; after all, they keep warm!

* * *

WELL DONE, REG.!

Caps off to Reg. Perks, Worcestershire's Hereford bowler (and not a bad bat either!). Reg has been bowling brilliantly lately and a little bird whispered that he is to be honoured this season by being picked for the Players against the Gentlemen. I wonder if he will play in the Test trial? Well done, Reg.!

NAME in full REGINALD THOMAS DAVID PERKS

ADDRESS 128, COMER ROAD. WORCESTER

DATE OF BIRTH Oct 4th 1911.

BUSINESS OR OCCUPATION Cricketsmen. and Professional Cricketer

AMOUNT TO BE INSURED AT DEATH
Note: Proposals are accepted up to £10,000 at proportionate premiums. £2000-0-0. £9-0-0

Do you require cover for Temporary Partial Disablement? (See additional premium.) No

DECLARATION

I declare that I am not physically disabled in any way and am in good health. I have never been declined for Life or personal accident insurance.

I warrant that the above statements and particulars are true and agree to give notice to the Company of any alteration in my profession or occupation or health, and I hereby agree that this Declaration shall be held to be paramount and shall form the basis of the Contract between me and The Vocational Insurance Company Limited; and I am willing to accept a Policy subject to the terms, exception and conditions prescribed by the Company thereto.

Signature of Proposer R Perks

Dated 5 May 19 54

known as a batsman, but was always a useful tail-end hitter. Reg was picked for the Players against the Gentlemen at Lords in 1931. He did not take a wicket, but bowled 8 overs for 7 runs. He was described in a national paper as 'Maurice Tate's successor'. He continued to play for Worcestershire until 1955. During his career he took 2,143 wickets at an average of 23.73, taking over 100 wickets in 16 successive seasons. He took a hat trick on two occasions – against Kent in 1931 and Warwickshire in 1933. Reg played only twice for England, the first time being in 1939 against South Africa in what was described as the notorious timeless test at Durban when he took 5 wickets for 100 runs from 41 8-ball overs. He also played against the West Indies. His career was sadly interrupted by the war when he was just coming to prominence. When cricket resumed after the war he was 35 and had clearly lost the best years of a fast bowler's life. Even so, he played in a total of 595 first-class matches and two test matches. Reg Perks had a sharp sense of humour, and did not miss an opportunity to create laughter. The County Ground at Worcester has always been susceptible to flooding from the River Severn and on one occasion a sharp cameraman caught him fishing from the side of

Much Marcle/Weston's
Henry Horton and Brian Farley coming out to
bat at the Racecourse in Hereford

Reg Perks fishing at the Worcestershire county cricket ground

the ground during a flood. When his first-class career was over he played Birmingham League cricket for West Bromwich, Dartmouth and Kidderminster. He died in Worcester on 22 November 1977 aged 66.

Joseph Horton was the eldest and least known of the three Horton Brothers. He was born in Colwall, on the edge of the Malvern Hills, on 12 August 1915. He played 62 first-class matches for Worcestershire between 1934 and 1938, scoring 1,258 runs and taking 5 wickets. He was a right-hand bat and right-arm medium bowler. Like many others, his career was undoubtedly cut short by the war. Joseph Horton died in Worcester on 6 November 1998.

Henry Horton was born in Colwall on 18 April 1923 and enjoyed a long and successful county career between 1946 and 1967. Henry's first-class career commenced in 1946 when he had a trial with Worcestershire. He played 11 games for Worcestershire between 1946 and 1949, but was not very successful. Luckily for Henry, he was also a professional footballer and that sport eventually took him to Southampton via Blackburn Rovers. His league soccer career ended when in 1955 he signed for Hereford United, then a non-league side. He had been playing some cricket in Hampshire during this period of time and made his first-class debut for that county in 1953, playing until 1967 at the top level. He played a total of 417 first-class matches scoring in excess of 21,000 runs. When he retired from the first-class game, Horton returned to Worcestershire as a coach for nine years and was then a first-class umpire for four years between 1973 and 1976, standing in 73 matches. Henry Horton had a peculiar crouching batting stance which was described by Brian Johnston as 'like someone sitting on a shooting stick'. Henry Horton died in Birmingham on 3 November 1998, just three days before his brother Joseph.

Peter Richardson (full name Peter Edward Richardson) was born in Hereford on 4 July 1931. His parents ran a butchers shop in Fownhope. He enjoyed his first competitive cricket at Hereford Cathedral School and played for Hereford during the school holidays. He also played invitation games for Much Marcle. On 18 May 1946 a report in the *Hereford Times* confirms that he enjoyed a stand of 177 runs with J.E. Hammond whilst playing for the Cathedral School when he was just 15 years old. On 8 June 1946 he scored 36 runs for the School against Brockhampton and on 25 August the same year he scored 53 for the School against Monmouth. In June 1947, when Guy Thornycroft was enjoying his one appearance for Worcestershire, Peter Richardson scored 97 against Brecon – no mean feat for a 16 year old who clearly had a natural talent. His batting that year came to the attention of Worcestershire and he was invited to go for a trial in the September. He joined Worcestershire in 1949 and immediately gained a place in the Worcestershire Minor Counties XI and also played four first-class matches batting between numbers three and seven. His natural batting position was to open, which he did successfully for his School and in Club cricket. He and his family moved to a farm just outside Worcester in 1950 and he was awarded his County Cap in 1951. Peter was a prankster at heart and had a fondness for sending false cricket records to E.W. Swanton, for publication in the *Daily Telegraph*. He had a long and extremely successful cricket career, playing in 34 Test

matches between 1956 and 1963. He made five centuries in his first 16 Tests, including 104 against Australia in Laker's Match at Old Trafford in 1956. He played for Worcestershire and Kent, and in 1957 he played alongside his brother Dick in the Trent Bridge Test. They were the last brothers to play in the same England side until the Hollioakes. In that match he shared what was then a record second wicket partnership with Tom Graveney – he scored 126 runs and Graveney scored a magnificent 258. He was Wisden cricketer of the year in 1957. He played a total of 454 first-class matches, scoring over 26,000 runs including 44 centuries. Richardson spent the last years of his first-class career with Kent and still lives there.

Peter Richardson at Worcester

England team for the Second Test against the West Indies in 1957. Peter Richardson top left.
(Dick Richardson did not play in this match)

Dick Richardson

Dick Richardson was born in Hereford on 3 November 1934. He joined Worcestershire as an amateur, turning professional in 1956, and was a successful member of the side until his early retirement in 1967. His one Test appearance was in the same side as his brother Peter against the West Indies in 1957 when he scored 33. During the time that he was at Worcester he played a total of 383 matches and scored 16,303 runs at an average of 27.39 per innings. He was an outstanding close fielder and held 412 catches during his career including a record 65 in 1961.

Leslie Robin Gardner was born in Ledbury on 23 Feb 1934. He had a reasonably long career for Leicestershire and played in 126 matches between 1954 and 1962. When his first class career finished he played for Hertfordshire.

John Chadd was born in Hereford on 27 October 1933. His family name is well known in Hereford because of the department store which has been the family business from inception. John Chadd has had a major influence on

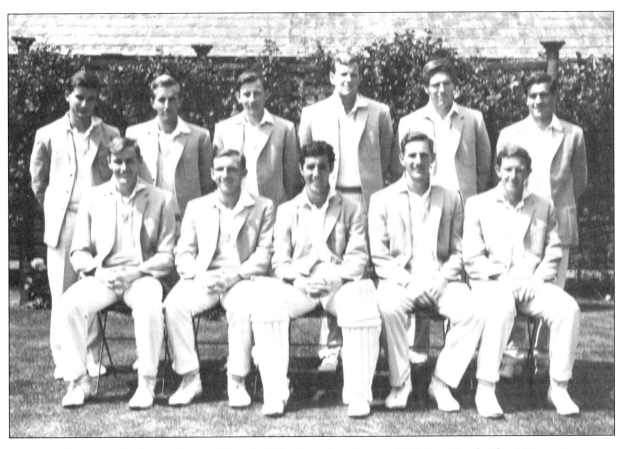

Mike Rose (back row far right) with Mike Brearley (front middle) at Cambridge University

Herefordshire cricket throughout his life. He has been President of the County team and has been President of Worcestershire County Cricket Club. His first-class career with the latter county was limited to two matches, both of which incidentally were captained by Herefordshire born players. He played against Scotland in 1954 under the captaincy of Reg Perks, and against Oxford University the following year when the captain of the side was Peter Richardson. John was a fine off break bowler who took a vast number of wickets in his career.

Michael Harrison Rose was born in Hereford on 8 April 1942. Mike played in local cricket and opponents noted his great potential when he batted against adult sides when he was only 15. He attended Cambridge University and between 1962 and 1964 played for the University team and also for Leicestershire. Whilst playing

for the University he was captained by Mike Brearley, the future England captain. Other notable cricketers in the same university side of 1963 were Richard Hutton, the son of Sir Leonard Hutton, R.C. Kerslake, and A.R. Windows, all of whom went on to enjoy first-class careers. Mike ceased playing cricket at an early age and now lives and works in Hereford.

Stephen Watkins was born in Hereford on 23 March 1959 and attended Lady Hawkins School at Kington where Robbie Richardson, the well-known Kington cricketer, coached him. On leaving school he played for Hereford City Sports Club where Eric Jenkins took charge of his development. During his time with Hereford he was very successful whether playing Three Counties League or in the Hereford Evening League. Whilst at Hereford City Sports Club he was selected to play many times for the Herefordshire

Representative XI and the Hereford Gentlemen.

In 1980 Steve was invited to play for Worcestershire in the Second XI. He was a member of the side that included Damian D'Oliviera and Richard Illingworth. The team won the Second XI championship on two occasions up to 1982. The following season he was honoured by being selected to play for the First XI against Oxford University. He opened the batting scoring a total of 105 runs including 77 in one innings. He was also chosen to play against Kent in a John Player League match when he scored 24. Unfortunately they were the only matches he played in the 1st XI. He spent a short time playing for Worcester City in the Birmingham League and, eventually, he played his cricket in the Welsh League in 1985 where he joined Croesycerriog as their guest player and coach. Steve holds the distinction of being the only player to have played in the First Minor Counties League Match for both Herefordshire and Wales. Steve Watkins is now married with a family and still lives in Hereford.

Justin Vaughan was born in Hereford on 30 August 1967 but, together with his family, he emmigrated to New Zealand when only 8 months old. He played in 6 tests and 18 one-day internationals for New Zealand. In 1992 he had one season with Gloucestershire as a U.K. resident, but says that he could not compete with Courtney Walsh as the overseas professional. Justin comes from a sporting family who lived at Kingsland, and his father was a good rugby player, being a Cambridge Blue. He also played for the R.A.F. and captained a Midlands XI. His uncle, Brian, captained England at rugby and also managed the British Lions tour to South Africa. Justin's brother Mark, who was born in 1961, played cricket for the Worcestershire Second X1 in 1982.

Despite the fact that Herefordshire has never had a first-class team, many cricketers have learnt the game in the county. Indeed, several Herefordshire-born players obtained their University Blues but did not play in County or Test cricket. They include Henry Arkwright and Frederic James Stevenson Moore who played for Cambridge University, and Charles Cooper-Key and Geoffrey Grasett who played for Oxford University. Mark Vane Millbank played one game for the Army in 1930.

CHAPTER II

Herefordshire Leagues & Associated Organisations

Hereford and District Cricket League

An article in the *Hereford Times* on 6 March 1920 quoted a letter from C.M. Dawes, the secretary of Mansion House Cricket Club, stating that there was interest in the county in the idea of forming a competitive cricket league. Support was received the following week when it was confirmed that if a league were to be formed then the *Hereford Times* would offer a shield to be competed for each year. There was a further article on 20 March confirming that interest had been received from Mansion House C.C., Hereford Y.M.C.A., R.A.O.C. Credenhill, and Canon Pyon.

On 17 April 1920 a meeting of the officials of the various clubs interested in forming a league was held at the Y.M.C.A. headquarters in Hereford. It was agreed that there would be no more than eight clubs initially, but that if there was more interest then another division would be considered. The representatives attending the meeting included Hereford Y.M.C.A., Great Brampton, Canon Pyon, R.A.O.C. Credenhill, Mansion House, Ivington, Frome Valley, and Withington. It was agreed that the entrance fee would be 10s. 6d. and that there would be no admission to the league after 1 May. Mr. W.J. Parrott was elected chairman, a full committee was appointed, and it was agreed to invite Lord Somers to be president. The Y.M.C.A. agreed to offer their premises as headquarters.

On 24 April 1920, the *Hereford Times* reported that Lord Somers had accepted the invitation to become president of the league. It was further reported that the following clubs had agreed to play in the league: Hereford Y.M.C.A., Great Brampton, Canon Pyon, R.A.O.C. Credenhill, Mansion House, Ivington, Frome Valley, and Wye Valley.

On 1 May the *Hereford Times* set out the rules of the league and confirmed that matches would commence on 15 May. Bromyard made a late application to join the league but they were not accepted at that time.

By 22 May the *Hereford Times* reported that the Y.M.C.A. had won the first match in the new league, beating Wye Valley by 119 runs, and on 29 May C. Powell of Canon Pyon recorded the league's first hat trick against Wye Valley. On the same day the R.A.O.C. were all out for 6 runs against the Y.M.C.A.

The first controversy in the new league was when Ivington fielded two ineligible players when they beat Frome Valley by one run. The matter was resolved by the league management who said that it was a clerical error and determined that the match should be a draw.

In August, Ivington were involved in another controversy when they could not raise a full team against Great Brampton because their players were working on the harvest. The same thing happened the following week in their match against Wye Valley.

The teams continued playing and on 28 August the *Hereford Times* reported that Hereford

Y.M.C.A. were league champions and had won the Hereford Times Challenge Shield, the runners-up being Frome Valley. The Hereford Times Challenge Shield, bats and medals were placed on display at Oswins jewellers in Hereford in October 1920.

The presentation evening for the year was held at the Cory Hall in Hereford. The secretary advised the full house that 185 players had been registered. The president, Lord Somers, presented the following awards:

Hereford Times Shield for the winners of the League – Hereford Y.M.C.A.
Jack Hobbs Ltd. bat for best batting to C.S. Davies of the Y.M.C.A., scoring 161 runs at an average of 20.50
Jack Sharp bat for the highest score to H.E. Rogers of the Y.M.C.A. who scored 74.
R.G. Pugh bat for the most runs to E. Griffiths of Frome Valley who scored 184 runs at an average of 16.72
John Wisden bat for the best bowling average to G.H. Shinn of the Y.M.C.A. who took 31 wickets at an average of 3.27.
Philip Mead bat for the most wickets to F. Jones of the R.A.O.C. who took a total of 61.

It would appear that the league was not a great success because in the following season there were only five teams competing: Y.M.C.A., Great Brampton, Frome Valley, Canon Pyon, and Withington, the others having dropped out. In 1921 the Y.M.C.A. won the league again, the joint runners-up being Frome Valley and Great Brampton. This must have been too much for the other teams and this early league folded shortly afterwards.

Evening League
Brief mention is made of the Evening League in this chapter because following the demise of the 1920 league the Evening League was the next to be formed. This league ran from 1927 to 1941 and then from 1946 until 2002. The Evening League is described in detail in chapter IV.

The Hereford Bulletin Unofficial League 1937
In 1936 a sports writer called 'Commentator' who worked for the *Hereford Bulletin* collected the results from weekend cricket and awarded points on a percentage basis. The winners in the first year were the Lads Club and the following year the winners were S.W.S. Power Co.

Orleton League
The Orleton League was started in 1950 by George Millichamp with the intention that it would be for local cricketers who were not first team players with each side being allowed one guest player. In the early years the teams playing were Eyton, Orleton, Broad Ramblers, Docklow, Ashford Carbonel, Bircher, Boraston and Nash, M.E.B., Ludlow, Kimbolton, Luctonians and B.B.C. Wofferton, Old and Bowled, Shobdon, Wigmore, Eye, Orleton and Brimfield, Wofferton Cadets, Richard's Castle, Torvale, and Weobley.

The Kimbolton team in 1951 won the Orleton League
Back row: Chris Bird, Harley Jones, Fred Morris, Geoff Morris, Jim Bird, Trevor Hodnett
Front row: John James, Dennis Parker, Jack Lewis, Keith Hodnett, Dennis Bird

Orleton League X1 1951 (game against Kimbolton 1951)
Back row: F. Hancorn, Ken Vale, P. Mumford, Bill Sparey, [-], Roy Gittens.
Front row: Gordon Davies, Walter Barker, [-], Peter Sparey, [-]

Games were played on Tuesday evenings and each side had 12 overs of 8 balls. There was also a knockout competition each year, the final being played at Orleton. After the match presentation there was a dance in the village hall. In later years, matches were played on the town pitches. One of the best known families who played in the League were the Spareys. Bill Sparey played for Eyton and allowed Broad Ramblers to play on his land at Broad Farm and Richard Sparey played for Broad Ramblers.

One of the most successful teams in the League was Kimbolton. Orleton are recorded playing from 1961 until about 1968. One of the oldest teams to play in the League was Bircher, recorded as playing from 1900 until the outbreak of the First World War and then from 1925

Orleton League Representative X1 versus Cromwell Sports 1950
Back row: Vince Tudge, J. Bird, [-], [-], Bill Sparey, Maurice Carpenter.
Front row: Ray Fortey, Jack Lewis, Dennis Poston, Geoff Smith, Alan Scriven

The problems besetting umpires are well displayed in this Mack cartoon

onwards. The Orleton League stopped when the foot and mouth epidemic broke out in 2000 and has not restarted.

Hereford Umpires' Association
The Association was formed in about 1958 with the main purpose of providing umpires for the Evening League. The first chairman was Tom Batho, a retired policeman who in his youth had played cricket in the Lancashire League and played for the police when stationed in Hereford.

It was agreed that the object of the Association should be 'to further the interests of cricket in Hereford, particularly the Hereford Evening Amateur Cricket League'. Neutral umpires being provided for league fixtures.

It was agreed that the following rules should be adopted:

1. Clubs reporting an umpire should do so to the league. Umpires reporting any club should do so direct to the Association.
2. A Management Committee (consisting of five elected members together with the officers), and the Committee and Officers all to be elected annually.
3. An Annual General Meeting is to be held before 31 January each year.
4. No alteration to the Rules to be made unless submitted to the Hon. Sec. seven days before a Committee meeting to which alterations will be submitted.

It was also agreed that the secretary should write to the M.C.C. to enquire into the possibility of obtaining instructional terms. It was further agreed that 50 copies of the book 'The Laws of Cricket' should be obtained and

Once upon a time in a far off land an umpire gave a batsman out. The great executive committee of that land was mightily displeased and ordered forthwith that the decision should be reversed. And it was so.

If this fairy story 'catches on' I can visualize a motorised unit of the Evening League Executive, in constant radio communication with headquarters, patrolling the various grounds frantically reversing the least popular of our umpires' decisions.

Or perhaps, judging by the excellent support we umpires have received from Evening League cricketers, Hereford – unmerged – may remain the last bastion of the traditional standards of good behaviour which make the name of the game synonymous with sportsmanship.

We, in the Umpires Association, are constantly striving by courses and discussions to improve our standards. Even so there will always be human error and mistakes will be made. Whatever decision is made the umpire must be the final judge. Reversal by an executive committee is not the answer.

Good luck in 1974.

K.B.Procter,
President.

Ken Procter's letter brought out the basic problem that beset umpires as early as 1974

lectures by qualified local umpires be arranged during the winter months for the benefit of the membership at large.

Whilst it is not possible to give profiles of all the members of the Umpires' Association, there are several who should be mentioned in more detail:

John Knill and Phil Noakes – a long standing umpiring partnership

Phil Noakes

Not many cricketers lived at the place where they played. Phil spent the early part of his marriage to Margaret at Harewood Park House and played cricket for Harewood End. He followed in his father Reg's footsteps playing cricket. Reg is shown on a photograph of the Post Office cricket team taken in the 1930s (chapter 10). Phil played school cricket for St. Owen's, then Hereford High School, and during his career in the police played for the Herefordshire Constabulary XI. When his playing days were over, Phil turned his hand to umpiring and was a prominent force in Herefordshire umpiring, including serving as an officer of the Association in many categories including being training officer. In 1979 Phil won the umpires' quiz trophy which was played for every year. Phil died tragically in a car accident in 1995 at the age of 71 whilst taking the Umpires' Association exam papers to Edgbaston to be marked.

Harry Miles

Harry Miles was one of the instigators of the Umpires' Association and was also umpire at Hereford City Sports Club for many years. Harry umpired many prestigious local matches and his achievements locally were recognised at first-class level when he was allocated three matches including a match between East Africa and Singapore. During his umpiring career he also

Umpire Harry Miles

Umpires Course Attendance Record

stood in one first-class match between
Leicestershire and Warwickshire. When he
retired in February 1980 the then president of
Hereford Umpires' Association, Ken Procter,
wrote a letter to Harry thanking him for his enthusiastic contribution to the Association for many
years.

In 1978 Harry Miles and Phil Noakes were
chosen to officiate when 15 associate member
countries of the I.C.C. competed in a tournament

PICKED TO UMPIRE IN PRU WORLD CUP

TWO Hereford umpires will officiate when 15 associate
member countries of the International Cricket Conference
compete in a tournament for a place in the Prudential
World Cup Finals.

They are Phil Noakes, secretary of Hereford Cricket
Umpires' Association, and Harry Miles, former secretary,
who are both members of the Midland Counties Cricket
Umpires' Association.

The countries taking part in the tournament are: Argen-
tine, Singapore, Canada, Malaysia, Denmark, Fiji, East
Africa, Papua New Guinea, Gibraltar, Netherlands, Israel,
United States, Bangladesh, Bermuda and Sri Lanka.

They will also be playing representative teams in the
Midlands and the final will be staged at Worcester on
June 21, with the winners going through to the Prudential
tournament.

Mr Miles has been allotted three matches and the first
will be at Hereford on May 15 when Bangladesh visit the
city to play a Three Counties League XI.

On May 28 he will go to Bromsgrove when the town
team also entertain Bangladesh, and three days later, on
May 31, he will umpire a match between East Africa and
Singapore at Shrewsbury.

Because of work commitments Mr Noakes has only one
match and that will be between Argentine and Wellington
at Wellington on May 27.

PHIL NOAKES   HARRY MILES

Phil Noakes & Harry Miles in a newspaper cutting about the 1968 Prudential World Cup

for a place in the Prudential World Cup finals. Because of work commitments Phil Noakes could only stand in one match at Wellington.

David James

David moved to Hereford in 1966 and played for the Herefordians until 1970 after which he became an umpire in the Evening League.

In the early 1980s he joined the Umpires' Association Committee, and later became chairman for four years. He then became Umpire Training Officer for the county and continues in that capacity. He umpired Hereford Evening League, Hereford Cricket Association, The Marches League, Three Counties League, Birmingham League, Welsh Premier League, and County Youth. He also stood in one Minor Counties Match when the official umpire did not appear.

It was in 1998 that he joined the Herefordshire Minor Counties Cricket Committee as the Membership Secretary. David has contributed to cricket in the county in the above capacities for over 40 years.

Umpire David James receiving the Rob Staite Memorial Cup from Mr. and Mrs. Staite

Ivan Bishop

The late Ivan Bishop, who passed away in 2004, moved from Yorkshire in 1949. He was a former player with Shop Assistants and become involved with Herefordshire cricket after a short playing career. He was secretary of the Evening League and the Umpires' Association for many years. In 1969, when he was an umpire he, suggested the idea of the good sportsman cup, which was presented by fellow umpire Ken Procter.

Umpire Ivan Bishop

Alan Taylor

Alan gave tremendous service to Herefordshire cricket being chairman of the Umpires' Association in 2005 and 2006. He was secretary of the Evening League for one year and was an umpire for fifteen years.

Mike Tidmarsh

Mike played for Frome Valley and for Shop Assistants, retiring from playing in 1982 when he then became an umpire.

He was umpiring a match on the King George Playing Field when one of the teams was the local S.A.S. Regiment. The Regiment was fielding and suddenly personal bleepers could be heard coming from the field. Within seconds the umpires and batsmen were standing alone on the pitch and shortly afterwards they could hear heli-copters taking off from the nearby army camp!

Many other former cricketers became umpires when they ceased playing and also held

Left: Bill Evans, umpire from Shobdon
Right: Jock McManus, umpire from Lads' Club

official positions in the Hereford Umpires' Association, including Paul Everall, Jock McManus, Ken Pole, John Knill, Tony Hehir, Ken Procter, Ernie Ridger, Cliff Rose, L. Savory, B. Staite, Bert Howells, R. Wood-Power, Peter White, Peter West, Les Gibson, Basil Watkins,

Alan Richards (Bringsty and Herefordshire and Worcestershire League umpire)

Clive Terry and Paul Everall
A long-standing umpiring partnership

Alan Holliday, Clive Terry, Ivan Bishop, Tony Capon, Alan Roberts, Ray Chillington, Chick? Nigel Cary, Alan Taylor, Eric Winchester, John Jones, John Chamberlain, John Burgoyne, George Field, Richard Styles, M. Furbor, Roy Jones, Simon Swancott, H. James, J.Worman, J. Roberts, C. Mince, A. Night, M. Keiser, R. Kendall, C. Kelly, A. Holloway, M. Heritage, F. Hawkins, D. Graham, B. Freeman, R. Davies, A. Davies, Ian Macklin, Roger Norgate, J Rivett, John Beaman, K. Platford, P Steele, B. Griffiths, K Davies, A Cooke, Ted Pearman, Tom Batho, and Derek Miles.

The Doug Procter Memorial Cup

This Cup was given by the Umpires' Association and was an award for sportsmanship. The first year was 1978. The two match umpires marked each game with five marks being the maximum per team under the following headings: punctuality, dress, acceptance of decisions and sportsmanship.

Hereford Lads' Club were the winners for the first three years.

The Lords' umpires cuff links show
Old Father Time from the
Lords Cricket Ground weather vane

Hereford Cricket Association

Mr. Peter Sutcliffe, the then National Cricket Coach, came to Hereford in 1974 and was concerned to note that Herefordshire was one of the few remaining counties without an association representing local cricketers. As a result, a meeting was held at Hereford City Sports Club, over 40 clubs having been notified. The following clubs were represented:

Ewyas Harold, Talybont-on-Usk, Canon Frome, Burghill and Tillington, Westfields, Golden Valley, Wayfarers, Wiggin, R.A.F. Hereford, Herefordians, Ledbury, Goodrich, Brockhampton, Titley, Presteigne, Weobley, Ledbury, Kington, Bulmers, Herefordshire Technical College, H.C.S.C., Bromyard, and Eastnor.

The following clubs confirmed their interest but could not attend the meeting:

Strollers, Painters, Leominster, and Luctonians.

It was agreed to form an association and as a result the Herefordshire Cricket Association was founded on 2 September 1974. A constitution was drawn up and sent to Lords, the home of the National Cricket Association. The Association was immediately recognised.

The Hereford and District Cricket League

In 1948 the Lads' Club proposed that a Saturday League, based on the one that had closed down in the 1920s, should be formed for the 1949 season, but nothing materialised. However, in 1975 the League was at long last formed. The League and Knockout Cups were sponsored in the early stages by local businesses including Stooke Hill, Flint and Cooke, Russell Baldwin and Bright, Andrew Morris, Bill Jackson, Bulmers, Bernard Thorpe, Chadds, and the Hereford Times.

The first year's winners were: Division One – Kington; Division Two – Brockhampton; and Division Three – Burghill and Tillington. At a meeting in 1988 there was a change in the points system to an average system. The proposal was

submitted by Brockhampton Cricket Club and carried unanimously. The Association became the Hereford Cricket Board in 1997 and is now linked to the English Cricket Board.

The League was extremely popular and teams from across the border in Wales participated, including Builth Wells, Brecon, Knighton, Talgarth, Talybont, and Monmouth. Monmouth are now strong in the Marches League, winning it in 2003, 2004 and 2005.

When Hereford teams ventured across the border they were greeted by great characters and fine cricketers and, whilst this book is about Herefordshire cricket, it would be wrong not to mention the Welsh sides. Some of the main players and officials from the Welsh clubs were Gerald Morgan, Rob Wall, Steve James, Tim Davenport, Peter Owens, Trevor and John Cooke, Ray Harley, Doug Williams, A. Ian (Tanner) Davies, Brian Francis, Gareth Davies, and Gareth Jenkins.

Flint and Cook Marches League and Cup

The League was formed by the Hereford Cricket Board in 1997 and is affiliated to the English Cricket Board. The League was formed out of the Hereford Cricket League for teams who could provide the appropriate standards and facilities. Independent umpires were appointed to officiate in the matches. Recently, a small minority of Herefordshire clubs, including Brockhampton, Eastnor, and Luctonians, have moved on to play in the Worcester County League with a view to progressing to the Birmingham League. Kington achieved this goal by winning the Worcester Division One in 2006.

Hereford and District Indoor Cricket League

In December 1974 discussions took place to form a Herefordshire Indoor Cricket League. It would be a six-a-side league and cup competition and the games would be played in a hangar at R.A.F. Credenhill. The hangar was 150ft. by 90ft. and the venue was made available thanks to the generosity of Group Captain Youdan. An annual fee of £12 per team was to be charged. The points system was

8 for the winning team and 4 for a tie. The games would be played with 5 overs each of 6 balls.

An exhibition match was held on 10 January 1975 to familiarize teams with the techniques of indoor cricket. Games were played on Monday and Friday evenings. Leominster and Bromyard also formed their own leagues on a similar basis at a later date. Because of security problems the venue was eventually moved to Broadlands Sports Hall. The competition proved extremely popular and had three Leagues and a Cup competition. The cup winners went on to play in area, regional and national competitions. Two of the most successful sides were Hereford City Sports Club and Burghill and Tillington. Burghill went through to the final stages on one occasion eventually being beaten by Weymouth.

At the end of each season there was a match between a Herefordshire representative team and a Worcestershire team.

One of the benefits of the League was that it kept players active and fit during the winter months, so ensuring that the summer game standards improved.

Pete Sykes and Phil Stock were umpires for every match in the first year when they were not personally participating in the cricket. They were also the main organizers of the competition. The League was sponsored by Bill Gross to advertise his carpet company.

Unfortunately, the Broadlands Hall became unavailable and the indoor competition moved to Bromyard in 1993 thanks to the efforts of Chris Graham. In about the year 2000 a new sports hall became available at Bridge Street,

Leominster, and the competition moved there and continues to thrive. Kington also formed their own local league in order to save travel; however it ceased after a few years.

Bromyard Indoor League
The league was formed in 1993, one of the main instigators being Chris Graham from Pencombe Cricket Club. The founder member teams were: Upper Sapey, Bromyard, Whitbourne, Bringsty, Bishops Frome, and Pencombe. The competition became successful and at one stage 18 teams competed. The competition is still active.

Herefordshire Cricket Society
Tim Lowe and Bob Hall, headmaster and deputy head of Hereford Cathedral Junior School,

Hereford Cricket Society logo by Peter Manders

founded the Society in 1997. The idea came after former pupil and England Test cricketer Peter Richardson had given a talk at the school.

The Society's first home was the Imperial Hotel in Widemarsh Street by courtesy of Windsor Jones. The first speaker was the Hereford sports writer, Frank Keating.

Speakers have included great names from the world of cricket including Tom Graveney, former Test cricketer and Worcestershire batsman, who refused to accept a fee stating that he did it for the love of the game; Sir Hubert Doggart, former test cricketer and Sussex player, who was also president of the MCC; Les Jackson, the England and Derbyshire fast bowler; Vanburn Holder, the West Indian and Worcestershire fast bowler who became a first-class umpire; Tom Moody, the former Australian test player; England Ladies' cricketer Barbara Daniels; Lord Maclauren, who was chairman of the England and Wales Cricket Board 1997-2002; TV personalities and avid cricket enthusiasts Nick Owen and Nicholas Parsons; and in 2007 one of the most well-known umpires in world cricket, David Shepherd.

The Society's current home is the Hereford Conservative Club, and local artist Peter Manders, has adorned the walls of the room with sketches of the various speakers.

Whilst finances are tight, the meetings provide wonderful evenings of warmth, comradeship and nostalgia, where around 50 cricket-loving members meet during the long winter months.

Hereford Cricket Society meeting February 2007
Left to right: Frank Bennett, Windsor Jones, Tim Lowe, Peter Manders, Ken Hook

Herefordshire Cricket Society

Previous Guest Speakers

1997-98
Frank Keating
Mike Vockins
Steve Watkins
Chris Old

1998-99
Vanburn Holder
Tom Graveney
Les Jackson
Tim Curtis
Barbara Daniels

1999-2000
John Jameson
Tony Wright
Phil Newport
Douggie Brown
Matthew Engel

2000-01
Stephen James
Mark Briars / Richard Skyrme
Bill Athey
Kevin Cooper
Jim Cumbes

2001-02
Derek Randall
Adrian Dale
Hubert Doggart
Tom Moody
Nick Owen

2002-03
Gladstone Small
Roy Palmer
Peter Walker
Martin McCague / The Earl of Darnley
David Leatherdale

2003-04
Nicholas Parsons
Richard Illingworth
Andy Stovold
Matthew Maynard
Lord MacLauren

2004-05
Steve Rhodes
Bob Taylor
Robert Croft
Nick Cook
Roger Tolchard

2005-06
Tony Cottey
Jack Simmons
Jeremy Lloyd
Neil Radford
John Barclay

2006-7
Stephen Chalke
Henry Olonga
Martin Ball
David Shepherd

CHAPTER III

Herefordshire Knockout & Challenge Cup Competitions

Numerous Challenge and Knockout Cup competitions were in existence in the county for the bulk of the 20th century. Many were restricted to teams in close geographical proximity to the organizers because of the obvious problems of transport at the beginning of the century. Whilst evidence has been found of the details of some of the competitions, in other cases little is known.

Hereford City Sports Club ran a popular six-a-side Knockout Cup which was presented by Col. Thornycroft in 1952. It was called the Coronation Cup to commemorate the forthcoming coronation of Queen Elizabeth II the following year.

It was an unusual competition and the rules were quite unique: 'Each team had five overs to bowl and each member bowled one over apart from the wicket-keeper and the last batsman standing; wides counted as four runs.' The competition was won by N.A.L.G.O. in its inaugural year. In 1953 the prize for winning the tournament was won by Hereford City Sports Club who beat the previous year's winners, N.A.L.G.O., in the final.

When on the field of play the teams were extremely competitive

– the main object of the competition was for local cricketers to enter into a competition that was also fun. The result was that sides were created purely to play this form of cricket. Some of the participating teams that were formed in this manner were:

The Courtiers

A team formed by Terry Court from Hereford City Sports Club. Other members of the team were Cedric Clinkett, Mick Haywood, Martin Shadsted, Bob Izon, and Bob Binnersley.

N.A.L.G.O. were the first winners of the six-a-side competition in 1952
Mr G.E.C. Higginbotham presenting to John Smallbone (captain)
rear: Reg Davies, Phillip Keyte, Neville Sandford, Brian Smith, John Terry and Vernon Grindon

HEREFORD CITY SPORTS CLUB

(Cricket Section)

SIX-A-SIDE TOURNAMENT

21st JULY, 1968 at 11.30 A.M.

on

RACECOURSE GROUND, GRANDSTAND ROAD, HEREFORD

Hereford City Sports Club v. Nalgo.   1967 Final

OFFICIAL PROGRAMME AND PRIZE SCHEME

Nᵒ   1199   1/-

PRIZES - 1. £3 Premium Bond.   2. £2 Premium Bond.   3. 50 Cigarettes.
4. Prize Value 15/-.   5. Prize Value 7/6.

Registered under the Betting, Gaming and Lotteries Act, 1963.

Promoter : E. B. SMITH, 5, Sollars Close, Whitecross, Hereford.

Hereford City Sports Club six-a-side programme 1968

Bromyard winning Foxes Six-a-side Competition
Back row: Tony Hope, Peter Jacques, Jeremy Paton-Williams
Front row Dave Frost, Ivor Lloyd, Norman Whittall

Hilldersley Casket

The origins of the trophy (above) remains somewhat of a mystery – save that it was presented to the runners-up of the Goodrich Cup. The only evidence that has been found of this particular competition is in the 1934 photograph of Brockhampton winning the cup (page 85). In that photograph the casket is in the centre and is flanked by the Perrystone and Brockhampton Cups.

Madley Bumpkins

The side was formed in 1973 and won the competition on three occasions. The captain was Mike Rose, the former Cambridge Blue and Leicestershire player; the other team members being Dennis Fothergill, Bob Gardiner, Martin Peek, Tracey Goodwin, and Neville Symonds. They dressed to suit their team name, but this did not detract from the quality of their cricket.

Other teams who played had their own descriptive names including Donglers, Ratters, Hay Makers, and Cavaliers.

Wood-Power Cup

Dr. R. Wood-Power presented a trophy for the Herefordshire and Worcestershire Representative XI's Annual Competition. It is current today although the Evening League is suspended from playing. The photograph (below) shows the team that beat Worcester at Malvern by 7 runs in 1980.

Kington 20-over Evening Knockout Cup

Robbie Richardson's father-in-law, Percy Biggs, presented the Cup in 1960. Robbie was one of the most respected cricketers in Kington and the surrounding areas for many years. It was a very popular tournament and drew some of the best sides in the county to compete. Two unusual regular competing teams were the Burgoyne XI (Chapter X) and the Ted Rees X1. Ted was a well-known insurance broker in Hereford who created his own representative team, ably assisted by his friend, Laurie Teague, a reporter from the *Hereford Times*. They invited some of the best local talent to play; thus the team was very successful. Ted also played for several other teams during his active days and can be spotted in several of the photographs in this book including the 1952 successful Lamputt's XI (Chapter IV). The Rees XI also competed in the Ross Knockout Cup for many years.

Knockout Cups in the South of the County

Brockhampton Challenge Cup

This is one of the oldest competitions in the county. The then president's wife, Mrs. A.W. Foster, gave the cup to the club in 1900. It was won, appropriately, by the host side, Brockhampton, in the first year. The format of the competition was altered in 1955 when it was

Hereford Evening League XI played Worcestershire in 1980 and were the winners of the Wood-Power Cup
Back row: Stuart Davies, Sam Griffiths, Alan Stokes, Dave Griffiths, Jim Apperley,
Richard Prime (manager and 12th man), Mike Kleiser (umpire)
Front row: Chris Smith, Alan Jones, Tracy Goodwin (captain), Ken Watson, Trevor Jones, Ken Hook

changed to a Twenty-over Competition, and it changed yet again to a Six-a-side Knockout Competition in 1963.

The creation of Challenge Cups at the beginning of the 20th century was largely because many of the clubs were created by the local Lord of the Manor. In addition to the Brockhampton Cup there was the Goodrich Cup, presented by Lady Moffatt from Goodrich Court, and the Hoarwithy Cup, presented by Lady Densham. Other Challenge Cups in the south of the county were the Longhope Cup and the Perrystone Cup.

Woolhope Six-a-side

Woolhope ran a successful competition during the 1960s and '70s. The photograph (previous page) shows the winning home side in the 1960s.

Many other clubs ran successful and exciting six-a-side competitions, including Canon Frome, Eastnor, Colwall, Fox at Bransford and the recently restarted Goodrich Cup. The photograph (bottom left) is of Bromyard winning the Foxes competition in 1980.

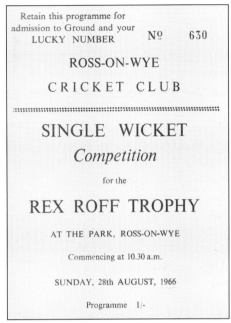

ROSS-ON-WYE

CRICKET CLUB

SINGLE WICKET

Competition

for the

REX ROFF TROPHY

AT THE PARK, ROSS-ON-WYE

Commencing at 10.30 a.m.

SUNDAY, 28th AUGUST, 1966

Programme   1/-

Left: The Brockhampton Cup
Right: Rex Roff Trophy, 1966 programme

Woolhope six-a-side 1960s team
Ron Gwilliam, Jeff Jones, Bill Lambert, Mike Waring, Maurice Bayliss, Selwyn Williams

Ross Knockout Competitions

Ross Cricket Club ran a Twenty-over Knockout Cup that was started before the Second World War and was still being run in the 1980s. Ross, like many other clubs, also ran a six-a-side competition. In 1974 Brockhampton, thanks to Roy Wargen who took a hat trick in the final, won the competition when they beat Ross Nondescripts. The Brockhampton club was the runner-up in the two previous years.

Ross, to the best of the authors' knowledge, was the first club to run an invitation single-wicket competition; it was called the Rex Roff Trophy, and began in 1966. The competition spread to all the clubs in the county, who ran their own single wicket competitions and the winner was entered in the Ross Finals. The winner in the first year was Royston Young from Goodrich who beat Roger Berryman from Wiggin in the final. Rex Roff presented the prize after J.F. McLean introduced him. The club raised £25 on the day.

The photograph (below) was taken at the end of the 1968 competition. A victorious Tony Hope from Brockhampton is being applauded off the pitch at Ross after he had beaten John Gurney from Dymock in the final. The original Ross Ladies Tea Pavilion is in the background of the photograph. Unfortunately the competition ran for less than 10 years.

Knockout Cups in the North of the County

Ludlow Knockout Cup

The cup was a very popular and prestigious one and was competed for by many of the main teams in the north of Herefordshire including Leominster, who

Tony Hope, Ross single wicket winner 1968

won it in 1949, and Bromyard. The Leominster team is shown in the photograph below.

Bromyard Twenty-over Knockout Cup.
The trophy was hard fought for especially by the North Herefordshire clubs, but they did not always have their own way as the cup was won by the Y.M.C.A. in 1969.

The Leominster team that won the Ludlow Cup in 1949
(Alec Haines is top left)

Y.M.C.A. winners of the Bromyard Knockout Cup in 1969
Ken Pole (captain) receiving cup, Dave Evans (on right in pads),others include
Simon Swancott and Nigel Yarwood

Leominster Twenty-over Knockout Cup.
The tournament started immediately after World War Two and proved very popular. There are records confirming that over 2,000 people have watched matches on the Grange – the former Leominster ground in the centre of the town. In 1951 the teams competing were Nondescripts, Stoke Prior, British Legion, Old and Bold, Bromyard, Old Luctonians, Dales, and Institute and Circle. Some of these teams sadly no longer exist.

The photograph on the next page shows the successful Bringsty side in 1957. Latterly, the competition reverted to a six-a-side tournament which Leominster won themselves in 1973. The competition continued throughout the century.

The jovial nature of the matches played under the above rules although still competitive, created some humorous incidents because of the characters that were involved on the field of play. On one occasion in a village Knockout Cup match the host club provided one of the umpires from their number. Like many cricketers who were still playing, he was watching the game from a slightly different perspective – that is as an admiring spectator. In this particular match the batsman hit a particularly fine cover drive and the fielder at deep extra cover glided round the boundary, picked up the ball single-handed, and threw it in flat. It went straight over the stumps, and the wicketkeeper flicked off the bails and there followed a loud appeal for a run-out. The cricketer acting as an umpire was not concentrating on the job in hand

Bringsty – the Leominster Cup Winners in 1957
Back row: Roger Burraston, Roly Powell, Simon Robinson, John Oliver, Colin Hawkins, Edwyn Green, John Sears,
David Barnes, Les Essenhigh
Front row: Don Essenhigh, Don Thomas, Eric Hawkins, Cecil Freegard (captain) Ted Oliver, Alan Mason, Gwyn Essenhigh

because, inwardly, he was admiring a fine passage of play and did not see the alleged run-out until very late. He therefore correctly called 'not out'. When the captain of the fielding side complained, indicating that the batsman was out by a yard, the umpire said 'Never, if at all he was only out by a foot!'

There was another incident in the same match. The batsman was Jim Apperley and it was said of Jim that if he hit a ball it stayed hit. Indeed, he was well known as one of the hardest hitters in the game at that time. When Jim strode to the wicket the opposition captain brought on a bowler who had achieved some success bowling at Jim in the past. The comment was 'Jim is no problem, bring P.Q. on, he will see to him.' When Jim received the first ball he hit a flat-bat six to cow corner. It went like a missile over the boundary through the car park, across the adjacent road and into the garden on the other side, only being stopped as it was still rising by the wall of the house. The opposing team's comments are not printable, but they knew that Jim was somewhat of a phenomenon, as his statistics in Chapter XIV will show.

CHAPTER IV

Hereford Evening League

This chapter is devoted in its entirety to one of the most important competitions in the history of cricket in Herefordshire in the 20th century. The League was formed in 1927 and ran until the outbreak of the Second World War. It resumed in 1945 but sadly folded in 2002 because of lack of interest. It is fascinating to see how it developed from small beginnings to host four divisions and then follow it through to its eventual demise.

The formation of the League really started with a meeting at the former White Lion Hotel in Hereford in April 1927; the clubs represented were Y.M.C.A., United Banks, George Mason Ltd., Post Office, City Police, and Hereford Times.

It was agreed that an Evening League would be formed and that the number of teams would be limited to eight. City Police decided not to join but, in addition to the remaining clubs who attended the original meeting, Eignbrook Congregational Church, Widemarsh, Boys' Club, and Hereford Second XI were all invited to join. There was less industry in Hereford in 1927 when the League was formed and this is reflected in the background of the teams that originally joined.

The following rules were made:

1. League restricted to eight clubs.
2. The players to be confined to the City area, and be members of the club concerned.
3. The entrance fee to be 7s. 6d. for each club.
4. Play to commence on 27 May and to start no later than 6. 30pm.
5. Each team to bat for one and a quarter hours.
6. Two points for a win and one for a tie.
7. Games abandoned because of bad weather to be re-arranged.
8. At the beginning of each season, Club Secretaries should send to the League Secretary a nominal roll of playing members by not later than 19 May.
9. Each side to provide their own umpire.

At a second meeting, N.V. Goddard of United Banks was appointed secretary and it was agreed that he should write to Col. C.M. Thornycroft, inviting him to be president.

Widemarsh had the distinction of fielding a future test player in their side when Reg Perks, who was still a schoolboy at Hereford High School, turned out for them and in June 1927 took 6 wickets for 22 runs against Hereford Times.

In July 1927 an article appeared in the *Hereford Times* taking issue with the current League rules. The author stated that in his view neutral umpires should be appointed and that the rule that the 11th batsman had to be dismissed must be abolished.

There was a League meeting on Monday 19 September 1927, again at the White Lion Hotel, chaired by Col. Thornycroft. Y.M.C.A. had failed to complete their fixtures so it was agreed that the points would be awarded to the teams they failed to play. As a result the League winners were United Banks. Y.M.C.A. still came second and George Mason Ltd. propped up the League.

The Chairman agreed to provide a trophy to present to the winning team. He said that because the League had no money there would not be a presentation of medals to the winning team. Discussion followed regarding employing neutral umpires who would be paid. It was agreed to leave this and other matters in abeyance until the next meeting in February 1928.

By 1929 the teams in the League were Hereford Banks, Hereford Lads' Club, the Labour Club, the Nondescripts, Hereford City Police, the Post Office, and the Y.M.C.A. There was a meeting at the White Lion on Wednesday 25 April 1929, chaired by Col. Thornycroft, when it was agreed that play that year would commence on 4 May and the following new rules were introduced:

A. An offending club would be fined 1s. if they failed to provide an umpire for the match.
B. Any player who played four games for the Hereford 1st XI during the season would not be eligible to play in the Evening League that year.
C. Visiting teams would bat first in every match.
D. Umpires must carry a spare ball.
E. No player could play for more than one team during the season.
F. All players signed on to play in the League, must be approved by the Committee. [This rule was silent on what circumstances would persuade the Committee to stop a player from playing.]

By 1930 the teams in the League were Banks, Post Office, Lads' Club A, Lads' Club B and Y.M.C.A., and by 1931 they had been joined by Rugby Club, N.A.L.G.O., and S.W.S. Power. The newly-formed Young Liberals side joined in 1932 and more teams joined later in the 1930s as the League became more popular.

The strength of the League at the end of its first decade is shown by a letter that was written to the League representative in 1937 asking him to select a League XI side. There were many fine cricketers playing at the time and the team chosen was: D.Wargent and S.C. Wright (High School Old Boys), R.W.P. Roff (N.A.L.G.O), D. Aston (Gas Works), A. Harris and R. Phillips (Lads' Club), F. Davies (Thynnes), G. Patrick and A. Savage (S.W.S.), R. Garrett (Y.M.C.A.), A.E. Hall (G.P.O.), 12th man S. Davies (G.P.O.).

In its heyday after the war the League had four divisions. The League was originally formed to accommodate players who worked at weekends and were therefore unable to play at these times. The playing rules were quite simple: there were to be 20 overs, each of 6 balls, with a maximum of 5 overs per bowler. The League was ahead of its time with the rules, which were very similar to those of one-day cricket that came into the First Class game several decades later.

To qualify for the League a team had to be situated within the Hereford City boundary. Players from teams outside the city limits joined the city teams purely to play in the Evening League. When the League started, sides were formed from work establishments and other social organizations in the city, and were intended to promote comradeship and to encourage work colleagues to socialise after a day's work. The League continued uninterrupted until September 1939 when it was agreed that it was not practical to carry on, although there was a limited League during the war. The teams playing during that period were Lads' Club, S.W.S., Y.M.C.A., and Herefordians.

The League proper started up again in 1946 and the teams who competed immediately after the war were Lads' Club (two teams), Hereford Sports Club, Y.M.C.A., P.O., S.W.S. Power Co., and Hinton Youth Club. The winners the first year were Y.M.C.A. and Col. Thornycroft presented the trophy to their Captain, Ken Procter. It was agreed that all games would be played on Widemarsh Common with the hope that later on in the season games could be played on the Racecourse.

In 1953 there were three Divisions of the League, indicating that at that stage it was going from strength to strength. One of the teams that was formed to play in the League at that time was Wyevale, who played on a pitch in Whitecross Road. Jerry Gilbert, who played for Wyevale, remembered that on more than one occasion barbed wire and cow pats had to be moved before the game could start. As the competition became more popular more teams were invited to join.

In 1955 teams that joined the League included H. Wiggins, Sankeys, Saracen's Head, Post Office, Hereford Light Infantry, and Cohen's, and B.T.H. Bradbury Lines joined in 1957 and Hereford Technical College and Accountants in 1958. By this time players from all walks of life were enjoying a game of cricket in the evening.

In 1956 the Knockout Cup was reduced to 16 overs of 6 balls. The first winners of the competition in this format were Thynnes (opposite).

A meeting of the Herefordshire Cricket Association was convened in January 1958 to consider the points system and it was agreed that, in future, there would be an average points system which would be calculated by dividing

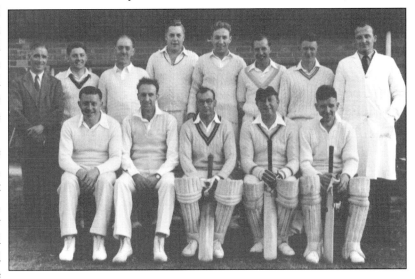

Thynnes – Knock Out Cup winners 1956
Back row: A. Smart, G. Kershaw, L. Beavan, D. Meredith, S. Chilvers, R. Wood, D. Preece, N. Morgan
Front row: F. Farmer, W. Jennings, E. Ridger (captain), V. Haylings, R. Ingram

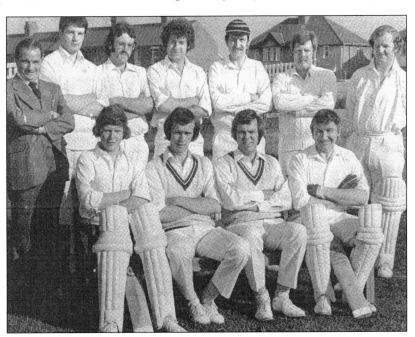

Herefordshire versus Worcestershire, 50th anniversary 1977
Back row: Roy Humphries (scorer), Gerard Flint, Trevor James, Ian Macklin, John Quinn, Ken Hook, Neville Symonds
Front row: Steve Watkins, Tracey Goodwin (captain). Norman Davies, Stan Marston

the total points accumulated by the number of games completed. This would deal with any unfairness caused by some matches being cancelled because of adverse weather conditions.

The 1960s was an exciting and competitive era for the League and many strong teams participated. One of the reasons was that many good players, who were members of the Hereford City Sports Club, were playing for their respective works and social teams. They returned to play for the Sports Club to form a very successful side that dominated the League for many years. During this period the League was in the hands of several experienced administrators including Dr. R. Wood-Power – president, Bill Morris – chairman, and Ernest Ridger – treasurer. Other very active members of the League were Ivan Bishop, and Ken and Doug Procter.

To commemorate the 50th anniversary of the League there was a match between a Hereford Evening League XI and their counterparts from Worcester. The photograph of the Hereford winning team retaining the Wood-Power trophy includes Steve Watkins who played a first-class

game for Worcestershire. In 1977 it was proposed by Mike Haywood, a former Hereford City Sports Club player, that the League points system be changed from two points for a win and one for a draw to ten points for a win, five for a tie, plus one batting bonus point for every ten runs scored, and one bowling bonus point for every wicket taken.

Shortly before the League ceased in 2002, the rules were changed once again with the games consisting of 16 overs, each of 8 balls, with a maximum of 7 overs per bowler. The Knockout Cup was different again, being 16 overs, each of 6 balls.

The social side was as important as the cricket and one of the highlights of the season was the annual League Dinner Dance. At one such occasion, held in the Shirehall, Len Sparrow, a police officer and well-known local cricketer with Burghill and Tillington, was asked to say grace. His mind was clearly on his work because he proceeded to say 'I swear by almighty God that the evidence that I shall give to the Court ...' etc. etc. He was nudged in the ribs by his wife and duly sat down to the general amusement of the assembled company!

Some of the participating teams have been mentioned in their respective chapters because they played in other leagues in addition to the Evening League. The following is a summary of some of the teams that have participated.

Hereford United Supporters Club
Back row: Mike Hibble, Tim Longworth, Brian Farley, John Rogers,
Roy Palfrey, Jock Handley
Front row: Dave Morris, Clive Terry, John Griffiths (captain),
Jack Stevens, Dave Bevan

Social Clubs in Hereford

Hereford United Supporters' Club
This cricket team was formed in the late 1960s. The founder members were Paul Everall and John Griffiths, who captained the Evening League and Weekend sides respectively.

One of the highlights of the season was a supporters' club game against the Hereford United football team. Some of the well-known Hereford United footballers of the time played cricket at the end of the football season, including Peter Spiring (whose son Reuben played cricket for Herefordshire and then for Worcestershire before injury cut his career short); Kevin Charlton; Dixie McNeil, who went on to manage Wrexham; Tommy Hughes; and finally Jimmy Harvey, the former manager of Morecambe.

One team member, Clive Terry, remembered going out to bat with Jack Stevens at the same time as a Lancaster bomber, a Spitfire and a Hurricane flew overhead on the way to an air show. The comment was rather inevitable: 'Not many batsmen have a fly past when they walk out to the crease.' The club had an active social side and played many other games such as darts and skittles in their night club.

Westfields

Westfields cricket club was mainly formed from the football team and played in the summer to keep their players together and, hopefully, to keep them fit. They are recorded as playing from 1973 until 1980, during which time they ran two Evening League sides and had a team in the Gloucestershire Saturday League. They also ran a team on Sundays playing friendly matches. All home matches were played on Widemarsh Common.

They were successful in the League during a three year period between 1973 and 1975 winning the Fourth, Third, and Second Divisions respectively. In 1977 they won the new Division Two, and the following year the new Division One. Keith Bullock hit two centuries in Division Three in 1974, one against the College of Education and the other against Saunders Valve. A century in the Evening League was quite an achievement in view of the limited overs available. One of the club's most memorable matches was during the 1972/73 season when they played the Hereford United giant killers team and over 500 spectators turned up to watch an evening game on Widemarsh Common.

Lads' Club

The Lads' Club is one of the oldest established of the city clubs and is recorded playing at the beginning of the 20th century. They played in the League before the Second World War and immediately after in 1946 when they won Division 4.

In the 1970s Paul Purchase was appointed captain and Tony Lowe was the secretary. Other stalwarts in the early years were Phil Donovan, Chris Lane, Arthur Richards, Phil Daw, and Les Campbell. In 1975 Graham Smith and Hedley Lawson were the co-founders of the weekend team which competed in the Second Division of the newly-formed Herefordshire Saturday League. The Evening League side won the Doug Procter Memorial Cup for four consecutive years from its inauguration in 1978. Philip Daw

Westfields team in 1973
Back row: Russell Jones, Nick Price, Alan Hartland, Phil Hallett,
Andy Morris, Barry Walters
Front row: Taffy Davies, Angus McIntyre, Rose Hartland (scorer), Chris Moore,
Keith Bullock, Ken Hedley

scored 108 runs in 20 overs in a Division Four match against the Gas Board

The Lads' Club won Division Three in 1968 and 1973, and Division Two in 1974. They won the new Division One in 1981, 1984 and 1986.

British Rail team, 1968
Back row: Ken Goodman, Sam Wilby, Trevor Jones, Bob Hughes, Brian Noden, Colin Woolley, Ernie Lloyd
Front row: Tony Meredith, Brian Jones (captain), Molly Jones, (scorer), Laurie Steele, Bill Fairclough

Denco, Evening League team 1964
Back row: Dave Gladwyn, Norman Davies, Ray Smith, Dave Jones, Des Williams
Front row: John Hall, Bob Thirtle, Keith Powell, Roly Howell (captain), John Coffee, George Hyde

Works Teams

Accountants XI

This team was formed in 1951 to play Evening League cricket. The founder and organiser was Peter Hill and the secretary in 1964 was R. Davies, who worked for F.H. Sunderland.

Anvil Cricket Club

This team, which was associated with Anvil Enterprises, is noted as playing between 1975 and 1978, but only existed for two years; Clive Morris and Gerald Bishop were involved. They won the new Division Two of the Evening League in 1978.

British Rail / B.R.S.A.

The team was formed in 1961 as a works team and stayed that way until about 1965, when players were recruited from outside. They played originally on the Bishop's Meadow and then Widemarsh Common. The club's secretary, Colin Woolley, also played cricket for Ross. They played friendly matches against St. Mary's and Garnons. They changed their name to British Rail Staff Association in the 1970s.

The team played in the Evening League and Railway Competitions and won the Western Region six-a-side competition in Swindon on more than one occasion. The successful six-a-side team in 1968 was Trevor Jones, Bob Hughes, Colin Woolley, Ernie Lloyd, Brian Jones (captain), and Laurie Steele. The full team photograph (top) was taken in 1968 when, as British Rail, they won the Evening

THE A.E.I. HEREFORD
SOCIAL AND ATHLETIC CLUB.

Cricket Section

ANNUAL

DINNER DANCE

THE IMPERIAL HOTEL
FRIDAY, 7th NOVEMBER, 1958
7.30 for 7.45 p.m.

*Above and left: AEI
Dinner Dance 1958*

The pavilion at Rotherwas

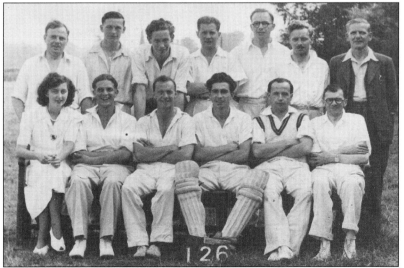

Ediswan 1950s team
Back row: Doug ?, [-], ? Morgan, Brian George, [-], Phil Godsell, [umpire]
Front row: Elaine Lamputt, Gordon Lamputt, Bill Plummer, Lee Hooper,
Vince Preece, Ernie Ridger

League Division Four title. They also won the Division Three title in 1972 and the Division Two the following year.

Cohen's

Not much is known about this team, which is recorded playing in 1954/5. Cohen's was a factory in Rotherwas grinding large shells for the Ministy of Defence and they only had a team for a short period of time.

Denco

The team played at Holmer, the current home of Pegasus Football Club, and is known to have played from 1956 until 1982. They won the Division Four league title in 1963 and were runners-up in 1969. They also won the new Division Two title in 1982. Norman Davies played a major part in the organizing and running of the team. They were the second side to win the Junior Cup in 1968, when they were too strong for Hunderton Youth Club. Roly Howell was captain and one of the main administrators of the team for many years. The photograph (far left)

Police versus Painter's 1952: Mr Wheeler (chief of police) bowling the first ball to Mr. Painter

includes the late George Hyde, who eventually became Mayor of Hereford.

Harcourts, Ediswan, B.T.H., A.E.I. etc.

The team in Hereford that can boast the most changes of name was a factory side originally called Harcourts who played at Rotherwas under that name in 1946, 1947 and 1948. The name was changed to Ediswan XI for the 1949/55 seasons and B.T.H. (British Thompson Houston) for the 1956 season when they were runners-up in the Coronation Cup.

An amusing incident occurred when they played Hinton in the Evening League on Widemarsh Common. Nag Welling, who was blind in one eye and played for Hinton, was fielding on the boundary. His attention was diverted from the game by a young lady spectator and he started to chat her up. He was called to attention by the bowler but took no notice. The inevitable happened and the batsman for B.T.H., Bill Plummer, struck the ball hard in his direction. There was a shout of 'Catch' from all the team and Nag, who saw it out of the corner of his good eye, nonchalantly caught

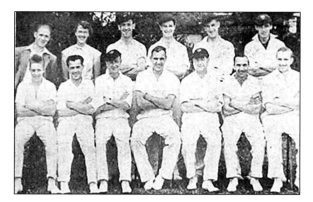

Sankeys c.1950
Back row: L. Preece, F. Morgan (scorer), D. Owen,
J. Powell, R. Davies, R. Marchant
Front row: G. Perkins, J. Powell, A. Kellard,
W. Davies (captain), C. Leek, D. Skyrme, L.C. Preece

it one handed and continued to chat up the young lady as if nothing had happened.

The team became A.E.I. from about 1957 until 1964; then Smart and Brown from 1965 until 1969; and, finally, Thorn Lighting, until the closure of the factory.

The original team to play on the Rotherwas ground was Harcourts. There was a rumour that during the Second World War an old railway engine was buried on the ground used as a pitch. The pavilion was built in about 1955 and was used until the field ceased to be a sports ground.

The team were playing in the Evening League in 1952 when they came second in Division Two. The club used the ground until about 1971, when Hereford United Football Club used it for training for about three years. Westfields Football Club became tenants in 1974 until they moved to their new ground at Widemarsh in about 2004.

Under Ediswan, they were runners-up in Division Two in 1950 and 1953 and, renamed A.E.I., were Division Two winners in 1960 and runners-up in 1958. In that year they had a dinner dance – the photograph at the dance (page 37 top) includes Nigel Yarwood, who played cricket in Herefordshire for many years and is described in more detail in chapter XIV. Eventually they won Division Three as Smart and Brown in 1968 and in 1971. The ground has now been sold for development within the industrial estate.

Painters

The team started in 1946 after the war and continued until about 1980. The ground was by the Denco factory near Mortimer House in Holmer Road and is now waste grassland and a car park. The photograph (opposite top left) shows Mr. Wheeler, the chief of police, bowling the first ball to Mr. Painter at the first match to be played on the new ground in 1952. The police won the match comfortably.

Painters won the Division Two title in 1954, 1967 and 1971; the Division Three title in 1964; and Division Four in 1974. They won the new Division Two in 1980.

Sankeys

Sankeys were a local works side that is recorded as playing from 1953 until 1971 but did not win any titles.

Sun Valley

Sun Valley is a major poultry processing plant situated behind Widemarsh Common. They were playing in the 1970s and '80s and were runners up in Division Two in 1978 and won the Junior Cup and Division Three in 1987.

Thynnes

The factory was a major tile manufacturer in the county. According to the *Hereford Journal* for June 1935 Thynnes Tile Factory works side had a team. In April 1939 the secretary placed an advertisement in the *Hereford Times* seeking opponents for the season. They played at Holmer on the

Painter Bros. 1963.
Back row: *John Sellars, Syd Caffles, Les Gambles, Bill Meredith,*
Clive Trenchard, George Hyde
Front row: *Roger Smith, Tony Meredith, Colin Morris, John Bradley, John Bevan*

Thynnes 1951 team
Left to right: *G. Marchant, R. Ingram, E. Ridger (captain), V. Haylings, I Lewis,*
W. Jennings, T. Davies, J. Handley, F. Farmer, L. Beavan, R. Leech

Pegasus Ground. One of the stalwarts of the team was Ernest Ridger who recalled that their pavilion was originally at Garnons. They were Division One winners in 1951 and 1953, and runners-up in the Coronation Cup in 1953. They went on to win the Coronation Cup in 1956. They were also Division Two champions in 1949. The team was dissolved in 1959 when Thynnes Tile Factory ceased trading.

Saunders Valve

The Saunders Valve factory was set up to manufacture aircraft valves. The team was formed in 1959 and entered the Evening League in 1962. They won the Division Four title in their first year, and the Hereford Six-a-side Knockout Cup. Three members of the successful side were Nigel Yarwood, Mick Carroll, and Ollie Tooze. They also won the Division Three title in 1963 and the Division Two title in 1964 and 1968. The club ceased to play in 1980. A team photograph in 1963 is shown in chapter VI.

Wiggin

The team was formed in 1955 specifically to take part in the Evening League and played until 1983. In the 1970s Wiggin players achieved individual successes in the League honours list. George Whittaker's score of 74 not out against South Wye was the highest individual score in Division Three and Selwyn Williams topped the same Division's bowling performance with 7 wickets for 15 runs against Denco. Wiggin also ran a weekend team during the same season.

Henry Wiggin had a superb social culture during the early years, boasting not only cricket but also football, rugby, tennis, bowls, table tennis, snooker, and darts.

Wyevale Evening League ,1950 team
Back row: Peter Buchanan, Mike Bryon, Les James, Tom Field, John Warley, [-]
Front row: John Causer, Trevor Roberts, George Warley, Gerry Gilbert, Ron Taylor

Gas Board Dinner celebrating winning the Leominster Senior and Junior Cups 1950
Back row: Ray G. Jones, Reg Griffiths, Ray Jones, John Godfrey, Tommy Hobson, Derrick Barlow, Cyril Williams, Barry Hill,
George Shutt, Ken Williams (not completely in original photograph)
Front row: Mr. Hobson (manager), Bill Griffiths, Don Preece, Bill Jones, (captain), Geoff Wood, Bernard Shaw

There were some fine sportsmen working for the company and it was often said that if Wiggins had fielded a representative team in football or cricket it would take some beating in the county. The company ran an inter-departmental cricket competition and a single wicket tournament, both of which were fought for tooth and nail. In 1971 Dave Hodges won the single wicket prize. In 1973 eighteen players took part and Dave Price beat Ken Hook in the final.

They won the Division Two title in 1965 and were runners-up in Division One in 1961 and '62. Wiggin A finished runners-up in Division Three of the Hereford Evening League in 1971. They were runners-up in Division Two in 1973 and 1974. They also won the Coronation Cup in 1968.

Peter Sykes ran the Wiggin Cricket Club during these halcyon days and Mal White oversaw the internal sports. Sadly, like many other company sports grounds, the Wiggins pitch has now been sold off for housing.

Wyevale

The garden centre team had two successes in the League, winning the Third Division title in 1953, the year that they were formed. They were extremely consistent during the 1950s, being runners-up in Division Two for two years before eventually winning it in 1956. One of their main players was George Warley who also played for Hereford City Sports Club. They ceased playing in 1965.

Services Teams

Fire Brigade

They are recorded playing from 1953 until 1969 and were runners-up in the Coronation Cup in 1960, losing to Hereford City Sports Club. They were the first Division Three side to reach the final. They were also runners-up in Division Four in 1966.

Gas Board

They played on the same ground as Painter's – behind Denco in Holmer Road and adjacent to a

N.A.L.G.O. team in 1950

Back row: B.Rutherford, E. Monkhouse, J. Terry, E. Pitt, R. Roberts, B. Cutler, J. Donaldson (scorer)
Front row: E. Johnson, J. Smallbone, R. Williams, B. Smith, N. Sandford

M.E.B. Evening League Cup 1979
Back row: Alan Stokes, John Worle, Pat Ellis, Nigel Yarwood, Len Sparrow, Simon Swancott
Front row: Paul Sparrow, James Worle, Clive Brazier (captain), Stan Marston, Dave Evans

1958. The Gas Board completed a unique double in the 1950s when they won the Leominster Junior Cup and were then invited to compete in the Senior Cup, which they promptly won by beating Bromyard in the final. They were reformed in the 1980s to play in the Evening League and continued until that League folded in 2002.

N.A.L.G.O.
The Local Government Officers team played Evening League cricket from 1931 until 1937 and was re-formed in 1946. They won the Division Two title in 1950. The team photograph (top left) includes Ted Johnson and Neville Sandford, who both played for Hereford City Sports Club at weekends.

In 1952 they won the inaugural six-a-side competition for the Thornycroft Cup which was presented to their captain, J. Smallbone, by Alderman Higginbotham. They also won the Coronation Cup in 1955 and were runners up in Division One. They ceased playing in about 1970.

M.E.B.
The team was formed from the old Midlands Electricity Board in 1953 and continued playing until the 1980s. They won the Second Division title in 1962 and 1970 and the Coronation Cup in 1974 and 1979. They also won the new Division One title in 1976 and the Hereford six-a-side competitions on at least two occasions.

large gasholder – perhaps Hereford's answer to the Oval. The team was formed in 1946 and played until 1965, being Division One winners in 1948 and 1950 and Division Two winners in

Police

The team is recorded as playing between 1921 and 1929, and then from the early 1950s until 1982. They played on the Essex Arms cricket ground in Widemarsh Street. an area that was bequeathed to the police force for sport. They had their own pavilion, and the building was still there in 2006.

Many members of the local police force played for the West Mercia Constabulary as well as the local Evening League side. The West Mercia photograph (below) shows Derrick Jones, who was secretary of the Evening League until it ceased in 2002. The over 40s side photograph (top right) has many well-known faces including

Police over 40s team – Evening League Champions 1969
Back row: John Peyton, Harold Cole, Philip Noakes, Mike Kidd, Mike Ovens
Front row: Bob Taylor, John Keyte, Jack Main, John Clinton

Police 1987. Playing in the Police Association Cup against Northampton at Kidderminster
Back row: Paul Davidson, Roger Powell, Andy Denton, Len Sparrow, Alan Ralph, Kevin Bayliss, Paul Sparrow
Front row: David Gower, Neil Preece, Paul Quested, Guy Thompson, Derrick Jones

Phil Noakes, who became chairman and training officer of the Umpires Association, and Bob Taylor, who was Coroner's Officer when he retired.

They won the League Cup in 1962, the new Division One in 1982, and the Junior Cup in 1989. Cricket is no longer played on the Essex Arms ground which is now used for dog training.

Post Office cricket team – photograph taken early 1900s

Post Office 1983. Sorting Office Winning Team
Back row: Steve Preece, Alan Wildig, John Hudson, Harold Lord, Keith Brisland
Front row: Brian Preece, Keith Bradley, Mick Ayres,
Julian Morris, Chris Gallagher

Hereford Post Office

There is evidence indicating that the Post Office had a team at the turn of the century, playing until the outbreak of the First World War. They played their home games at Widemarsh. On 14 May 1914 the *Hereford Times* reported that the team was in its 13th year and that in the previous year they had won 11 out of 15 matches. The early photograph (top left) taken at Holmer includes Reg Noakes, the father of Philip Noakes of Hereford Police and prominent member of the Umpires Association. The team is recorded as playing again from 1921 until the outbreak of war and then from 1946 until the end of the Evening League.

The Post Office had one success in the Evening League when they won Division Three in 1970. In the mid 1970s the original Post Office team ceased to play under that name, and two other teams were formed from the original members. The telephone engineers section played as **Telesports** and won the new Division Two in 1985. The sorting office played as **P.O.S.O.** (Post Office Sorting Office) and in 1983 were winners of the Herefordians Invitation Knockout Cup, beating Herefordians. The photograph (bottom left) shows the winning team in the final. In about 1990 another side was formed called the **Royal Mail Tigers** which entered the Evening League. This created a great friendly rivalry between the three teams. Audrey Legg was a loyal supporter and was the Post Office canteen cook. She volunteered her services to be scorer and tea lady when the team played weekend friendlies.

Shop Assistants

The team was formed in 1952 by Ivan (Ivor) Bishop, Ernie Preece, Danny Wright, and Roy Powell. They started playing friendlies on Sundays so that Saturday workers could play. They joined the Hereford Evening League in 1954 and won Division Three in their first year; they won the Third Division again in 1967 and the Second Division in 1969. They also won the League Cup in 1972 and 1973 and the Leominster Knockout Cup in the early 1960s. One of their least notable performances was in 1966 when they were bowled out for 7 runs by Wiggins in an Evening League match. Steve Bishop, son of Ivor, boasted that he was top scorer with 2!

The team included not only the two playing members of the Bishop family but also Ivor's wife Gladys, who was the tealady for many years.

P.I.M.

The managing director of Plastic Injection Mouldings, Brian Tutchenor, was a keen cricket supporter who, in the late 1980s, sponsored Burghill and Tillington. He went on to form his own works team which played in the Evening League, winning Division One in 1989.

S.W.S. Power Company

The team was successful in the 1930s and won the Unofficial League in 1938. They played Evening League cricket from 1937 until 1941 and again in 1946 and 1947.

Wayfarers

They were formed in 1962 and continued until the 1990s, winning the new Division Two title in 1983 and the new Division One in 1990. There is a further reference to this team in chapter VI.

Pub & Club Sides

Saracen's Head

The team played from 1953 until 1988, but not continuously. They joined the Evening League in 1955 and won the Third Division title in 1957. The first secretary was Les Lamb and he was followed by Bob Lovering, who continued until the club finished, and provided the information for this book. The team was latterly made up from members of the Lichfield Vaults darts team. During their second spell they re-joined the Evening League in 1983. They played their first game against B.R.S.A. and were skittled out for 31. They were runners-up in the Evening League Junior Cup in 1983. One of their best players was Brian Preece, who was a footballer with Hereford United. He scored the first 50 for the club in 1983 and was top scorer in 1984 with 46 runs. Brian also had a good season in 1987, scoring 119 and two further 50s.

In 1983, Julian Morris had the best bowling figures of 6 wickets for 8 runs, and Chris Gallagher took 4 wickets for 2 runs. In 1985 they were runners-up again in the Junior Cup.

Saracen's Head Team.. Division Two winners in 1987
Back row: Frank Edwards, Les Powell, Steve Keen, Eddie Pritchard, Chris Gallagher, Roger Eames, Keith Brisland
Front row: Clive Eames, Steve Deem, John Marston, Dave Brooks, Chris Lea, Brian Preece

Chris Gallagher was top scorer that year with 52 not out and Julian Morris had the best bowling figures with 5 wickets for 14 runs. They had no honours in 1986, but 1987, when they won Division Two, was their most successful year. Chris Davies had remarkable figures of 4 wickets for 5 runs.

The team folded at the end of 1988 when they finished bottom of Division One. Some of the players went on, rather appropriately, to play for the Crusaders and others for the Treacle Mine Inn.

Richmond Club – formerly the Labour Club

The club is in Edgar Street, the present team being formed in around 1975 when they amalgamated with the Gas Board team to play Evening League cricket.

The Richmond Club started a weekend fixture list in 1979/80. No photograph of the team has been found, but some of the players were Geoff Foster, Tony and Bob Main, Norman and Keith Rees, Gerald Marchant, Bert Mann, John Wood, Mick Reece, Wayne Williams, Taffy Beddows, Bob and Ashley Brown, Bob King, Pete Morris, and George Whittaker. The side continued to play until the end of the Evening League.

One of the most influential members of the team was Robin Buchanan, who played from the start. His uncles, Peter and Alwyn, played for Wyevale and his grandfather, Alf, was an umpire. The family produced many fine local sportsmen and were related to Dennis Buchanan, who started the local bus company that bore his surname. Mention must be made of the stalwart tea ladies who kept the team operational – Anne Buchanan, Carol Rees and Jeanette Foster.

Welsh Club

Two of the prime movers in the formation of the Welsh Club were Bill Griffin, a former Mayor of Hereford, and local solicitor Gary Davies, who worked actively with the first secretary Arthur Farmer. The club, which was officially opened on 24 May 1966, was intended to provide a home-from-home social club for the many men from the Welsh Valleys who came to Hereford to work for Henry Wiggins.

The cricket team is recorded between 1969 and 1976 and was sponsored by Eric Jay, a local businessman. They did not win any honours, but former player Roy Joshua remembered playing for the club in the Evening League.

Invitation Sides

Lamputts XI

Gordon Lamputt is very much a Hereford man who was born in Barroll Sreet and, during the Second World War, served with distinction in the R.A.F. He came out of the Air Force in 1947 and ran the A.T.C. Squadron in Hereford. Gordon always had a passion for cricket, and it was a

Lamputts XI, Division Two winners 1952
Back row: Les Pope, Nelson Carter, Sid Gunstone, Stan Kaye, Ted Woodriffe, Bob Delahaye, Ted Rees, Mr. Bates (umpire)
Front row: Elaine Lamputt (scorer), George Emerson, Derek Evans, Gordon Lamputt, Ray Grist

natural progression for him to take his cadets on to the King George Playing Fields for a game of cricket. One day in 1947 he was walking in the playing fields with a young lady (who eventually became Mrs. Elaine Lamputt) and started to talk to some local lads who were playing cricket. He was always losing his cadets to National Service and to help rectify the situation he eventually formed the Lamputt XI. They had no ground of their own and Gordon recalls booking Widemarsh Common for 10s. a day. The reputation of the team increased and they were able to play stronger opposition. Gordon was a good local cricketer who also played for Hereford City Sports Club, M.E.B., and Ediswan. The biggest obstacle was the lack of a home ground which meant that they were unable to play in the Evening League which was very strong at that time.

Early in 1952, Gordon Lamputt was approached by Hereford City Sports Club who suggested that, because the Lamputt XI had no home ground, they should amalgamate with the Sports Club. However, Gordon had been running a successful team for some years and was unwilling to lose its identity. There was a meeting at the Kerry Arms and it was eventually agreed that the Lamputt XI would retain their identity and name until they won the League. This they did in 1952 and they then became part of the Sports Club.

Charlie Thompson, the Hereford United foot-baller, played for the Lamputt XI in 1953 when they were renamed Hereford City Sports Club A. Gordon remembered playing in the same Sports Club team as the future test cricketer, Peter Richardson; he also played football with him for Canon Pyon.

When the Lamputt XI won their first trophy in 1952 they celebrated with a dinner at the Imperial Hotel in Widemarsh Street. It was a memorable fun occasion which emphasised the philosophy of the team. In May 1979 Gordon and Elaine Lamputt traced all the people who were in the photograph taken in 1952 and there was a 25th anniversary dinner held at How Caple Grange, and the photograph taken some 25 years earlier was recreated.

Adult Educational Sides

Hereford Technical College
The team was formed in 1954 for the benefit of teachers and students. They started playing evening friendly matches before entering the League. Eric Williams, a lecturer at the college, was involved with the club throughout its existence and was captain for much of the time. They were runners-up in Division Four in 1973 and runners-up in Division Three in 1974. An unusual tie occurred when they played Almeley and dismissed them for 26. To make the match more interesting, the captain decided to reverse his team's batting order. The result could hardly have been predicted for they achieved exactly the same total as Almeley! The club ceased to play in 1980.

Hereford High School Old Boys
The team played pre-war and joined the League soon after the war was over becoming Division One winners in 1952, 1954 and 1963. As well as old boys, the team included teachers from the school. One of the players was Bill

Lamputts XI celebrating winning Division Two in 1952
Back row: Mr Bates (umpire), [-], Andy Davies, Ted Rees, Les Pope, Stan Kaye
Front row: Gerry Franklyn, Johnny White, Sid Gunstone, Gordon Lamputt,
Ray Grist, Derek Evans, Nelson Carter, Ted Woodriffe, George Emerson

Morris, who played for Hereford City Sports Club and, at one stage, was chairman of the Evening League. The school produced many fine local cricketers but not all of them played for the old boys. These included the Warley twins, Ken Pole, John Keyte, and Phil Noakes. The team finished playing in about 1970.

Whitecross Academicals

The club was formed in 1973 when Angus Macintyre, who was on the school staff, suggested that a cricket team be formed because many of the staff were young and already played other games. The first match was a friendly against the Lads Club. During the first season they fielded some parents and senior pupils. The team had to leave the ground at Woolhope rather hastily during a friendly match in the early days when the wicketkeeper, who later became an umpire, was spotted by the opposition tapping the base of the stumps with his foot as the ball went past!

The club played on King George's Playing Fields until 1987 when they then played their home matches on a new artificial wicket at Whitecross School. A match was played to celebrate the opening of the artificial wicket. Two first-class cricketers, Steve Rhodes and Graham Dilley from Worcestershire, played in the game.

The club had some success in the Evening League. They were Division Three runners-up in 1986 and the following year were runners-up to Sun Valley in the Division Two/Three Cup. The match was played on the Bulmer's ground off King's Acre Road. Success was finally achieved in 1988 when they won the Division Two Cup beating B.R.S.A. in the final. They won the Hereford Evening League Junior Cup in 1988, and the team is shown on the photograph (below). Two founder members of the club, Dave Roberts and Dave Riley, played throughout the club's existence until it folded in 2004.

Whitecross Academicals 1958
Back row: Mark Lawrence, Dave Riley, Simon Barton, Stuart Wigley (captain), Martin Skirrow, John Harries,
Roger Norgate, Andy Lawrence
Front row: Dave Roberts, Pete Hobbs, Wayne Barton, Paul Lavis

Old Collegiates (Cartoon by Peter Manders c.1980)

Old Collegiates
In 1974, when the Evening League was in its prime, Adrian Davies and Eddie Phillips (two Teachers' College lecturers) formed a team to play in the League, which they did for 10 years. After the College closed in 1978 the team continued to play until 1983 when they gained promotion (see cartoon above). Several well-known local sportsmen played for the team, including Selwyn Vale, who had a successful football career with Hereford United.

Youth Clubs

Garden City
The team was formed in 1953 from the members of a youth club based in Bulmers Avenue, and continued playing until about 1969. They were successful in 1964 when they won the Fourth Division and the following year when they won the Third Division and then the Second in 1966. In 1968 they won the Third Division title once again. They repeated their success in the 1970s, for three years running. They won the Fourth Division title in 1972, the Third Division the following year and the Second in 1974.

The successful side in 1966 was Rodney Grinnell, R. Lewis, Alan Watkins, Roger Jenkins, Phil Donovan, P. Hall, Bill Lucas, K. Syed, A.C. Nash, N. Bell and Trevor Roberts.

Hinton Cricket Club / Hinton Youth Club
There was a meeting at The Duke's Head Inn, then in St. Martin's Street, on 22 February 1947 with a view to forming a new team to be called St. Martin's Cricket Club. The formation of the team went ahead, but not under the proposed name,

becoming the Hinton Cricket Club. The team played on the King George VI Playing Fields, which was originally part of the Hinton Court Estate, the Court being situated where Hinton Crescent now stands. The estate was sold after the Second World War and the Hinton Housing Estate was built in about 1949. The team eventually became Hinton Youth Club. The headquarters of the Youth Club, which was formed in 1946, was a First World War Nissen Hut in Hinton Road, which was situated on the site currently occupied by the Welsh Club car park. Jock Thomson, who turned out for the team occasionally with his father-in-law Bill Inight, recalled that he held his wedding reception in the hut and that the cost was 7s. 6d. per head. They then moved to a room at the former Redhill Hostel on a temporary basis, and moved to their present premises in Ross Road in the 1950s.

They played their home games on the Bishop's Meadow and won Division Four in 1961 and Division Three in 1966.

A former player, Bob Gardiner, recalled an amusing incident that happened during a match on the

Garden City Youth Club c.1955
Back row: J. Rogers, D. Bridges, B. Bridges, B. Parry, N. Jones,
D. Gagg, M. Knowles (umpire)
Front row J. Palamountain, J. Chamberlain, A. Wainwright (captain),
J. Powell, J. Tyler

Hinton Youth Club c.1949
Back row: L. Preedy, [-], Tommy Mann Middle row: ? Elcox, Eric Jay, , Les (Keki) Davies, Don Bateman, [-]
Front row: Harry Inight, Eric Hurd, Peter Buchanan, Sam Waite, Jim Baker, [-]

Y.M.C.A. Cup winners in 1954
Back row: Mr. Daw (umpire), Tony Day, Alan Rudge, Pete Daw, Arthur Harris,
Charlie Layton, Jim Preece
Front row: Alan Griffiths, Cliff Reese, Eric Griffiths (captain), Ken Pole,
Ken Procter, Chubby Daw

Bishop's Meadow. He was bowling at an aggressive batsman and moved his long on fielder to cow corner and told him to look out for the last ball of his over. He intended this to be a slower one to tempt the batsman to have a go at him. The plan almost worked – the ball was hit in the air in the direction of cow corner, the fielder ran in towards it and dived forward to make the catch. Unfortunately, as he fell to the ground on his stomach, the impact caused the ball to slip through his fingers; his false teeth shot out and they ended up firmly lodged in his hands!

The Buchanan family, of Richmond Club fame, were also very much involved with Hinton. The family emigrated from St. Kitts and produced some fine sportsmen in the county. Tony Buchanan not only played cricket locally, but also played first-class football for Chelsea. Peter played cricket for Hinton and Wyevale and also played football at a high level for Arsenal. Alwyn played cricket for Wyevale and Robin played for the Saracen's Head and the Richmond Club. Molly Buchanan married Archie Phillips and their son, Stewart, was a professional footballer for West Bromwich Albion and Hereford United.

The team won Division Four of the Evening League in 1961; and they were Division Three runners-up in 1965, winning that Division the following year. They were also runners-up in Division Two in 1968 and 1971. They ceased playing in 1974.

Y.M.C.A.

The Young Men's Christian Association team is recorded as playing as early as 1910. They entered the newly formed Hereford and District Cricket League in 1920 and emerged as champions, winning the Hereford Times Trophy. At the A.G.M. the following year the treasurer revealed that they had a credit balance of £2 1s. 7d. In 1925 they applied to play their home matches at Widemarsh Common, mainly as a result of their success the previous year.

They were founder members of the Evening League in 1927 and the team won the League's Division One trophy in the first season of its reformation in 1946. They won the same title nine years later, and were also League winners in 1959 and 1960 and were cup winners in 1954, 1959 and 1963. The photograph (above) shows the victorious 1954 side. Included in the side was Ken Procter, who became a Hereford umpire after his playing days.

Also in this side was one of the best known players in Hereford cricket circles – Ken Pole, a former High School pupil, who was very much involved with the team and, following his playing career, became a long-standing successful umpire until he died in 2006. They never lost their

Division One status, but the club was disbanded due to lack of interest in 1972.

Nomads

The Nomads played cricket from 1967 until 1985. They were Division Three winners in 1969 and they won the Coronation Cup the following year. A newly-formed Nomads B won the Evening League Junior Cup in 1985, whilst the A team won the Senior Cup the same year. In 1986 the A team won the Senior Cup and in 1988 the B team won Division Two and the Senior Cup. Some of the players in the early years were, Malcolm Hughes, Viv Thomas, Stewart Blyth, Jim Knipe, Dennis Jackson, and Terry Morgan, who was the captain.

Other Teams

The following teams are known to have played in the Evening League from time to time, but despite research no additional details have been found.

Hereford Academicals

This team won the new Division Two championship in 1984 and Division One in 1985.

H.C.S.O.S.

They won the new Division Two in 1976.

Belmont Abbey

Belmont Abbey School entered a team in the Evening League between 1991 and 1993.

Hunderton Youth Club.

The Youth Club had two successes in the League, winning the Division Four titles in 1967 and 1969.

Bartonsham

This team is recorded playing in the inaugural year in 1927.

Berrows Newspapers

Berrows, owners of the *Hereford Times*, had a team that played from 1927 to 1929.

British Legion

This team played in 1978 and 1979.

Cavanagh's

This team played between 1985 and 1988.

College of Education

The College appears to have played only in 1972.

Hergarr

An oddly-named team that played from 1985.

Midland Red

The team from the 'bus company, Midland Red, were runners-up in Division Three in 1954.

Mother's Pride

The bakery team was active from 1967 to 1973.

Pegasus

This team has been playing since 1985.

South Herefordshire District Council

This local government team played in the 1980s and won Division Three in 1986 and the Paul Levy Knockout Cup in 1984.

South Wye

This team was active in the 1970s and was runners-up in Division Four in 1972.

Spread Eagle

This pub team played in 1985 and 1986.

Tesco's

The supermarket team played from 1985 until 1994.

Treacle Mine

This team took players from the Saracen's Head team when it folded in 1988 and was active from 1985 until 1998.

Widemarsh

This team played from 1975 until 1980.

Wyedean

This team has been playing since 1985.

Ambulance Service

Nothing known.

B.N.S. (South Wye)

Nothing known.

Hereford Taxis

Nothing known.

CHAPTER V

Herefordshire County Cricket Club

Cricket is first recorded in Hereford in 1836 when there is a report that the City Cricket Club was formed. In 1850 an England XI came to Widemarsh Common and played a Herefordshire XXII; the match was watched by 3,000 spectators who cheered a 14-run victory by the home county. W.G. Grace played in the county in the 1860s and in 1896.

The first part of the 20th century proved to be an encouraging one for the county. Home and away fixtures with Worcester Club and Ground were arranged and the driving force behind this was P.H. Foley from Stoke Edith. Matches were played against the M.C.C. in the early part of the century as well as against local teams. The *Hereford Times* on 30 April 1904 reported that the Club & Ground had fixtures against E.C.S at Garnons, the Cathedral School, Ledbury, Bromyard, Leominster, Ross, and A.W. Fosters XI at Brockhampton.

The Pavilion on Widemarsh Common in 2006. The pavilion was originally thatched

W.G. Grace (seated, third from right) playing in Hereford in the 1890s

The home ground at the beginning of the century was at Widemarsh Common. In 1907 there were problems with the pitch at Widemarsh, which was used by several clubs more or less at the same time. The ground was covered with molehills and local children used it as a play-ground. It was suggested that the club endeavour to find an alternative venue for their home matches and the Racecourse was suggested. The matter was brought to a head at the A.G.M. in 1908; however, there were other problems within the club in 1908 apart from the pitch at Widemarsh. The playing season did not start until the end of May and the Club & Ground Team played Ledbury at Widemarsh on 4 June – for the record the home team won.

In 1908 the treasurer was Mr. T.W. Allen of Lloyds Bank and the members' subscription was £2 10s. per annum. In the same year the club sent a circular requesting donations in order to purchase a cricket ground on the Racecourse consisting of about 10 acres. The circular stated that £400 was needed and that subscriptions should be sent to Mr. Allen of Lloyds Bank or Mr. G.A. Denny of Yarsop. The circular informed readers that the following monies had already been promised: Sir James Dinham £25; 'an old cricketer' £25; A.W. Foster £25; Farrar Eckroyd £10; Sir Joseph Verein, Bart. £10; Rev. A.E. Green Price £25 G.A. Denny £25; Capt. Rolleston 5 guineas; C.J. Gwyer £10; and C.W. Hazlehurst £25.

Matters improved for the Club in 1909 when they made the move from Widemarsh to their new home on the Racecourse. The opening game on 1 May 1909 was an invitation match, arranged by the Dean of Hereford, between H. Leveson Gower's XI (the Surrey captain) and H.K. Foster's XI. Leveson Gower and Foster were in the same Oxford University side in 1895. Henry Leveson Gower, whose nickname was Shrimp, was knighted in 1953 for his services to cricket as a legislator and Test selector.

A new groundsman was appointed in 1910. He was Thomas Perks, the father of Reg Perks, who was born in Worcester on 2 October 1883. He was a wicket-keeper and played one game for the M.C.C. in 1902. He spent most of his life in Herefordshire and played for Holmer Cricket Club. He died in Ledbury on 15 January 1953. He is seated on the right-hand side of the photograph of Holmer cricket club taken in 1910 (page 69).

The First World War took its toll on normality even after it finished. Cricket did not start in earnest until 1920. H.K. Foster was appointed captain and he held that post until 1922.

On Whit Monday 1922 there was a match between Hereford A and Gloucester A. The Hereford team won thanks largely to an unbeaten 115 from H.K. Foster, who had not lost his form despite not having played much cricket of late. In addition to his Herefordshire duties he was appointed to the board of England Selectors in 1921 and appointed to select the England team to play Australia. He was at the same time an estate agent practising in Broad Street, Hereford. He had settled in Tarrington after 12 successful seasons as captain of Worcestershire.

Foster's team included a man who was going to have a great influence on Herefordshire cricket up to, and after, the Second World War – Lieutenant-Colonel C.M. Thornycroft D.S.O. C.B.E., who was captain from 1922 until 1925 and then from 1930 until the war broke out in 1939. He had moved to Herefordshire after a successful military career. As secretary and treasurer, he reported at the A.G.M. for 1927 that more support was needed for the club if it was to survive. The members subscriptions for that year totalled £224 14s. Col. Thornycroft also reported that the new evening league matches were successful, and advised that applications to play on the ground had been received from the Post Office and Hereford Times teams, and the Secondary and Elementary Schools. The Chairman, H.K. Foster, expressed concern at the proposal to have the Three Counties Show on the Racecourse. He said that if it went ahead it would mean an end to Cricket Club activities. The club

had spent £600 on laying out the ground and irreparable damage would be done to the pitch so cricket would not able to be played for some time after the show had finished. He also expressed concern at the future of schoolboys playing cricket if the facility was lost. He said that 30 to 40 youngsters played there every night of the week.

In 1928 Herefordshire County Cricket Club entered into a 14-year lease with Herefordshire County Council for nine acres of ground at the Racecourse, the rent being £60 per year. Thus the problem of a permanent home for the county's premier side was solved.

The years between the wars can be summarized as the Foster and Thornycroft years because of the input they both put into Herefordshire cricket, both on and off the field of play. During this period Col. Thornycroft's three sons all played cricket. Towards the end of the 1934 season, H.K. Foster made a presentation to Colonel Thornycroft at the County Cricket Club. It was a portrait of the Colonel, which was to be hung in the cricket pavilion at the Racecourse.

On 24 October 1939 the Hon. Secretary wrote to members saying that, following an extraordinary meeting, the club would terminate its activities owing to the impossibility of carrying on under war conditions. Cricket resumed after the war and in 1953 Hereford City Council turned down the Estates Committee recommendations that the cost of playing on the ground be: £1 weekdays; 25s. Saturdays; and 30s. Sundays. The Council obviously favoured cricket as it was agreed that the cost would be 15s. for any day. Several weeks later a letter was sent to the parks superintendent stating that lives had been put at risk by the introduction of the uniform charge of 15s. because of the poor playing surface.

Efforts were made to form a Minor Counties side from the 1950s onwards. During this time Herefordshire Representative sides played against Shrewsbury, Monmouthshire, Radnorshire, Breconshire and a Worcestershire League XI. They also played in national knockout competitions and travelled as far as the Isle of

Wight to play and to advertise the County's cricket ability. Latterly the games were organised by the Hereford Cricket Association, Peter Sykes and the late Eric Jenkins being the main motivators. The sides included many good local cricketers including Ken Watson, Steve Watkins, Paul Sparrow, Ian Macklin, Phil Hunt, Tracy Goodwin and many others. Many other fine cricketers have influenced the County during the last century, including:

J.F. Mclean, who was born in Aclington, Northumberland on 1 March 1901. He played first-class cricket for Gloucestershire and Worcestershire between 1919 and 1932. He died at Ross-on-Wye on 9 March 1986.

Colonel C.M. Thornycroft, who has already been referred to, was involved in Herefordshire cricket after he settled in the County in 1922 following a distinguished army career both in the Boer War and the First World War. He played regularly between the wars and when cricket started up again after the Second World War, he wrote to the *Hereford Times* on 15 September 1946 deploring the fact that there was not a decent cricket ground in Hereford. Col. Thornycroft had three sons all of whom were involved in Herefordshire cricket between the wars – N.M. Thornycroft, C.G.M. Thornycroft and, the most successful of his sons, Lieut. Col. Guy Thornycroft. Guy took a touring team to India in January 1946 and in one match scored 31 and took 5 wickets for 74 runs. His one match for Worcestershire was in June 1947 when he appeared for the County, undoubtedly as a guest player, against the Combined Services XI in a 3-day match on Hereford Racecourse. He was clearly excited by the match because he wrote to the *Hereford Times* on 2 August 1946 asking Hereford cricket enthusiasts to support the match because it was the first first-class match that had been played in Hereford since 1919. The Worcestershire side also included Henry Horton and Reg Perks, who were both born in Herefordshire and enjoyed successful and long careers in the first-class game.

On 2 August 1947, shortly after his appearance for Worcestershire, Guy Thornycroft was playing for Herefordshire Gentlemen against a South Wales Hunt Cricket Team and scored 203.

It is interesting to note that Peter Richardson, who went on to play for Worcestershire and England, scored 2 in the same match. Guy Thornycroft died in Reading on 8 January 1999.

Sir Derrick Bailey was born in London on 15 August 1915. He played 60 times for Gloucestershire between 1949 and 1952. He captained Herefordshire when his first-class career was over. As there was no first-class cricket on Sundays in the 1940s and '50s, he was free to play on Sundays in Herefordshire and did so on many occasions. At the A.G.M. in 1951, which was chaired by Sir Derrick, discussion took place regarding the possibility of Herefordshire entering the Minor Counties League. Four games were arranged to assess the strength of the county. They were against Glamorgan Seconds, Worcestershire, Gloucestershire, and Shropshire. It took the county some 40 years to bring to fruition the dream of the previous generation and in 1992 Herefordshire joined the Minor Counties League, replacing Durham, who were promoted to become a first-class county.

Sir Paul Getty, who was awarded the freedom of the city of Hereford because of his association with the retention of the Mappa Mundi in Hereford, was also a keen cricket supporter and became a patron of the club.

The first competitive game in the Minor Counties League was played at Brockhampton on 24 and 25 May 1992 and was against Wales. Herefordshire won the exciting match by 5 wickets off the last ball of the match. The captain was Herefordshire born Richard Skyrme and the side included six other Hereford born players. The County was runner-up in the Holt Cup at Lords in 1995, losing to Cambridgeshire in the final. In the following years they played first-class Counties Somerset, Yorkshire, Worcestershire, and Middlesex in the NatWest Competition.

One of the club's greatest achievements was beating Middlesex in 2001. They won the championship in the same year. The Minor Counties side's first competitive match against a first-class county was against Yorkshire in 1999. On 30 August 2000 the Herefordshire Minor Counties side achieved one of their greatest

Minor Counties Championship
HEREFORDSHIRE v WALES M.C.
Played at Brockhampton C.C. on 24th & 25th May 1992

WALES M.C.	1st innings		2nd innings	
A. Jones	not out	100	ct. M. Robinson b D. Robinson	25
A. Harris	ct. Fowles b Holland	15	ct. & b. D. Robinson	46
D. Hemp	not out	127	ct. Sparrow b. Abberley	33
R. Moore			l.b.w. b Abberley	18
J. Derrick			ct. Skyrme b D. Robinson	23
A.C. Puddle			not out	13
B.J. Lloyd	DID NOT BAT		ct. Mokler b D. Robinson	4
Shaw				
A. Smith			DID NOT BAT	
R. Wiseman				
G. Edwards				
	Lb 10, w 2, nb 4	16	b1, Lb 10, w 2, nb1,	14
WALES M.C. WON TOSS	TOTAL (1dec) 258		TOTAL (6 dec) 176	

21,

M.F.D.Robinson	8.1 - 1 - 47 - 0	53, 96, 127, 136, 168, 176
E.R.M.Holland	15 - 2 - 68 - 1	M.F.D.Robinson	8 - 1 - 25 - 0
S.D.Verry	14 - 6 - 39 - 0	M.G.Fowles	11 - 2 - 26 - 0
M.Fowles	8 - 2 - 24 - 0	D.C.D.Robinson	14 - 3 - 84 - 4
D.C.M.Robinson	18 - 2 - 70 - 0	E.R.M.Holland	5 - 0 - 17 - 0
		M.C.Abberley	5 - 0 - 13 - 2

HEREFORDSHIRE	1st innings		2nd innings	
S.G. Watkins	ct. Hemp b. Derrick	4	ct. Harris b. Smith	70
M.C. Abberley	ct. Puddle b. Edwards	7	(4) run out	31
J.W.D. Leighton	ct. Hemp b Lloyd	44	(3) run out	70
R.P. Skyrme	st. Shaw b. Edwards	29	(5) not out	1
P.L.J. Sparrow	ct. Hemp b Lloyd	32	(1) l.b.w. b. Smith	13
M.F.D. Robinson	run out	1	(6) not out	64
S.D. Verry	b. Derrick	9		
M.G. Fowles	ct. Jones b Derrick	5	DID NOT BAT	
D.J. Mokler	not out	10		
E. Holland	not out	10	(2) ct. Edwards b. Wiseman	0
D.C.M. Robinson	DID NOT BAT		DID NOT BAT	
	Lb.12, w 4, nb2	18	Lb 17	17
	TOTAL (8 dec)	176	TOTAL 5 wkts	266

12, 72, 110, 112, 128, 141, 142

J. Derrick	26 - 5 - 62 - 3	3, 128, 154, 184, 264,
G. Edwards	23 - 7 - 48 - 2	R. Wiseman	9 - 2 - 24 - 1
B.J. Lloyd	21 - 12 - 40 - 2	J. Derrick	11 - 1 - 99 - 0
A. Smith	2 - 0 - 7 - 0	G. Edwards	3 - 1 - 16 - 0
		A. Smith	17 - 1 - 82 - 2
		B.J. Lloyd	11 - 1 - 68 - 0

HEREFORDSHIRE WON BY 5 WICKETS, OFF LAST BALL OF THE MATCH.
Herefordshire's first Minor Counties Championship Match.
umpires S. Kuhlmann, W. Morgan

Herefordshire Minor Counties versus Wales. First match 1992. Played at Brockhampton

Back row: S. Verry, P. Sparrow, M. Abberley, M. Fowles, E. Holland, J. Leighton, M. Robinson

Front row: E. Jenkins (coach), D. Mockler, R. Skyrme (captain), S. Watkins, E. Robinson

successes when they went to Lords, the home of cricket, and beat Cheshire by 42 runs in the final of the 38 County Cup. Herefordshire amassed 291 runs for 6 wickets off their 50 overs whilst Cheshire was restricted to 249 runs for 9 wickets. Derek Hince, the match manager of the Minor Counties team, received the Sports Council Service to Cricket Award on 8 Feb 2001. In 2002 they were the joint Minor Counties champions, winning the western division of the Minor Counties League.

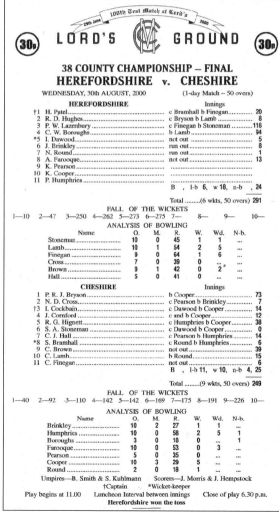

LORD'S GROUND
(MCC)
100th Test Match at Lord's
29th June — 2000
30p. 30p.

38 COUNTY CHAMPIONSHIP — FINAL
HEREFORDSHIRE v. CHESHIRE
WEDNESDAY, 30th AUGUST, 2000   (1-day Match – 50 overs)

HEREFORDSHIRE	Innings	
†1 H. Patel	c Bramhall b Finegan	20
2 R. D. Hughes	c Bryson b Lamb	8
3 P. W. Lazenbury	c Finegan b Stoneman	118
4 C. W. Boroughs	b Lamb	94
*5 I. Dawood	not out	5
6 J. Brinkley	run out	8
7 N. Round	run out	1
8 A. Farooque	not out	13
9 K. Pearson		
10 K. Cooper		
11 P. Humphries		
	B , l-b 6, w 18, n-b ,	24
	Total ....(6 wkts, 50 overs)	291

FALL OF THE WICKETS
1—10   2—47   3—250   4—262   5—273   6—275   7—   8—   9—   10—

ANALYSIS OF BOWLING

Name	O.	M.	R.	W.	Wd.	N-b.
Stoneman	10	0	45	1	1	...
Lamb	10	1	54	2	5	...
Finegan	9	0	64	1	6	...
Cross	7	0	39	0	...	...
Brown	9	1	42	0	2	...
Hall	5	0	41	0	...	...

CHESHIRE	Innings	
1 P. R. J. Bryson	b Cooper	73
2 N. D. Cross	c Pearson b Brinkley	7
†3 I. Cockbain	c Dawood b Cooper	14
4 J. Cornford	c and b Cooper	12
5 R. G. Hignett	c Humphries b Cooper	38
6 S. A. Stoneman	c Dawood b Cooper	0
7 C. J. Hall	c Pearson b Humphries	14
*8 S. Bramhall	c Round b Humphries	6
9 C. Brown	not out	39
10 C. Lamb	b Round	15
11 C. Finegan	not out	6
	B , l-b 11, w 10, n-b 4,	25
	Total ....(9 wkts, 50 overs)	249

FALL OF THE WICKETS
1—40   2—92   3—110   4—142   5—142   6—169   7—175   8—191   9—226   10—

ANALYSIS OF BOWLING

Name	O.	M.	R.	W.	Wd.	N-b.
Brinkley	10	2	27	1	1	...
Humphries	10	0	58	2	5	1
Boroughs	3	0	18	0	...	1
Farooque	10	0	53	0	3	...
Pearson	5	0	35	0	...	...
Cooper	10	3	29	5	...	...
Round	2	0	18	1	...	...

Umpires—B. Smith & S. Kuhlmann   Scorers—J. Morris & J. Hempstock
†Captain   *Wicket-keeper
Play begins at 11.00   Luncheon Interval between innings   Close of play 6.30 p.m.
Herefordshire won the toss

*Herefordshire beating Cheshire at Lords in the
ECB 38 County Cup Final in 2000*

Above top:
Back row: J. Shaw, P. Thomas, A. Farooque, I. Dawood
Middle row: D. Hince, M. Morgan, J. Chadd (President),
E. Morgan, K. Cooper, P. Lazenbury, K. Pearson, J. Brinkley,
R. Hughes, N.Prabhu, P. Humphries, J. Beaman, P. Sykes,
Gwynne Jones, D. Wood, J. Morris
Sitting:. N. Round, N. Nenadich (chairman), H. Patel
(captain), B. Smith (chairman of cricket), C. Boroughs,

*Above: The players balcony at Lords
on 30 August 2000*

Left: The scorecard for the match

58

In May 2003 the newly-formed club played their inaugural match against Worcestershire 2nd at Wyeside, the home ground of Hereford Cathedral School.

In the early days the county club was able to employ the services of some exceptionally fine former County players including:

Alvin Kallicharan, who was born in British Guiana in 1949. He played in 66 tests for the West Indies and played for Warwickshire in the County Championship. At the end of his first-class career, he played for Herefordshire in the Minor Counties.

Neal Radford was born on 7 June 1957 in Northern Rhodesia. When Neal came to the U.K. it was to South Wales because of his love for rugby. He was spotted playing local cricket and ended up in the Lancashire League. He then signed for Lancashire, but his stay there was not very successful and he then went to Worcestershire where he enjoyed a first-class career that lasted some 17 years. He played in three test matches and six one-day internationals for England. Neal was Wisden Cricketer of the Year in 1986. He took more than 100 wickets in a season on three separate occasions. When he retired from the first-class game he had taken 994 wickets at an average of 26.86. After leaving first-class cricket he represented Herefordshire with distinction in Minor Counties cricket, forming a formidable opening bowling partnership with Kevin Cooper.

Kevin Cooper was born on 27 December 1957 at Sutton-in-Ashfield, Nottinghamshire. He enjoyed a first-class career that lasted 20 years, playing for Gloucestershire and Nottinghamshire. He played in 305 first-class matches and took 817 wickets at an average of 26.94. He was one of the most influential cricketers to play for the club. He played for the County team from 1996 until 2003. In his career with Herefordshire he bowled 1,535.3 overs including 472 maidens. He took 221 wickets at an average of 14.79. He was a true clubman and his experience was invaluable to the County. He was awarded his County cap in 2000.

Martin McCague was born on 24 May 1969 in Ireland. He was raised in Australia but chose to play for England. He had a successful first-class

Kevin Cooper receiving his County Cap from Nick Nenadich.

career playing for Kent and Western Australia and also played in three test matches for England. Martin enjoyed a successful time playing for Herefordshire.

Reuben Spring was born in Southport, Lancashire on 13 November 1974, but was brought up in Hereford when his father joined Hereford United. He was a gifted cricketer and after enjoying much success in local cricket he signed for Worcestershire in 1994. He played in 45 matches scoring 2,237 runs at an average of 32.89. He scored four centuries and 13 half-centuries. His career came to a premature end because of injury in 2000. Reuben's father, Peter Spring, was a footballer and also a useful cricketer.

The cricket authorities in Hereford are satisfied that young talent is coming through in the county to ensure that a good standard of cricket will be maintained. For instance, Ashley Nahorniak followed in his sister's footsteps by playing youth cricket at Brockhampton. He then progressed to the county schoolboys team and from there to Swansea University Cricket Team which he captained. In August 2006 he made his debut for the Minor Counties side.

All clubs are dependent on the back-room boys and the County must certainly be indebted to Jim Morris who has acted as scorer for many years.

Herefordshire Gentlemen

The 1935 Herefordshire Gentlemen
Back row: E. Morris (scorer), A.E. Brooks, H.A. Picton, N.M. Thornycroft, C.G.M.
Thornycroft, C.M. Thornycroft, S. Morris
Front row: G.L. Clay with Benjamin, C.K. Foster, Col. C.M. Thornycroft (captain),
R.E.H. Bailey, S.T. Freeman

Herefordshire Gentlemen playing at Worcester
Back row: D. Pash, D. Berisford, D. Bourne, J. Chadd, R.C. Brinstead
Front row: J.W. Steele, G.L. Clay, W.J. Foley, G.M. Thornycroft, J.S. Pitts

This team has been an integral part of Herefordshire Cricket for more than a century and many prominent Herefordshire cricketers have played for them.

In the first part of the century the Fosters, Foleys and Colonel Guy Thornycroft (who ran the team before the Second World War) dominated the team. G.L. Clay was in charge for 15 years after the war and recounted in the Herefordshire County Cricket 150th Anniversary book that they played about 12 matches a season. They played for about 10 consecutive days in in one season in early August playing two-day matches. Their opponents included the Suffolk and Shropshire Gentlemen.

In 1947 Colonel Thornycroft hit 203 runs off the South Wales Hunt XI, the second hundred coming in less than 30 minutes. When G.L. Clay retired in the 1960s Ernie Morgan took on the job of secretary. Harry Ellam helped organise the club through the 1980s. At various times they have played Worcestershire Gentlemen at Bransford near Worcester; Gloucestershire Gypsies; Shropshire Gentslemen at Shrewsbury School; and Warwickshire Imps at Edgbaston.

Cricket in the county continues to flourish at all levels and with the encouragement of local talent, plus the influx of talented outsiders, the future is indeed promising.

CHAPTER VI

City Clubs & Military Cricket

The City Clubs

There is obviously a limit to the number of teams that can play within the city limits because of the number of pitches available. The main grounds that have been used are the Racecourse, Widemarsh Common and King George VI Playing Fields, although some of the teams – especially works teams – were lucky enough to have their own grounds. Many teams played Evening League Cricket and are described in chapter IV.

In the years following the end of the Second World War, a cricket match could be watched on Widemarsh Common or on the King George VI Playing Fields most summer evenings.

Hereford City Sports Club

The Club is based in Grandstand Road adjacent to the Racecourse. On 14 March 1946 there was a meeting at the Town Hall when it was unanimously agreed that the Hereford City Sports Club should be formed. The meeting was so successful that, by the start of the 1946 cricket season, the Club had a First and Second XI both with full fixture lists, 43 fixtures having been arranged for that season. Their first match was on 24 May when they played the Lads' Club at Widemarsh and won by 104 runs. Jack Goodwin was the first post-war captain from 1946 until 1949 and was a fine all-round cricketer. In 1946 the club played an Australian United Services XI. The Australians were a high standard team that toured the country after the war.

In November 1946 there was a report in the *Hereford Times* on the progress of a financial appeal for the club to develop part of Hereford Racecourse – £3,000 was needed.

Hereford City Sports Club 1947
Back row: Charlie Capper, Alan Morgan, Ted Johnson, Cliff Carr, Terry Collins, Geoff Morris, Ted Gallimore, Robbie Richardson, Ron Deacon, Roy Humphries (scorer)
Front row: Peter Richardson, Hugh Jenkins, Jack Goodwin, Vernon Grindon, Ted Strange

During the late 1940s and early '50s players were so keen to play for the club that they were willing to pay for their cricket. On one occasion when the club's First XI was due to play a match at Colwall the Hereford team arrived at the ground during a downpour and the match had to be abandoned. One Sports Club First Team player drove straight back to Hereford, crossed the palm of a Second team youngster with half-a-crown and took his place in the team. Such nefarious methods demonstrate how keen cricketers were immediately after the war years.

The photograph of the 1947 team (previous page) includes Peter Richardson, who just 10 years later was playing for England, and Robbie Richardson, his uncle, who was 'Mr. Kington' for many years. Also in the picture is Ted Johnson who was a well-known architect in Hereford for many years.

In the 1950s a young man who came to Hereford to work was Peter Harrison. He asked the club if he could play for them and the captain, John Chadd, gave him a run in the second team. Peter turned out to be one of the finest batsmen to play for the club. In his first two innings for the second team he scored a century on successive days. He was promoted to the first team immediately and scored four centuries in his first five innings.

The photograph of the successful 1977 team (bottom right) shows Steve Watkins, Mike Rose.

Hereford City Sports Club 1956
Back row: W. Morris, R. Birkett, N. Sandford, P. Harrison (captain), G.Gilbert, D. Evans, R. Humphries (scorer)
Front row: E. Jenkins, E.A. Johnson, B. Pike, J. Goodwin, N. Pritchard

Hereford City Sports Club 1977
Three Counties League Challenge winners
Back row: Roy Humphries (scorer), Steve Watkins, Mick Hayward, Derek Stowe, Tracy Goodwin, Mike Rose, Harry Miles (umpire)
Front row: Neville Symonds Ernie Morgan, John Chadd (captain), Keith Edwards, Norman Davies, Eric Jenkins

Ernie Morgan, John Chadd, Norman Davies, and Eric Jenkins, all of whom have had a great influence on Herefordshire Cricket over the years.

City Sports Club 2nd. c.1970
Back row: Stewart Hince (scorer), Mick Carroll, Duncan Sedgwick, Brian Tipper,
Derek Hince, Mike Bradley, Dennis Fothergill, Cedric Clinkett, John Hall (umpire)
Front row: Vic Jones, Harry Ellam, Terry Court, Bob Binnersley,
Dave Keyte, Paul Griffiths

Hereford City Sports Club. Three Counties League Winners 1983
Back row: David James (umpire), Roy Humphries (scorer), Andrew Chadd, Richard
Skyrme, Tracy Goodwin, Phil Hunt, Bob Flack, Norman Davies, John Knill (umpire)
Front row: Ernie Morgan, Keith Edwards, Ken Watson, [-], Rob Watkins

When Mike Rose, the Hereford-born former Cambridge Blue and Leicestershire player, joined the club he was one of the most successful players and in 1969 won the award for the best batsman. The bowling award for the same year went to Keith Edwards, another local businessman, who played for the club for many years.

The club joined the Three Counties League when it was formed in 1971 and during the 1970s and '80s they were a force to be reckoned with, becoming champions from 1972 to 1977 and then in 1980, '81, '83 and '85 respectively. The photograph of the 1983 successful side includes many stalwarts of the club including Richard Skyrme, Norman Davies and Keith Edwards.

They were one of the most successful teams in the Hereford Evening League, winning the Division One championship on no fewer than 14 occasions between 1947 and 1975. They were also successful in the League cup on nine occasions between 1953 and 1975. In the 1960s and '70s much of their success was due to the opening bowling partnership of Keith Edwards and Brian Smith. On more than one occasion they each took nine wickets in an innings and they consistently had superb economical bowling figures. Norman Davies and John Chadd ably supported them. When the Evening League Division was re-organized in 1976, the club was placed in the Premier Division, which they duly won eight times between 1977 and 1985; they also won the

John Chadd, a well-known Hereford businessman, captained the club from 1960 until 1979 (see chapter XIV).

The first time they played weekend league cricket was when they were founder members of the Seven Counties League in 1968. This League did not last long, disbanding in 1970.

Coronation Cup on seven occasions between 1977 and 1983. Mention must be made of Derek Hince, another stalwart of the club, who played for many years and who, after his playing days were over, became the fund-raising secretary for Herefordshire Minor Counties, a post he still holds in 2007, 16 years later. There is also Roy Humphries who officiated as an umpire and scorer for a period of 40 years, and Tom Langford who, in addition to playing for the club, was such a fine groundsman for many years that he was snapped up by Worcestershire after they had experienced playing on the pitches that he had prepared. He became assistant groundsman at Worcester until his retirement.

The club used to organize an annual tour, called the Mercian Tour, to South Devon during the late 1960s. They have supported the county players from Worcestershire on more than one occasion. Indeed, one match was played against a Worcestershire XI on the Racecourse ground in support of Herefordshire born Dick Richardson's benefit. The Worcestershire side included two England players – Tom Graveney and Basil D'Oliviera. The first-class side batted first and found themselves 30 runs for 5 wickets. Herefordshire's opening bowling partnership of Brian Smith and Keith Edwards took the wickets between them. When Tom Graveney was dismissed, he is rumoured to have said to Herefordshire's captain, John Chadd, on his way back to the pavilion 'If you want to make a game of this I suggest that you replace those two opening bowlers.' Regrettably the match was abandoned because of rain but that did not detract from the ability of Messrs. Smith and Edwards.

On another occasion, the team hosted a benefit match for the Australian batsman Bill Alley, who was playing for Somerset at the time. At the end of the game Alley was handed £175. He had

enjoyed himself so much that he ended up in the bar with the Hereford team and stayed until about 3 o'clock in the morning. He left without the proceeds of his benefit match and a little the worse for wear. This obviously did not affect him as the following day he scored 190 for Somerset against Warwickshire. He had a successful season scoring 3,019 runs for his county.

In 1977 John Chadd was on a West Country tour of the Caribbean and had the idea of taking a Sports Club side there. On his return to Hereford, a committee including Norman Davies, Ernie Morgan, Alan Jones, and John himself, was set up. The tours to Barbados were extremely successful for the next ten years, playing against cricketers of the calibre of Desmond Haynes and Malcolm Marshall, two well-known West Indian Test players.

The old pavilion and changing rooms were eventually demolished and John Warr, the England and Middlesex player, opened the new clubhouse in 1990. The club amalgamated with the Herefordians in 2002 and the newly-formed club used the new facilities. All league and cup cricket were played under the name of Hereford City Cricket Club, with other social competitions under the name of Herefordians.

Old Herefordians 1957
Back row: Cecil Lilley, Paul Hill, Kit Danby(Scorer) Terry Morgan, Pete Morris, Brian Thomas, Randy Langford, Frank Wall, Laurie Teague, Malcolm Millichip
Front row: Dave Jones, Pete Johnson, Johnny Kettlewell (captain), Mike Hughes, Ted Rees

Old Herefordians / Herefordians

The original team – Old Herefordians – played at Widemarsh and Holmer. They are recorded playing at Widemarsh Common in 1910 and up to the outbreak of the First World War. They reformed in 1929 and continued playing until the Second World War.

Herefordians, Evening League Team 1980
Back row: Chris Smith, John Burgoyne, Richard Evans, Rob Johnson,
Rob Staite, Malcolm Hughes
Front row: Dave Keyte, Maurice Emburey, Richard Prime, Ted Amos, Sam Griffiths

Herefordians 1984. Invitation game for opening of pavilion
Back row: Robin Michael, Richard Prime, Terry Mason,
Gary Bendall, Richard Thorne
Front row: Phil Knight, Eric (Matey) Jenkins, Andy Brace, John Pritchard

After the war they won the Division One championship in 1962, 1964 and 1965, and the new Premier League in 1976. They won the Division Two championships in 1959 and 1963 and the League Cup in 1957. In the same year they were the first club outside the First Division to win the Coronation Cup when they defeated Division One runners-up, Y.M.C.A. They also won the Cup in 1964, 1965, and 1971. They won the new Premier Division in 1976.

Some of the stalwarts of the side were Randy Langford, Ted Amos, Trevor James, Terry Morgan, Ted Partington, Cecil Lilley and Malcolm Hughes.

Terry Mason and Keith Fortey started Herefordians Grafton in 1984. They played at the Grafton Inn on the A49 between Ross and Hereford. In their opening season they fielded an invitation team to commemorate the opening of their new pavilion which was originally a canteen that they had obtained from the S.A.S. Regiment at Bradbury Lines. They won the Division Three title in 1988. They also had a fine weekend side that travelled all round the county under the supervision of Ted Rees and Laurie Teague.

In 2002, because of problems with long term security at Grafton, they joined forces with Hereford City Sports Club in a bid to form a stronger club.

Hereford Doctors' XI

The team grew from an annual doctors' game against Burghill that was arranged by Dr. Anthony Evans. Friendly matches have been played since 1976, when all five matches were lost – after that the only way was up. Over the years the

Hereford Doctors' XI
Back row: Adrian Thomas, David Malins, Mike Allen, Tim Coleman, John Wood, Ian Reynolds,
Peter Johnstone (Lords Taverners. Hon, Doctor for the day)
Front row: Peter Richards, Steve Watkins, Henry Connor, Peter Wilson, Julian Wheeler, Andrew Corfield.

team has encouraged hospital staff, and especially junior doctors, who could only play irregularly because of their medical duties and training, to play cricket again. It has included medical and non-medical hospital staff, general practitioners, sons of doctors, and occasional ringers.

Until 1980 the side played on rough bumpy municipal pitches on Bishop's Meadow, opposite the old Hereford General Hospital. In 1981 the team began to use the Hereford Cathedral School ground at Wyeside. The long reign of groundsman Brian Goode ensured that the pitches and facilities were excellent, and the presence of a pavilion with a telephone (in pre-mobile days) enabled doctors who were on call to play. No less than three of the annual matches against the Cathedral School staff ended as ties.

Most matches were played at home, on Sundays or Thursday evenings, and opponents at different times included Worcester, Cheltenham, Abergavenny, and Sandwell hospital teams, plus some Herefordshire villages. One such was Harewood End, whom they played in alternate

years on Harewood End's hilltop concrete strip surrounded by a ring of tall decaying pine trees. This small ground formed a slightly sinister setting for cricket where they played against an effective fast bowler with an artificial leg, and where they had to deal with a serious ground invasion by a flock of sheep. Once they lost a ball, clearly visible but totally inaccessible, in a high fork of one of the dead conifers. Another rustic fixture was at Bodenham, where all players had to change behind an oak tree.

The side's most distinguished opposition were members of the Lords Taverners teams who played the hospital side in aid of charity in 1995 and 1997 in a splendid rural setting at Fownhope. The Taverners included cricketing stars plus other national celebrities – Ray East of Essex, who scored a century in the 1995 match; John Price of Middlesex and England; Fred Rumsey of Somerset and England; David Allen of Gloucestershire and England; musician and author Sir Tim Rice; and Rugby International J.P.R. Williams. Bill Frindall, encyclopedic contributor to Test Match Special, gave the public commentary. The hospital side led by physician Henry Connor invited a few local celebrities including jockey Peter Scudamore. One doctor was even asked for his autograph, no doubt mistaken for a star of stage or screen! The hospital side discovered that Taverners' matches have certain conventions – Taverners field first so that the spectators can straight away see the stars take the field (strange to a hospital side which, at best, might expect one or perhaps two unusually besotted girlfriends). In the second match they discovered that all Taverners bat when necessary, so the hospital side had to take 15 wickets to complete the visitors' innings.

The hospital team has its own style and conventions – and each year appoints a new captain, alternating between a member of the hospital staff and a G.P. For the last few years many of the players have been Indian, Pakistani or Bangladeshi doctors training at the County Hospital and bringing with them much talent and enthusiasm. The existence of the side has been good for hospital morale and companionship. Julian Wheeler and John Wood, two of the original players, still turn out occasionally thirty years after the club started.

Bulmer's / Woodpeckers

Cricket was played at the company's own sports ground in King's Acre Road. The cricket team shared the facility with the football, bowls, and archery teams. The club was formed in 1932 and Fred Jones, a former player, recalled that the original pavilion was burnt down in 1939 and a new one built. The new pavilion was a fine building which incorporated the club-house. The club resumed in 1946 after the war.

When Arthur Morris left the Royal Navy and joined the factory as Personnel Manager, anyone applying for a job was virtually guaranteed employment if he could play cricket. Morris was a much-respected man of good nature and played his cricket wearing a cravat. He was a good medium-pace bowler and will be remembered for his skilful organisation of matches against other brewery companies including Evan Evans from

Bulmer's 1970
Back row: Alf Marston (umpire), Dave Pullen, Stan Marston, Nigel Yarwood, Kenny Davies, John Chamberlain, Taffy Beavan (scorer)
Front row: Dave Long, Gerald Marchant, Jerry McManus, John Bullough, Mike Hands, Phil Donovan, Hedley Lawson

Bulmer's 1972
Back row: Dave Evans, Ronnie Burbeck, Dave Llewellyn, Jack Roberts, Kenny Gladwyn, David Gilbert Smith, Alf Marston (umpire)
Front row: Stan Marston, Clive Brazier, John Worle, Ken Davies, Nigel Yarwood

Neath, Bents of Stone, Stroud Brewery, Rhymney Brewery, Buchan of Oxford, and a local derby against Weston's Cider from Much Marcle.

They only played in the Evening League for two seasons winning Division Two in 1948 and the First Division the following year.

The best season was 1968 when Stan Marston totted up several centuries, Dave Long took 141 wickets at an average of 7, and Dave Marchant scored 1,400 runs at an average of 66. The following year Dave had two outstanding individual bowling figures of 9 wickets for 60 runs and 9 wickets for 17 runs.

They reformed as Woodpeckers in the Evening League in 1970 and won the new Premier Division in 1986, '87, '88 and '89. They also won the new Division One title in 1992.

Imperial Cricket Team

The manager of the Imperial Hotel in Widemarsh Street, Windsor Jones, formed the Imperial cricket team in 1984 because of his passion for the game. He decided to form his own team with the idea that any money raised would be given to charity. The team members were customers of the Imperial and the matches were all played on Sundays at away venues. They played local teams including Wormelow, Burghill and Tillington, Woolhope, and Leominster Grange. On one occasion they played the First Team players of Hereford United Football Club who were then managed by John Newman. Younger Imperial players went on to play for established teams in the Hereford Leagues. The Imperial was the meeting place for the Hereford Minor Counties Cricket Clubs and was also the first home of the Hereford Cricket Society. Windsor Jones has now retired from the Imperial, but still plays an active part in local cricket.

Wyesiders

Jack Roberts and Alan Taylor formed Wyesiders cricket team in

The Imperial

1977. They played at Aylestone School ground, formerly the High School. The team folded in 2002 and the side merged with Marden a year later. The photograph, taken in the 1980s, includes a second generation of players apart from Jack Roberts, Bruce Freeman and David Bird, who were in the original team. The 1977 team was picked from teachers and pupils from the Sixth Form College and Aylestone School.

Holmer

The team was playing in the early part of the 20th century and in 1910 included Tom Perks, the father of Reg Perks who went on to play county cricket

Wyesiders, late 1980s

Perks senior seated on the far right at Holmer cricket club in 1910

for Worcestershire. He is seated bottom right in the photograph (above) whilst F.H. Sunderland, who founded and gave his name to the local firm of estate agents, is the second one from the left on the same photograph. In 1910 Holmer played 19 matches, winning 12 and losing 5. In 1913 and '14 the team was playing their home matches at Widemarsh. The *Hereford Times* indicates that the club was playing once again in 1935, but they appear to have ceased playing sometime thereafter.

The former headmaster of Holmer School, D.V. Hopkins, recounted a nostalgic occasion that he witnessed at the Cheltenham Cricket Festival in about 1965. He was sitting near an elderly gentleman who was approached by a journalist. The gentleman was Michael Grace, the younger brother of W.G. Grace, who had played in Herefordshire on more than one occasion.

Lads' Club

The club's home ground is at Widemarsh Common, the original home of Herefordshire Cricket. The pavilion, which still stands, is one of the oldest in the county and can be traced back to the end of the 19th century. There are reports in local newspapers confirming that the team was playing at the beginning of the 20th century. They won the Thornycroft Knockout Cup and the Perrystone Challenge Cup in 1930 and were immaculately turned out in the photograph taken with the two cups (page 70).

The club played on and off in the Evening League in the years following the Second World War without a lot of success, but became a force in local cricket both in the League and the soon to be formed Saturday League, when it was established in 1972. They won Division Four in the first year.

Paul Purchase was appointed captain and Tony Lowe was the secretary. Other stalwarts in the early years were Phil Donovan, Chris Lane, Arthur Richards, Philip Daw, and Les Campbell. In 1975 Graham Smith and Hedley Lawson were the co-founders of the weekend team which competed in the 2nd Division of the newly-formed Herefordshire Saturday League. The Evening League side won the Doug Procter Memorial Cup for

Hereford Lads' Clubhouse

Lads' Club 1930s
Back row: [-], Geoff Marchant, Roly Hill, Arthur (Ally) Harris, [-], Dick Haymes,
Reg (Stodger) Williams, [-], [-]
Front [-], [-], [-], John Bolton, Fred (Tubby) Lawson, Edgar Hill,
Harold (Chubby) Daw, [-]

Lads' Club 1980
Back row: Arthur Richards, [-], Brian Robinson, Graham Smith, Hedley Lawson,
Phil Donovan, [-]
Front row: Philip Daw, [-], Garth Lawson, Arnie Palmer

four consecutive years from its inauguration in 1978. Philip Daw showed his batting prowess when he scored 108 runs in 20 overs in a Division Four match against the Gas Board.

The Lads' Club won Division Three in 1968 and 1973 and Division Two in 1974. In 1978 they won the new Division One title and won it again in 1981, '84 and '86. They also won the Brockhampton Cup in 1985.

Three families have provided players for more than one generation with Geoff Marchant, Chubby Daw and Fred Lawson continuing family connections with the club.

Saunders Valve

Saunders Valve is a good example of a works side formed in the years after the war. It was formed in 1959 and entered the Evening League in 1962. They won the Division Four title in their first year, the Division Three title in 1963, and the Division Two title in 1964 and 1968. They won the Brockhampton Cup in 1965. These were their glory years for the club folded in 1980.

Shop Assistants

Until relatively recently, Thursday was half-day closing in the retail trade in Hereford and, to compensate, shops were open all day Saturday but now many shops are open seven days a week. Sportsmen formed mid-week leagues and played friendly matches on their half-day and on Sundays to compensate for Saturdays. Shop Assistants was formed in 1952 by Ivan (Ivor) Bishop, Ernie Preece, Danny Wright and Roy Powell. They joined the Hereford Evening League in 1954 and won Division Three in their first year. They won the Third Division again in 1967 and the Second Division in 1969. They also won the League Cup in 1972 and 1973. The photograph (opposite page) shows the side at the

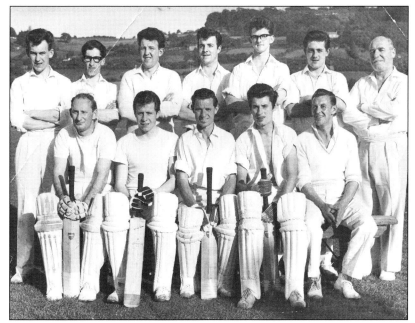

SAUNDERS VALVE
CRICKET CLUB

CRICKET FIXTURES
SEASON — 1959

Hon. Secretary—Mr. L. J. Christian.

Hon. Treasurer— Mr. W. J. Aston.

Address :-

c/o Saunders Valve Co. Ltd.,
Blackfriars Street,
Hereford.

Home Fixtures to be played at Holmer
Sports Ground (late Thynnes Sports Ground)

Left: Saunders Valve team c.*1963   Right: Fixture card 1959*
Back row: Bob Downes, Tony Body, Mick Carroll, Ray Phillips, Simon Swancott, Mick Williams, Arthur Ridler
Front row: Ken Perks, Ollie Tooze, John Dewey, John Badham, Nat Cartwright

Shop Assistants late 1950s
Back row: [Henry ?], Doug Meredith, Ray Mewies, Mike Cronin, A. Davies, Ivan Bishop (umpire)
Front row: Ken Davies, Ken Dallow, Jock Handley, Norman Stokes, Danny Wright   Inset: Steven Bishop

71

Racecourse in the late 1950s. They won the Leominster Knockout Cup in the early 1960s. One of their least notable performances was in 1966 when they were bowled out for 7 by Wiggins in an Evening League match; Steve Bishop, son of Ivor Bishop, one of the founder members of the club, acknowledged that he was the top scorer with 2!

The team not only included the two playing members of the Bishop family – Gladys Bishop, wife of Ivor, was the tea lady for many years.

Hereford United
There was a Hereford United Cricket Club when the football team of the same name was called Hereford Thistle. The rules of the team issued in about 1900 show that John Williams was captain, P.R. Spencer was treasurer and Samuel Cole secretary. The rules were:

1. The club be called the Hereford United Cricket Club.
2. Managed by a committee of seven, including the Captain, Secretary and Treasurer.
3. The annual subscription shall be 2/6d. And no person shall be allowed to play until he has paid the same.
4. Tuesday and Saturdays be special practice days.
5. That any member shall be permitted to use the property of the club, on the production of his cheque, and that he be held responsible for the return of the same to the place appointed. That any member wilfully damaging the property of the club shall make good the same, or be expelled.
6. That any member using profane or abusive language shall be fined 6d. for each offence, and shall not be permitted to play until he has paid the same.
7. That all matches be made by the committee, the players to be chosen by the Captain, subject to the approval of the committee.
8. That any member consenting to play in a match and failing to do so, shall find an approved substitute or pay 2/-

9. That the committee has power to pay part, or all of the expenses of a match, should the funds permit.
10. In the event of the misconduct of any member, complaint to be made in writing to the committee, such complaint to be investigated by them, and if found necessary, such member to be fined or expelled.
11. That at the close of the season, the Secretary shall call a meeting, when the Treasurer shall present the accounts, which shall be audited by the committee and the property of the club shall be delivered over to the treasurer until the following season.

N.B. Persons desirous of becoming members are requested to apply to the secretary.

Some footballers from Hereford United have also contributed to local cricket in recent years. They usually played against local sides in charity matches. The players included Peter Isaac, Charlie Thompson (who also guested for Westons Cider), Sammy Chivers, Dixie McNeil, Roger Griffiths, Steve Emery (who also played for Ledbury), Brian Preece, Jimmy Harvey, Keith Hicks, Ken Volpe, a former manager of the club, Ian Bowyer, and his two sons Gary and Paul.

Tupsley and District / Hampton Bishop
There is no record of the team playing prior to 1912, but in 1913 Tupsley and District played at 'The Field, Hampton Bishop' according to an article in the *Hereford Times* dated 9 August. The ground was next to the Bunch of Carrots public house and is shown on a contemporary Ordnance Survey map. The club also had their own pavilion.

At the A.G.M. in March 1914 the chairman reported on a successful year and confirmed that the club were looking forward to the following season.

Hereford City Council
The City Council ran a side in the 1920s. One of their most distinguished players in 1929 was Tom Perks, the father of Reg Perks, the Worcestershire and England player. Tom Perks qualified as a member of the team because he

Above: Wiggin's former pavilion in 2006

Centre left: Wiggin A 1964 League knockout cup final

Back row: George Whittaker, [-], Peter Sykes, Stan Davies, Dave Hodges, [-]
Front row: Russell Jones, Pat Ellis, Roy Preece, Derek Allison, Bob Watkins.

Below left: Wiggin's inter-departmental cup 1971
Sheet Rolling team (left)

Back row: G. Rachel, R. Plant, B. Grocutt, S. Hull, J. Perry, W. Lucas
Middle row: R. Thwaites, M. Phelps, A. Preston
Front row: D. Watkins, R. Beare, J. Preston

Melting team (right)

Back row: J. Carter, G. Harbottle, L. Jenkins, M. Smith, R. Lewis, G. Whittaker
Front row: D. Price, R. French, A. Griffiths, P. Cleeton, G. Jones

Wiggin

The works team was formed in 1955 and played regularly until 1983. The original playing field has now been reduced in size and the ground and pavilion are used by footballers. The team enjoyed its main successes in the 1970s. Wiggin A finished runners-up in Division Three of the Hereford Evening League in 1971. Their players also achieved individual successes in

was the groundsman at the Racecourse which was owned by the Council. In June 1929 the side played Widemarsh Lads' Club at Widemarsh.

the League honours list – George Whittaker's score of 74 not out against South Wye was the highest individual score in Division Three, and Selwyn Williams topped the same Division's bowling performance with 7 wickets for 15 runs against Denco. Wiggin also ran a weekend team during the same season. In 1973 they finished third in the Division. Cricket was so strong in the 1960s and '70s that places with large work forces had their own cricket competitions. Henry Wiggin and Co. was no exception and the company, like many others, produced fine cricketers who enjoyed competitive internal competition. The photograph (bottom, previous page) records such a competition, when the Sheet Rolling team beat the Melting team by 16 runs in the 1971 final. In 1973 a single wicket competition was introduced by the club – 18 players took part. Dave Price beat Ken Hook in the final of the competition.

Prudential Insurance Company

It was the practice of many national companies to hold cricket competitions within their own organizations and the Prudential was no exception. The Hereford branch of the company played friendly games in the city during the late 1980s, treating them as practice matches for their inter-departmental competition. Hereford won the competition in 1989 – the winning trophy being proudly displayed by the manager in his office.

The photograph (below) shows the side that reached the quarter-finals in 1990, but lost to the eventual winners.

Prudential six-a-side 1990
Back row: Ken Hook, Brian Pederson, Bill Lucas,
Kevin Williams
Front row: David Cope, Haydn Phillips, Graham Hawkins

Wayfarers

The club was formed in the early 1960s as a Hereford Schoolteachers XI. Two of the most influential teachers in the formation of the club were Alan May, a physical education teacher, and his colleague at Red Hill school, Glyn Jones, a music teacher. Many pupils and former pupils

started their cricketing careers with the team and they benefited from their former master's experience. These included Derrick Jones, who played for many years and then undertook countless committee positions in Herefordshire Cricket; Stuart Blyth, who played for Wormelow and was one of the main men behind the development of their new pavilion; and Ken Hook, one of the authors of this book, who found Alan May's coaching to be of great benefit to him.

The side eventually joined the Evening League and in 1982/3 they won the Paul Levy Knockout Cup. They also won Division Two of the Evening League in 1983 and 1989.

Hereford Insurance Institute

The Insurance Institute was an organization formed for the benefit of all employees in the insurance industry in Hereford. The team, which started in the late 1970s, was the brainchild of Andy Head from the Royal Insurance Company. Friendly matches were played between the branch members of the various offices based in the area. This not only gave the participants an excuse for an afternoon out of the office on a nice summer's day to play cricket followed by a good steak in a local hostelry, but also gave the members of the industry an opportunity to meet and to discuss matters that affected them all. Three of the main participants were Brian Tipping from

W.J. Bond and Co., Malcolm Harris from Eagle Star, and Nigel Barrington from Rees and Co. The cricket ceased in the early 1990s following the closure of many local insurance offices.

National Westminster Bank

National Westminster Bank 1977
Back row: A. Johnston, [-], G. Meyers, M. Powell, K. Dye, K. Brimble
Front row: R. Simmonds, W.A.O. Salter, D. Heale, R. Moseley, T. Partington

The Hereford branch of the bank played friendly matches, inter-bank competitions and in the Evening League, and were prominent in the 1970s and '80s. In 1977 they won the Bank Regional Final for the West Midlands and Wales area at Goodrich. They won the new Evening League Division Three title in 1985, their first year in the competition, and played in that league from then onwards, winning the Junior Cup in 1986.

Other City Teams

Other teams that were based in the city in the early part of the 20th century included:

Hereford Excelsior, who in 1910 had a fairly successful season, winning nine out of 14 matches played, losing only three.

Hereford Constitutional, who clearly had a frustrating season in 1910, as they were unable to play six arranged matches because their opponents were unable to raise a team.

Hereford Men's Club Thursday XI, who were playing in 1910 when they played 12 matches, winning six of them.

Cavaliers and **Roundheads** were both off-shoots of Hereford City Sports Club. In later years the Cavaliers played in the Evening League and were successful three years running, winning the Division Four, Three and Two titles in 1970, '71 and '72. Roundheads were also successful in the Evening League in the 1970s – they won the Division Three title in 1975 and Division One in 1977.

It is almost certain that other teams came and went very quickly. As a result they were not around long enough to be reported in the local press and are thus lost forever as they disappear beyond living memory. The above teams with but brief references are those that the authors have been able to identify from a perusal of local newspapers of the period.

Wartime Cricket and Military Teams

Military cricket in general is included in this chapter with city clubs because many of the military sides were based in the city. The first evidence of a military team is in 1902 when Burton Court took on a Hereford Militia team (see chapter IX) but, in the main, cricket was played by the military sides during the two world wars when men, usually not from choice, were deprived of normal civilian life and tried to compensate by resuming their passion for cricket under the umbrella of the armed forces. The teams did not usually last long and, for obvious reasons, there was no continuity of personnel.

Because civilian domestic cricket was virtually non-existent during the wars the teams quite often played friendly matches against local schools and the larger club sides that were still able to raise a team, as well as competing against each other.

The Evening League was the only competitive cricket during the Second World War, continuing until 1941. There were only four local teams competing: Y.M.C.A., Herefordians, S.W.S. Power Co., and Lads' Club. There was some friendly and fund-raising cricket played during the war years, mainly between the forces' sides including the Military XI and the R.A.F. who played Ross, Hereford, Leominster, and Ledbury. There is also some evidence of a team at Aeroparts who played the R.A.S.C.

In August 1941 Lt. Col. Thornycroft fielded a side against the Military XI in a fund-raising game for the County Welfare Fund. It is not surprising that the Thornycroft Invitation XI was successful because included in the side was Reg Perks, the Hereford born Worcestershire player. R.W. Roff from Ross, and J.M. and C.G. Thornycroft were also in the side. In another August Bank Holiday charity match between Col. Thornycroft's XI and R.A.F. Hereford, Reg Perks played alongside another Worcestershire player – Jack Singleton. The R.A.F. team was the winner and £10 4s. 6d. was raised for the Merchant Navy.

There was hardly any senior cricket during 1942 and 1943 and the game was limited to the schools including Hereford High School and the Cathedral School. On 10 June 1944 the Hereford Recreation Society organized a knock-out cup with the final to be played on 23 August. The teams competing were S.W.S., R.A.F., Col. Thornycroft's XI, Ledbury Road Camp, R.E.M.E., Hinton Youth Club, R.A.O.C., Prospects, Aeroparts, P.D.C., Cathedral School, and South Wales District XI. The competition was won by the R.A.F. who beat P.D.C. by one run in the final over. A collection on the night raised £1 17s. for the local wounded soldiers fund.

Keith Miller, the post-war Australian all-rounder, played in an Australian Services side against a Hereford XI at Widemarsh Common in

Peter Manders' cartoon of Keith Miller

1946. The father of Mike Rose, the former Leicestershire and Hereford City Sports Club player who was born in Hereford, organized the game.

Corporal Hitler and his army could not stop the ingenuity of Ross man R.W.P. Roff, who, according to his son Rex, refused to allow petrol rationing to stop him from keeping the cricket pitch in tip-top condition during the war. He laid his car up for four years and removed the wheels. This allowed him to use his precious petrol ration to feed the cricket mowing machines. Rex recalled wartime matches against military sides including K.S.L.I., R.A.F., Homeguard, and the A.T.C. Some information has been garnered regarding the following teams which have been located playing in the county at different times.

King's Shropshire Light Infantry
The team is recorded in 1952 when they played against Hereford Gentlemen. Three of the players for the Hereford team were Bill Bullock, Jack Goodwin and Dr. Wood Power. Local man W. Griffin played for K.S.L.I.

R.A.F.
The side is recorded playing until 1930 and then during the war when the team was strengthened by the inclusion of two Yorkshire second team bowlers – Arch and Goode. After the war they played from 1946 until 1975. By 1985 the R.A.F. in Hereford was represented by Credenhill who are recorded playing against the Lords Taverners in 1988 (opposite).

Bradbury Lines
The team, which was formed in 1940, played a few games each season as morale boosters. Not many clubs could raise a team during the war, but

R.A.F. Credenhill 1988
Known team members: Middle front: Gary Kaye (captain)
Top left: umpire Mike Heritage; Top right: umpire Ray Chillington

they played Ross, Monmouth, Leominster, Hereford, Withington, and Ledbury. They ceased to play in 1955. The groundsman was Tom Perks, Reg Perks' father. Tom's playing career was with Holmer some 30 years earlier.

R.A.F. Shobdon

The team at this rather remote air force station was active from 1939 until 1951. They played Hereford High School in 1946. On 22 May 1952

they played Dilwyn, unusually on a Thursday, in an exciting game when they beat them by four runs. The R.A.F. team then was L.A.C. Boddy, L.A.C. James, L.A.C. Measham, Cpl. Batho, F/O Riach, S.A.C. Tanner, A.C. Quinsey, L.A.C. Burgess, A.C.Avent, A.C. Astley, and L.A.C. Chappell.

Hereford Light Infantry

This team was formed in 1946 and the photograph (below) is of the Division One side in about 1961. They were successful in their first year in the League in 1955 when they won the Second Division championship. They won the Division Three championship in 1960 and repeated their Division Two success in 1961. The club ceased in 1965.

R.A.O.C. Credenhill

In 1920 the club joined the newly-formed Hereford and District Cricket League, but in 1921 they agreed that they would not be running a team for that year.

Falcons Touring Cricket Team

Whilst this team is not strictly speaking a city side, they are included in this chapter because of the numerous times over many years that they have played in the city and in the main towns in the county. As their name indicates, they were a touring side but always played in the county during the August Bank Holiday weekend. It is believed that the team members were Quakers.

It has been established that they played throughout the last century against Hereford, Ledbury, Leominster, Colwall, and Ross. In 1904 they had a busy weekend schedule playing

Hereford Light Infantry, 1961
Back row: [-], W. Healey, K.J. Vale, [-], E. Saunders, [-], C. Clinkett
Front row: J. Sullivan, T.A. Matthews, D. Miller, C.Cleland, G. Miller

Left: The Falcons Touring Team at Ross in 1932
Above: The Falcons at Ledbury in the 1930s

Leominster on the 1st of August, Ross on the 4th, and Ledbury on the 5th. In August 1973 they were involved in a close, low-scoring game against Ross, which Ross won by 10 runs thanks to some fine bowling by Bob Hughes who took 6 wickets for 27 runs.

The photographs provide some indication of the team's contribution to cricket in the county: top left – a visit to Ross in 1932; top right – a batsman returning to the pavilion at Ledbury; and left – Henry Southall sitting at the pavilion in Leominster during a match against the Falcons in 1930.

Henry Southall at the Falcons match in
Leominster in 1930

CHAPTER VII

Ross & the Surrounding Area

Ross Cricket Club

Ross-on-Wye is the most southerly major cricket town in the county and Ross Cricket Club can boast one of the most picturesque grounds, situated as it is between the Wilton bridge and the town and close to the River Wye. The club is recorded as playing at Weir End in 1837, the year they were formed. By 1908 the team had moved to The Park – their current ground – and where the old pavilion built in 1837 still stands, has recently been renovated, and is now in immaculate condition. A report in the *Hereford Times* stated that they had a fairly successful season in 1910 when they played 15 matches winning nine times.

At the turn of the century the president was Mr. H.C. Moffatt of Goodrich Court. However, he resigned his post as he believed that sport was unequally taxed and so refused to subscribe to the club. He was objecting to taxes being levied on owners of shooting rights when other sports were allowed to practise tax-free. He promised to renew his subscription when the tax was removed from the shooting rights.

Ross was not the only team to play at the Park that year. In August 1910 there was a representative match between Mr. J.P. Morgan's XI and Mr. Harry Webb's XI. The game was unusual as it

The 19th-century pavilion at Ross which has recently been refurbished

ended in a tie and was reported in the *Hereford Times* as follows:

Local cricketers will not have forgotten the match between Mr. J.P. Morgan's XI and Mr. Harry Webb's XI played at the Park, Ross, in August which ended in a tie. They will be interested to know that in order to record this unusual result, and to show their appreciation of Mr. Webb's hospitality, the gentlemen who played in the match have subscribed together and had a silver shield mounted on the ball which was used, and a brief report of the match engraved on the shield. The ball,

Members of Ross Cricket Club in 1906. The 19th-century pavilion is in the background

together with a silver-mounted ebony stand bearing this inscription. 'Presented to H Webb. Esq., by the players', has been sent to that gentleman as a memento.

At the A.G.M. in May 1914, the chairman confirmed that the work done to enlarge the pavilion was a great success and that it provided better facilities for the players. He advised that the cost, which was not specified, would be paid over a period of three years. At the 1920 A.G.M. the president, Mr. Adair Righton, informed the members that the subscriptions for the forth-coming season would be 10s. 6d. for senior members and 5s. for juniors under 18.

Ross played in tour matches in the 1920s. At the A.G.M. in February 1927 it was agreed that the team should go on tour out of the county and Mr. R.W.P. Roff arranged three one-day matches in Kent for the forthcoming season.

In 1931 Ross appointed their first profes-sional, Mr. R.G. Preece who came from Leominster. In the same year the Ross ground was sold by its owners for £1,470. Fortunately the new owners confirmed that the club could remain at the ground, continuing to pay the same rent of £30 per annum.

Two of the finest batsman for the club in the 1930s and '40s were Don West and Don Ruck. In the 1940s Ross had an invitation Challenge Cup Competition. The pavilion was moved to the Park about 1957 and in the same year Ross cricket, rugby and football teams, whilst keeping their own individual names, all came under the umbrella of the Ross Sports Centre.

Doc Lewis, an ex-player for Ross, recalled an event in the early 1950s when they played Dudley Casuals in a friendly match. He recalled dropping Tom Graveney, the England batsman, when he had yet to break his duck. Tom was qualifying for Worcestershire after leaving Gloucestershire and he went on to make a century. The openers for Dudley in the same match were George Headley, of West Indies fame, and his son Ron, who played for Worcestershire for many years.

In 1962 John Notley became the first Ross player to score 1,000 runs in a season since 1949. His best performance was 150 not out against Lullington Park at Ross on August 7.

In 1964 a former Gloucestershire fast bowler, George Lambert, who was manager of the Prince of Wales Inn in Ross, played Sunday

In 1964 a former player, J.H. Moore, wrote to the Ross Gazette *reminiscing about his playing days for the team forty years earlier*

games for the team. His first-class career, which was interrupted by the War, was between 1938 and 1960. He scored 6,375 first-class runs and took 917 wickets and was a tremendous asset to the club. In the same year a Ross XI played a Worcestershire XI in a benefit match for the Worcester captain and opening batsman, Don Kenyon. Between 1964 and 1976 the captain of the side was Paul Notley who played for the club for 40 years until he retired in 1991.

The new Ross Sports pavilion was opened in September 1965 by Brigadier A.C. Clive, Mrs. Simmonds initially donated £500 towards the cost of the building and at a later stage another £1,000. The total cost was £22,000, much of which was raised by the chairman, Albert Porter, who obtained donations locally. The photograph of the 1976 team shows the new Sports centre in the background.

The team ran a 20-over Evening Knockout Cup which started in 1970. They then ran a six-a-side competition until 1976. A Ross XI played the Worcestershire Championship side in 1964; the county side including Basil D'Oliviera, who was qualifying to play for the county at the

The Ross team in 1976
Back row: [-], Alan Matthews, Alan Johnson, Mark Newton, Gerald Horlick, Robert Brain, John Howls, Nigel Peters
Front row: Rex Roff, Mike Burrows, Paul Notley (captain), Peter Plomley, Dave Hodges

Ross 1964. Rrepresentative side versus Worcestershire Championship side
Back row: W.R. Hill, I.C. Aubrey, J.C. Notley, A.P. Notley, K.A. Higton, E. Elliott, D. Bevan, N.J. Davies, A.H. Matthew
Front row: J.B. Mortimore (Gloucestershire), H. Stephenson (Somerset), G.E. Lambert (Gloucestershire),
B. Langford (Somerset), D. Constant (Kent and first class umpire)

time. The representative team photograph (above) was taken in front of the original ladies' tea pavilion, which was tucked under the trees on a bank overlooking the wicket. Traces of the foundations are all that now remain.

Ross achieved national publicity between September 1965 and March 1966 when eight members of the team had obviously bowled a few maiden[s] over because they all became fathers! The event was reported in the local paper and the national press picked up the story. The unusual event was described in the *Ross Gazette* on the 40th anniversary in March 2006.

In 1969 the speaker at the annual dinner was Tom Graveney, who was no stranger to the club. He received a cheque towards his benefit year from the Ross Club captain, Rex Roff. Tom presented the award for the top batsman for the year to Paul Notley who had been a prolific player for the club for many years. He scored some 15,000 runs in his career including 42 centuries. In 1969 he scored 14 consecutive

The 150th anniversary dinner and dance

half-centuries. He won the club batting averages for 14 consecutive years between 1964 and 1978. In one season he won a national award for the most wicket-keeping victims for the year.

The team won the Three Counties League in 1983 when Bob Hughes and Eric Jenkins were two of the most successful members of the team. When the club celebrated its 150th anniversary in 1987, the members held a dinner dance at the Chase Hotel in Ross. The compere for the evening was Bryn Phillips, a local man and round table member. The guest speakers were Peter Parfitt, the England and Middlesex player, and Jack Bannister, the BBC commentator and former Warwickshire player. Jack was an evacuee during the Second World War and was billeted in Ross. During the evening, Terry Court, an auctioneer from Russell Baldwin and Bright and himself a local successful cricketer, carried out an auction for the club.

Rex Roff recalled an incident when he was playing for Ross against Gloucester Nondescripts at the Ham cricket ground in Gloucester. Rex was positioned at long on, and as the ball was struck in his general direction he chased around the boundary to field it and ran into another player. On getting up from his fall he enquired of his victim, 'Where did you come from?' The chap replied 'From long on.' The players looked at each in total confusion until they realised that they were playing in two different games and that there was a joint boundary. Rex was a stylish left-hand bat and was also an accurate medium pace bowler and an excellent fielder.

The current groundsman at Ross is Steve Earl who is also president of the club. He follows Jim Reeves in the 1960s, Horace Lewis in the '70s and Charlie Ford in the '80s.

The club continues to prosper and has an excellent youth project in operation so the future looks bright.

Ross United Services

The team was originally called Ross United Football Club Cricket Team, and played as Ross United Services. They won the Ross Knock Out Cup in 1948.

Ross Nondescripts

This team was formed in about 1962, the members being known as the Nondies. The team originally comprised members of the Ross Football Club and only played in the Ross Knockout competition. They always had a strong team mainly because Ross Cricket Club provided many of the players. The side used to vary from week to week and played by invitation from the captain, John Notley. In 1971 they won the Ross Six-a-side Knockout for the first time and also captured the Ross Knockout Senior Trophy. In that match Bob Hughes took 7 wickets for 14 runs including a hat trick. Two other important members of the side were Peter Plumley and John Howells, both being automatic selections.

Ross Nomads

Little is known about the team apart from the fact that they were playing in the 1960s and '70s. At some stage they played league cricket in Gloucestershire.

Ross United Services Team, 1948
Back row: George Arrowsmith, Fred Hill, Harold Smith, Colin Fowler, Elmo Clarke, [-], Nobby Griffiths, Dennis Drinkwater, Alan Matthews, Bert Porter
Front row: [-], David Wellington, Jim Bacon, Don West, Bill Hill (captain), Stan West, Don Ruck

Brockhampton

Above: A.W. Foster 1897. (Portrait by the American artist J.J. Shannon)

Right: Club card for 1929

BROCKHAMPTON

CRICKET CLUB.

SEASON 1929.

President—
Colonel A. W. Foster,
M.A., D.L., J.P.

Vice-Presidents—
Mrs. A. W. Foster, J.P.
A. Blain, Esq.
Major H. J. Allfrey.
Rev. F. G. Knott, M.A.
Rev. J. Hodgson.
D. Elkington, Esq.
J. Wyndham Smith, Esq.
G. W. Hunt, Esq.
W. T. Bennett, Esq.
H. Bellamy, Esq.

Officials and Committee.

Captain—
Mr. H. Hudson.

Vice-Captain—
Mr. H. Powell.

Committee—
Mr. G. Mineay.
Mr. J. Lilley.
Mr. J. Yarnold.
Mr. H. Greening.
Mr. E. Clarke.
Mr. I. Hudson.

Hon. Treasurer—
Mr. M. T. Hall.

Hon. Secretary—
Mr. H. C. Dredge.

Headquarters—
Brockhampton.

Brockhampton

Brockhampton cricket club plays on one of the prettiest grounds in the Wye Valley. Situated close to Brockhampton Court, the ground nestles between two wooded areas on the Brockhampton Estate and is about 8 miles from Ross-on-Wye. The cricket club was formed on 20 March 1897 when Col. Arthur Wellesley Foster, who married Alice Madeline Jordan, the daughter of the owner of Brockhampton Estate, was in the chair. He was elected president and captain of the club, a position he held until just before the First World War. Foster was not a direct relative of the Fosters who played for Worcestershire, although it is generally believed that there is some distant family connection. The early days of the club are known because, thankfully, the original minute book has survived. During the first year, 37 subscriptions were paid and it was agreed that there should be practice evenings three times a week. There was no pavilion when the club was formed and the kit

had to be locked in a box on the field of play. It was agreed that the annual subscription would be 2s. 6d. and labourers and boys under 16 paid 1s. The accounts for the first year showed a profit of £2 2s. 9d. Payments for the year included one to a Mr. Griffiths for a horse and trap to Perrystone, and another to Fawley Station. When the club was first formed it relied on players who happened to work on the Brockhampton Estate, hence the different annual subscriptions for labourers. The standard was not very good in the beginning and in 1903 they lost by three runs to Perrystone despite bowling them out for 26. In 1900 Col. Foster's wife presented a challenge cup to the club which is still played for every year. Brockhampton won it the first year and they have also won it a further 32 times out of the 74 times it was played for during the century.

There was no cricket during the First World War, but it was agreed in April 1920 to revive the club. R.H. Simpson and E.J. Griffiths were

BROCKHAMPTON CRICKET CLUB

FIXTURES 1955
1st and 2nd XIs.

President :
G. L. CLAY, Esq.

Hon. Secretary :
MR. G. TOWNSEND,
THE TUMP, BROCKHAMPTON.
NR. HEREFORD.

Hon. Treasurer :
MR. B. SIDAWAY.

Captain :
1st—Mr B. Howells.
2nd—Mr. H. Parry

Vice-Captain :
1st—Mr. E. Williams.
2nd—Mr. F. Hudson.

Groundsman :
MR. J. C. HOWELLS
Practice Tuesdays and Thursdays

Brockhampton Club card 1955

appointed as joint secretaries. It was also agreed that the Brockhampton Cup would be revived on similar rules to the pre-war days.

One of the reasons for the success of the club is the continuity of people at the helm. They have only had four presidents since 1897:

1897-1928	Col. A.W. Foster
1929 -1931	Mrs. A.W. Foster
1932-1997	G.L. Clay
1996	J.P.F. Clay

Brockhampton cricket ground is now owned by the Clay family who have been involved since the 1930s and is one of the oldest grounds in the county in continuous use.

The Club can boast an old traditional pavilion which started life as a hunters' lodge for the Clay family. The cricket ground was ploughed up at the outbreak of the Second World War to help with the war effort and was re-laid in 1946. In the minutes of the A.G.M. for 1946 it was recorded that Mr. Clay had received the appropriate permits for the tackle and that it would be left to the secretary to apply for the

Brockhampton Club with three trophies in 1934
Trophies, left to right: Perrystone Cup, Hilldersley Casket, Brockhampton Cup
Back row :H. Dredge, M. Hall, G. Townsend, J. Avery, E. Clark, E. Avery,
G.L. Clay, J. Lilley, A. Preece, F. Haines
Front row: A. Skyrme, I. Hudson, R. Yarnold, H. Powell,
(Bengie, Mr. Clay's dog), J. Gibbons, H. Hudson, C. Hall

The Brockhampton Cup

Brockhampton
Top: The traditional pavilion. Bottom: The permanent sponsorship tent

and joined the Hereford and District League Division 2 in 1975 and won the league during the first season. Roy Wargen had a very successful season – he took 46 wickets at an average of 7.13 runs each. In 1977 they won the league and cup double.

1980 was another successful season when they won the Canon Frome, Woolhope, Brockhampton, and Ross Six-a-side Knockout Cups. In 1981 Brockhampton was the first village side to host an Australian Touring side when they played the Manley Warratahs Cricket Club from Sydney. In 1988 they won the 1st Division League and Cup and the Goodrich Cup.

In 1988 the club photograph (opposite) demonstrated that Brockhampton was then very much a family club. Five fathers and sons are in the photograph – they are David and James Price, Peter and David Howells, Michael and Guy Best, Peter and Simon Children, and Gerald and Steven Howells.

Another first was achieved in 2003 when they became the first village club to engage an overseas cricketer – Mahmood Malik – who helped them win the Worcester League Division 2 in that year. In 2005 they signed Mohammed Ali and were runners-up in Division 1. Ali signed professional terms with Middlesex in 2006.

Two of the most influential players during recent years have been Tony Hope, who took 150 wickets in 1958, and Roy Wargen, who joined the club in 1974 as a young, raw pace-bowler. He has twice taken over 100 wickets in a season. He has been club captain on a number of occasions and in 1992 he became club chairman.

The club is proud that it hosts Herefordshire Minor Counties matches and continues to prosper.

necessary permits for rations. At the same meeting club membership was set at 5s.

In a match against Golden Valley in 1954, the team fielded 11 players whose surname started with the initial 'H' namely: the Hope brothers – Tony, Vernon, Tom, Bill, Jack and Dave; and the Howells brothers – Bert, Gerald, Peter, Reg and Jack. All were left-handed batsmen!

The club numbers amongst its Vice-Presidents and supporters Brian Huggett the golfer and former Ryder Cup captain who lives locally, and Bill Frindall, the Test Match Special statistician who lived in the area briefly and played a few games for the club and was also a guest speaker at an annual dinner dance.

The Club has had many successes over the years. They won the Ross Knockout Cup in 1974

Brockhampton 1975 team. The first winners of Division 2
Back row: Jean Howells (scorer). G. Howells, R. Evans, G. Williams, R. Hood, R. Wargen, J. Yarnold, C. Lilly, P. Howells
Front row: V. Hope, R. Phillips (captain), D. Howells, J. Hope, J. Hudson

Brockhampton 1988 with their many trophies
Back row: M. Sharman, B. Caffelle, T. Cawley, R. Roberts, J. Jones, J. Lamont, J. Hudson
Middle row: N. Harper, P. Children, B. Hope, G. Best, R. Williams, J. Price, P. Hodges, K. Williams, J. Cook, T. Hope,
D. Howells, D. Price
Front row: T. Price, T. Goodwin, D. Jones, R. Howells, B. Howells (chairman), G.L. Clay (president) M. Best (club captain),
P. Howells (treasurer), R. Wargen, N. Nenadich

Perrystone

Perrystone is recorded playing between 1900 and the late 1950s, being based at Perrystone Court. The team was run by the owner of the Court, Lieutenant-General Sir Sidney Clive.

Perrystone 1935 team in front of the pavilion with the Perrystone Cup
Back row: Percy Brown, Bill Allsop, Fred Sollers, Tom Gibbons, Reg Turner, Harry Davies, Chris Powell
Middle row: Walter Moss, Charlie Clark, George Francis, Jack Loveridge, Albert Davies
Front row: Ted Lerigo, Jack Griffith

Perrystone 1946 team winning the Brockhampton Cup
Back row: Jim Clarke (umpire), Alan Teague, [-], Jim Roberts, Bill Steadman, John Roberts, Trevor Clinton, Trevor Manning
Front row: Harry Davies, Fred Sollars, Stan Young (captain), Ivor Jones, Jack Davies
Inset: Jeff Clarke

The social side was as important as the cricket in the 1920s. The *Hereford Times* reported a match that took place in August 1920 between the Perrystone Ladies and the Gentlemen. The match was organized by Mrs. Snell of Home Farm to raise money for the club. Teas were taken in the garage by courtesy of Mrs. Clive. £8 10s. was raised for club funds and, for the record, the Ladies won the match by 9 runs – they scored 29 and the Gentlemen replied with just 20, but perhaps the cricket seemed immaterial to the occasion.

In the early years they won the Brockhampton Cup in 1906, 1908 and 1909. Cricket ceased at the Court during the war years and Perrystone was home to the Land Army Girls. When cricket resumed after the war they won the Brockhampton Cup again in 1946, together with the Perrystone Cup. The photograph (below) shows them proudly displaying their trophies in front of the pavilion.

Jim Clarke worked on the estate for many years and gave considerable help in confirming the above details. He played cricket for Perrystone with his father Chris Clarke, his uncle, and his brother Jeff. Jeff also played for Brampton Abbotts. Other players of note were James Roberts Senior, his brother John, and Harry and Jack Davies. The captain was Stan Young.

Sir Sidney Clive tragically died when the Court was burnt down in

Above: Perrystone Court, the home of Sir Sidney Clive, after the fire
Right: Woolhope fixture card for 1962

1958. Cricket ceased after this sad event and many of the players moved on to play for Brampton Abbotts.

Woolhope

The team played on a pitch perched up on a bank on the left-hand side when entering the village from the Fownhope direction. The first meeting to form a cricket club at Woolhope was held at the local vicarage on 5 June 1950. The following officers were elected: president – C. Maclaverty; chairman – Rev J.C. Williams (who sadly passed away in the following September); secretary – G.Peters; treasurer – W. Darby. It was agreed that the subscriptions for the season would be 5s. for senior members and 2s. 6d for those under 18. Practice night was each Thursday. The club's equipment was as follows:

```
2 bats at 35s. each...........................£3 16s. 0d.
2 pairs batting gloves at 11s. each...£1  2s. 0d.
1 ball (plastic)......................................10s. 6d.
1pr. batting pads.............................£1  5s. 0d.
1pr. wicket keepers pads.................£1 18s. 6d.
1pr. wicket keepers gloves..............£1 16s. 0d.
1 set bails........................(price not in records)
```

The club, as can be seen by the amount of equipment, started in a modest fashion. The first A.G.M. took place on 31 Oct 1950 when the treasurer announced that the funds amounted to approximately £4. He was clearly happy with the finances because he recommended that the subscriptions remain the same for the following season.

On the playing side, the club did not make a very good start to the 1951 season when they played Canon Frome on 26 May 1951 and were all out for 7 runs. At one stage they was only a single run for 8 wickets, but thanks to V. Hoyes batting at number 9, and D. Bayliss at number 10, both scoring 3 runs, the final score did at least reach 7.

In the 1960s '70s and '80s they ran a successful six-a-side competition. The club's successes include the Brockhampton Cup in 1968 and the Andrew Morris Cup and the Hereford Times League Division 4 in 1990.

Woolhope enjoyed a unique success at local level when they produced Colleen Rogers, the daughter of long-standing Woolhope cricketer Colin Rogers. She was the first lady cricketer from Woolhope to play in the Hereford League. Colleen gained international status when she played for England Ladies and toured Sri Lanka. Another lady cricketer, Jo Greaves, also played for West of England Ladies alongside her club colleague Colleen.

Woolhope, early 1950s, with the Lady Densham Cup
Back row: [? Woolhope schoolmaster], Harry Davies, Colin Rogers,
Norman Williams, - Peters, - Bayliss, Fred Bayliss
Front row: Maurice Bayliss, [-], Jack Davies, Godfrey Davies, [-]

Brampton Abbotts team winning the Perrystone Cup in 1933
Back row: Rev. Brind, C. Goode, A.A. Matthews, G. Broad, J. Whitaker,
G. Morris (umpire)
Middle row: J.C. Snell, R. Pragnall, - Pragnall (captain), J.B. Sainsbury, A. Matthews
Front row: E. Morris, G. Thomas

Brampton Abbotts

The team played before the Second World War between 1927 and 1933 and won the Perrystone Cup in 1933. No cricket was played during the war and they reformed in 1946. The original ground belonged to the Snell family, who donated it for cricket, and a pavilion was erected. The team played on that ground until 1960 and two of the Snell family played in the team. The team won the Goodrich cup in 1953 and '59, but ceased playing in 1962. For the final two years they played at Phocle Green.

On one occasion, not to be forgotten by those present, a local man who lived in a property adjacent to the ground was cutting some rough grass with a hook. He became so engrossed in the cricket that he missed the grass and cut his wrist very badly. He held up his hand, which by then was covered in blood, and shouted for help. One of the cricketers shouted to his colleagues: 'Look chaps, he has found a cricket ball.'

Eaton Bishop

Eaton Bishop had a team in the early 1950s and were playing as Madley and Eaton Bishop at Blenheim Farm in 1952. By 1953 the team played as Madley. The known players involved were Phil Skyrme, Malcolm Hughes (who later played for Herefordians) and Keith Bishop of Holme Lacy. It is believed that the club folded in about 1961.

Bridstow

Ray Court, the landlord of the Kings Head public house at Wilton, near Ross, and several members of the local football club, formed Bridstow Cricket Club in 1953. The football club played on the same ground. The club existed for 13 years until 1966. The ground was about 300 yards from the Wilton roundabout near to Wilton Castle. Until one was built, the pavilion was the pub! The new one was a wooden frame with corrugated iron sides and roof, the only window being a lift-up flap.

The picture of a Hoarwithy batsman returning from the field of play to the pavilion at Wilton quite clearly shows the long grass (below left). A hand mower originally cut the square, and the outfield was left uncut apart from grazing sheep and cattle. There was a little path cut from the pavilion to the square, and certain batsmen became adept at steering the ball along the path for a four, otherwise the scoring shots were either a six or a one. The average team score was 70.

The long grass in the outfield provided a natural habitat for wildlife, and on one occasion a batsman deposited a snake that appeared on the field of play into the nearby brook.

The captain was Geoff Watkins; Ray Court was secretary, and Charles Peachey was treasurer. The first match was an away game at Goodrich and the club hired a coach from Llangrove Coaches to take the players and a number of enthusiastic supporters to the game. Unfortunately, Bridstow were dismissed for 12. The treasurer's son, Mike Peachey, recalls that his father was run out for a duck.

Other captains included Tim Rubery, Charles Peachey, Terry Court, Les Hammond, Alan Holliday and Ken French. Terry Court recalled one match when he was bowling to Godfrey Farr, who unfortunately forgot to take his box of matches out of his top pocket when he came in to bat; a short, rising ball hit him on the pocket and the matches burst into flame, leaving Godfrey with a permanent scar on his chest.

One of the stalwarts of the club was a local builder called Charles Peachey. His son, Mike Peachey, also played for the club. Other long-standing players were Cecil Evans, Graham Gwynne, Charlie Price,

Bert Davies, Frank Jones, Keith and Mervyn Probert, and John Howells. When Cecil Evans recorded the team's first half century against Weston under Penyard, he was rewarded with a 10s. note from a local retired farmer, Bert Sainsbury, whose house overlooked the ground. In 1956 Bridstow played Llancloudy and Mike Peachey remembered that the changing room was a shelter made of bales of hay. It is assumed that no ladies were present at matches before haymaking.

When the club ceased to play in 1966 Terry Court went on to play for Hereford City Sports Club; John Howells, Charles Peachey and Guy Sainsbury went to Ross; and Mike Peachey went to play for Tewkesbury Cricket Club.

Sellack

The ground, which was part of the Caradoc Court Estate, was opposite the village hall. The club did not have a pavilion, but changed on the opposite side of the ground in a green hut with a sloping

Above: Returning to the pavilion at the Bridstow pitch.
Ross on Wye is in the background

Right: A young Mike Peachey in 1953

Inset: His father, Charles

roof. Their first match was against Weston under Penyard. The captain of the club in the 1950s and early '60s was James Roberts who is in the middle of the front row of the photograph holding the Goodrich Cup (below). They won the Cup in 1950 and 1954 and again in about 1960. John Notley was captain from 1951 to 1954 and his brother, Paul, played for Sellack before transferring to Ross, where he enjoyed a long and successful career.

Sellack team in 1950 – winners of the the Goodrich Cup
Back row: Alan Morris (umpire), Charlie Morris (secretary and grounds man),
Bill Davies, Leo Whittall, Kenny Hull, Rex Seaborne, Steve Davies,
Godfrey Lewis, Alan Matthews (umpire)
Front row: John Notley, Sid Seaborne, James Roberts (captain), Dick Price, Jim Eckley

Cricket played between village sides in the 1960s was mainly a social affair, and James Roberts recalls that he always made a point of welcoming the visiting team during the tea interval. He failed to play in one game because when he was tossing-up before the match he was hit between the eyes by a cricket ball and ended up in Hereford General Hospital. James went on to play for Strollers; he played in their first match and then went on to captain the side and became president for a time. The club played until 1963.

Lea

The team played first of all at Castle End Corner. The ground was well known for the oak tree on the edge of the square. The outfield presented a challenge to the fielders with long grass, thistles and the odd cowpat. The occasional chicken or sheep complemented the fielding side. There was a celebration match played between Lea and the President's XI in the 1950s, but not all the team members are known.

There was no pavilion, and according to Les Barker, the teams changed either before they got to the ground or out in the open. John Gurney, one of the players, said they were active from the mid 1950s until about 1964.

Lea President's XI versus Lea in the 1950s
Back row: 3rd from left, Charles Peachey, 2nd from right, Bill Robins, 3rd from
right, Stan Young.
Front row 1st on left, Bill Hill, 2nd on left, Les Barker

Weston under Penyard

It is believed that in the early days one of the world's best known players, W.G. Grace, played on the ground, which is in the centre of the village. The team is recorded as playing from 1900 until the Second World War, and then from 1952 to 1972. They won the Brockhampton Cup in 1907 and 1920. They also won the Goodrich Cup in 1924, and the Longhope Cup in the 1930s and again in 1947.

A fête was organized to raise funds to develop the ground. The pavilion, which is now used by the football teams, was opened in July 1959. Gwen Berryman, who at the time played Doris Archer in the long-

Weston under Penyard 1947
Back row: Denis Robbins (scorer), [-], Ray Goode, [-], Phil Evans,
Edgar Phipps, Edgar Marfell
Front row: Ronnie Smith, Bill Robbins, Les Barker, Bert Barker, Eddie Clarke

Whitchurch about 1990
Back row: Tony Fletcher, Mike Payne, Adrian Howard (captain), Alf Ransom, Daniel Whyatt, Nick Whyatt, Roy Stevens
Front row: John Perrott, Paul Murtha, Julian Hazel, Pete Murtha, John Wall

running radio serial 'The Archers', opened the fête. The sum of £171 3s. 6d. was raised on the day. Before the new Village Hall was built in 1985 the team changed in the old tin reading room (built in 1898), before it became uneconomical to maintain.

The Robins family were involved in the club for several generations. Indeed, it is believed that at the turn of the century a Mr. Robins was the master of the local workhouse.

Whitchurch

A team can be traced at Whitchurch as far back as 1859 when they are recorded as having a team in Edwyn Anthony's *Hereford Cricket* published in 1903. In 1866 W.G. Grace, when still a teenager, played near Whitchurch for a West Gloucestershire XI.

Whitchurch is recorded as playing in 1942 and from 1958 until 1968. The most recent team in the village was formed in 1988. In the initial stages the team was formed from the locals at the Crown Inn in Whitchurch. They were a 'jeans and trainers' side and played a few local pub teams. In the early stages they played on the concrete and matting pitch at Harewood End. Thereafter, home fixtures were played at Monmouth Comprehensive School, again on an artificial wicket. Janet Howard, Jen Hazel and Jean Murtha provided the teas, which were made at home, there being no pavilion, and brought to the ground when they thought that the first innings might be over. As time went on the team improved and then played stronger village teams. Regrettably, after about 10 years 'active life, the club folded after

the 1997 season because the original players were getting older and there was no interest from local youngsters. The kit was donated to near neighbours, Goodrich.

Longhope

The club was formed in 1886 when the subscriptions were: new members 2s. 6d.; old members 2s.; junior under 16, half-price. The pitch was on

Longhope 1923. Brockhampton Cup Winners
Back row: Harold Wright, P. Williams, L.Williams, Bill Bowen, Walter James, W. Bowkett, Arthur Miles
Front row: Jack Bradley, Walter Sterry, Mr. Bowell, Bert Brown, Harold Bowkett

Longhope 1966. Huntley Cup Winners
Back row: Ian Davidson, Gerald Wyman, Tony Davies, Harold Wilson, [-], Christian Westmacott, Wilf Jones, Mr. Peachey (scorer)
Front row: Percy Yemm, Dave Cox, Harold Gurney, Geoff Sterry, Geoff Gurney

the recreation ground and the rules were strict on discipline:

> Any member using improper language or disobeying the Captain would be disciplined as follows, 1st offence fine 3d, 2nd offence fine 6d and 3rd offence expelled from the Club.

The first cricket balls used cost 5s. each and the scorebook 2s. They won the Brockhampton Cup five times in the first part of the century. In 1923 they ran two teams and in a game for the Brockhampton Cup the reserve side scored 44 against Brockhampton, who were all out for 33 (opposite). Influential members were Ian Cameron, who also served the club in an administrative capacity, and Harold Gurney, who on one occasion took 8 wickets for 11 runs despite being hit for four off his first ball. He was presented with a tankard for this unusual feat. He also received an inscribed cricket bat, presented to him by Ron Nicholls, the Gloucestershire opening batsman, for completing the season with a bowling average of 8 runs per wicket. Percy Yemm was an outstanding batsman for the club. In 1966 they won the Huntley Knockout Cup and in 1986/7 they won the Gloucester Indoor League Knockout Cup. The club ceased to play in their own right in 1989 and amalgamated with Huntley Cricket Club.

Goodrich / Bishopswood

The Moffatt family from Goodrich Court gave the land for the ground to the club, and in 1903 Goodrich played the first recorded game against Bishopswood. The two clubs amalgamated in 1904, playing at Goodrich under the name of 'Goodrich and Bishopswood', and in 1913 they won the Ross Cricket League. In 1914 there was a match between the team and a representative team selected from the remainder of the league. In 1909 Lady Moffatt presented the club with the

Goodrich Challenge Cup, which has been played for every year.

After the First World War both teams played under their own names from 1925 until 1932 after which Goodrich carried on alone.

The photograph (below), with the bearded gentleman in the second row, was found behind a cupboard in the old pavilion when it was being knocked down to make way for the new one that was being built in 2005. It is not known who the team is, but the bearded gentleman is either W.G. Grace (who played in various matches in the county between 1866 and 1896) or someone who looked exactly like him. The scorer in that photograph is also in the Goodrich

Goodrich Court in the early 1890s

A photograph that was found behind the panelling of the old pavilion at Goodrich. Is it really W.G. Grace in the middle row?

The Goodrich team in 1909 with Mrs. Moffatt from Goodrich Court

photograph dated 1909 (left).

The club won the Brockhampton Cup three times before the Second World War. The cup has been played for each year since 1909, the only breaks being the war years. Overall, Goodrich has been a very successful club, winning the trophy 45 times out of 98; other successful sides have included local teams Weston's, Hoarwithy, Brampton Abbotts, Sellack, Moreton and Lyde, Wormelow, Brockhampton, Bromyard, and Canon Frome.

Goodrich 1976 Cup winners
Back row: Mr. W Evans, Eric Winchester, Des Samuels, Gerald Hughes, Sam Birt, Richard Hope, Bill Marfell, Nick Reeves, Michael Evans, [-], Fred Browning (scorer)
Front row: Chris Young, Royston Young, Sam Herbert (chairman), Des Evans, Brian Nixon

Mrs Moffatt was president of the club until 1939, when Mrs. Trafford succeeded her. Transport had obviously presented somewhat of a problem in 1925, but it was resolved at the A.G.M. when it was agreed that the surplus of £6 in the account should be split between Mrs. Moffatt, Mr. C.C. Ibbitson and Mr. M.R.A. Herbert for lending their cars to transport the team to away matches.

One of the club's most loyal servants is Eric Winchester, who joined as a player when he moved to the county in 1952. He captained the club for six years in the 1960s and has

Goodrich old pavilion with Eric Winchester and Royston Young

also served the club as secretary, treasurer and chairman, and has been president since 1998. When his playing career was over Eric joined the Gloucester Umpires Association and was the club umpire for 25 years.

Sunday fixtures started with the entry into the Haig Village Knockout Competition in the 1970s. The club also entered into evening knockout competitions over the years. The most important change was in 1976 when they joined the Hereford and District League. In that year they achieved notable success, winning the Goodrich Cup, the Third Division Championship, and the Ross Junior Knockout Cup. The club has achieved other successes in competitions with many promotions and championships over the years; Division 4 of the Hereford and District League in 1975; the Ross Junior Cup in 1939 and 1959; and the Dymock Cup in 1999. Like many other teams, Goodrich joined the Marches League in 1996. They won the Hereford and District Cup in 2002.

In the 1990s, junior cricket was started at the club and the response was exceptional,

several juniors having progressed through the ranks to the first XI.

The club is now purchasing its own ground and the new pavilion will hopefully be completed by the end of 2007. In the course of the work many modern facilities have been added to the ground. The photograph (above) shows the old pavilion being knocked down in September 2005 with the president, Eric Winchester and chairman, Royston Young, overseeing the work.

Goodrich, under the captaincy of Andy Brown, was successful in the Marches League in 2006, winning the League and then the Cup when they beat Kington in the final. This was the first time that they have completed the double.

One of the main stalwarts of the team in recent years, both on and off the field, has been Richard Hope. He joined the club in 1970 and has been captain for 7 years. He was vice-chairman under Royston Young and took over the job of chairman in 2006. He still plays cricket and is now in the 2nd XI. He has been a

Upton Bishop. Brockhampton Cup winners 1920
Back row: Percy Browne, George Francis, Walter Moss, Walter Jones, Gilbert Price, George Payne
Front row: Cyril Lockwood, Charlie Clarke, Bill Thornley, Bill Stocker, Jack Gibbons
Sitting: Don Gardiner, Jack Loveridge

great help in providing much of the information relating to the club for this book. Other stalwarts of the club are Eric Winchester, who has held every office in the 56 years that he has been with the club; Royston Young, who has been with the club for 50 years; and Mike Evans, who has been with them since the 1960s and has been secretary since 1985. Clearly the club has a wealth of experience at the helm and the future looks bright.

Upton Bishop

The team was operational from 1909 until the late 1920s and also in 1960 and 1961. They won the Brockhampton Cup in 1920. One of the players in the photograph is Charlie Clarke, who later joined Perrystone, where he was eventually joined by his brother Jeff and the next generation.

CHAPTER VIII

South of Hereford

Bryngwyn / Wormelow

The team was originally known as Bryngwyn Cricket Club and played under that name between 1904 and 1910. They played at Bryngwyn Manor, the home of Sir James Rankin, the M.P. for Leominster, who formed the club. Wormelow Cricket Club was reformed and financed by a local racehorse breeder, Mrs. Simmonds, in the early 1930s. With the permission of Sir James Rankin, the reformed team played in the grounds of Bryngwyn Manor on a site called the Park until 1938.

The club had a fixture against the South Hereford Hunt cricket team and the Gas Board in 1935. When they played the Gas Board the wicket clearly favoured the bowlers. Wormelow scored a total of only 69 but still managed to win – 19 of the batsmen were clean bowled and A. Sharland took 6 wickets for just 12 runs.

The team met at the Wormelow Reading Room and travelled to away games in a lorry owned by their benefactor, Mrs. Simmonds, who was also the president of the club. In 1939 the team moved to their present ground called the Kennel Field, situated behind the Tump Inn in the village. The 1939 photograph (page 101) was taken at the first match played on the new ground. Activities ceased at the end of the 1939 season and did not start up again until 1965, when the club was reformed by Handley Scudamore,

Wormelow new pavilion which was opened in 1998

David Beaumont, Dave Verry, and Richard Crossman.

Richard Crossman was master of the South Hereford Hunt and loaned the Kennel Field to the club for the first year. There was no pavilion on the ground and he brought a large horsebox for the players to change in. The first match was appropriately against South Hereford Hunt, a regular fixture that had started in the days of Bryngwyn some thirty years earlier. In 1966 David Beaumont gave the club a summerhouse, which was used as a pavilion. The summerhouse was used until 1977 when the club purchased a large site hut from John Laing for £30. With the assistance of Stewart Blyth and Roger Colcombe, a club member transported the hut from Newport in South Wales to the ground. The old summerhouse was given to Harewood End who used it until they ceased to exist as a team. It was in a sorry state in 2006 and was demolished shortly afterwards (page 104).

Wormelow joined the Hereford and District League in 1979. The club were able to buy their ground at Kennel Field in 1982, thanks to negotiations carried out by Handley Scudamore, and this is their present home. They played Bangladesh in the 1960s and are one of the few village sides to host a national side.

Throughout the 1960s and '70s the club had two annual social fixtures against National Hunt Jockeys organized by local jockey, Michael Scudamore, and the Trevor Williams Removal Company. Whilst the games

Wormelow 1983
Back row: R Gummery (scorer), Chris Knock, Richard Evans, David Boulter, Mark Wadelin, Ted Amos
Front row: Stewart Blyth, Richard Prime (captain) Arthur Swain, Dave Verry, David Edmunds

Wormelow 1965
Anthony Morgan Hughes, Walter Davies, D. Williams, Trevor Whittaker, Tom Cook, Dr. Maurice McGinn, Dennis (Doc) Worthing, Guy Hughes, Bill Voyce (hidden), Roger Smee, Handley Scudamore, Richard Crossman (Master of South Hereford Hunt)

Wormelow 1978
Back row: John Colcombe, Dennis Hands, Geoff Prime (president), Ken Hook,
Clive Wadelin, Mark Wadelin, Martin Bowe, John White, Tom Cook
Front row: Chris Knock, Stewart Blyth, Dennis Pepper, Richard Prime,
Mike Stayte, Dave Verry

Wormelow 1939
Albert Sharland, Dave Sharland, Eric
Howe and young lady at Kennel Field

The club became founder members of the Marches League in 1992 and in 1998 a new pavilion was built at a cost of £125,000 (page 99). Stewart Blyth, a former player and life member, was instrumental in raising most of the cost through local events and a national grant and, in addition, he managed the building work. It was opened by one of England's finest test bowlers, Freddie Trueman, who is now sadly deceased. Wormelow won the Hereford and District League Cup in 2001 and the Worcester Division Three title in 2006.

National Hunt Jockeys
The team was formed by a local man, the former National Hunt Jockey and Grand National winner, Michael Scudamore, in 1956. The first game played was against Much Marcle and District Farmers being organized by Michael Scudamore and a local farmer, Roy Blandford. The game was played on Weston's Sports Ground behind the Slip Inn at Much Marcle. Included in the team were well-known members of the racing fraternity – Robin Knipe; David Nicholson and H. Nicholson; Peter Scudamore's grandfather, Michael Duffield; and three local amateur jockeys, Basil Mullins; Dave Sharland; and Harold Thompson. For the

were played competitively, the after match socialising in the local hostelry was in the right spirit. Two of the most successful weeks in the club's history were in 1968 when one weekend they won the Goodrich Cup and on the following one they won the Rockfield Knockout Cup at Monmouth. They ran a 20-over Knockout Competition in the early 1980s, but it only lasted for a short period of time. The first winners were local rivals Burghill and Tillington. On one occasion in one of these matches the fielder at extra cover was somewhat surprised to have a hang-glider make an emergency landing right by him. Wormelow embarked on a number of tours out of the County including Liverpool in the 1960s, Somerset in the 1970s and the Gower coast in the 1980s.

National Hunt jockeys and cricketers
Above: Michael Scudamore   Right: Robin Knipe

record the Jockeys won by 7 runs. The main contributors to the match were Dave Sharland, who scored 55, and Harold Thompson and H. Nicholson, who both took 4 wickets to seal the victory. Other team members were Victor Speck, Derek Ancil, and R. Hamey. Several other jockeys, some of them nationally known, played on various occasions for the team, including George Slack, Paddy Cowley, James Knipe, Frenchie Nicholson (David's father), Rex Hamey, and Stan Mellor. Some of the local teams they played were

Wormelow, Moreton and Lyde, and the North and South Hereford Hunts. The team only play the odd game nowadays and play in the Lambourn area.

Michael Scudamore also played local cricket for Wormelow and Hoarwithy. His first winner was for Mrs. Amy Simmonds, the president of Wormelow Cricket Club and master of the South Hereford Hunt. He clearly loved playing cricket, but he was an outstanding jockey, in which sport he made his career, winning the Grand National and the Cheltenham Gold Cup. One of the most famous

National Hunt Jockeys' team
Back row: Hunter Rowe, L. Ensten, W. Bonner, N. Elliott Brooks, J. Elliott Brooks, P. Hodgkinson, M. Hillman, J. Bracey
Middle row: N. Goddard, Josh Goddard, V. Dartnell, J. Knipe, N. Williams, A. Porter, G. Dartnell, B. Hillman, [-]
Front row: M. Wylie, Terry Biddlecombe, J. Arters, R. Nicholson, D. Nicholson, W. Murstoe, M. Scudamore, J. Meads

National Hunt champion jockey and local cricketer Peter Scudamore.

owners that he rode for was Sir Freddie Laker. When Michael Scudamore retired from cricket, his son Peter took over the 'reins' as captain and manager of the jockeys' team. Colin Cowdrey, the former England captain, saw Peter playing at Arundel and described his bowling as 'interesting little tweakers'.

David Nicholson, the well-known jockey and trainer, who was a stalwart of the jockeys' cricket team, sadly died in 2006.

South Hereford Hunt Cricket team
It is believed that Mrs Amy Simmonds, master of the hunt and local racehorse breeder and trainer, formed the team in the 1930s. Michael Scudamore rode his first National Hunt winner for her yard. Before Wormelow played at the Kennel Field, the South Hereford Hunt XI used it periodically. On the re-formation of Wormelow Cricket Club in 1965, Wormelow adopted Mrs. Simmonds racing colours. In 1939 Mrs. Simmonds took a side to play Hereford Cricket Club, appropriately, at the Racecourse. She is pictured in the middle of the photograph (below left). Some of their regular opponents were North Hereford Hunt, Wormelow, Harewood End, Hoarwithy, and the Merry Millers. It is understood that the side still plays social cricket.

Harewood End / Harewood Park
A cricket team has been in existence at Harewood from as early as 1892 and is recorded playing between 1900 and 1909. The team was formerly known as Harewood Park and there is a report of a match between Harewood Park and Wormelow in the *Hereford Times* dated May 1892.

The team re-formed in 1946 after the war and played at Elviston Drive on farmland occupied by Harold Badger, who also played cricket for the South Hereford Hunt side. The ownership eventually passed to Sid Williams. Harewood End Sports was formed in 1947 and incorporated cricket, football, darts, and cribbage. The cricket team moved to their final ground, close to the A49 and half-a-mile from the village, in 1952. The field was on a mound surrounded by trees and behind a stone lodge at the entrance to the drive of the now demolished house. A local innkeeper, Percy Kinch, and his brother, Ebor, took an active part in the club in the 1930s and local farmers Godfrey and Frank Davies were involved in the club after the Second World War.

In 1953 Frank Spendlove was appointed captain but, very regrettably, broke his arm prior to the season starting and never played serious cricket again. Dave Sharland was appointed captain instead and remained in the post

South Hereford Hunt 1939
Back row: Harold Badger (umpire), Colin Howe, [-], Harry Lucas, E. Watkins, [-], Percy Kinch, J. Fisher
Front row: Bill Beeks, Bert Sharland, Mrs. Amy Simmonds, (master of hunt), Eric Howe, [-]

Harewood End, Married versus Singles 1962
Back row: Aubrey Innes, Arthur Moss, Fred Cotterill, Roger Partridge,
Percy Kinch, Godfrey Davies
Front row: Bernard Curtis, Jim Rainsford, Ted Harris (umpire), Mr. Prosser

for many years. The original pavilion was a tin shed, the replacement, an old summerhouse, being a gift from Wormelow in 1970.

On one memorable occasion the team was playing the St. Mary's Hospital side at Burghill. Two players, Godfrey Davies and Tony Cotterill, needed to answer a call of nature. They asked directions and were dutifully led to the lavatories. The door was unlocked and they were let in, but once inside they heard the door being locked from the outside. After much shouting they were rescued by a member of staff and advised that one of the mental patients had locked them in!

In about 1962 a player was hit on the head by a cricket ball and knocked out. The pavilion door was removed and used as an improvised stretcher.

The club won the Brockhampton Cup in 2001 but folded shortly thereafter. The pavilion (bottom left) stood empty for several years and was eventually demolished in 2006.

Hoarwithy
The club was founded in 1919. When Hoarwithy dismissed Broomsgreen for 14 runs in the final of the Brockhampton Cup in September 1925, they must have been confident of winning the trophy, but their hopes were dashed when they were dismissed for a total of 8. They made amends when they won the Goodrich Cup in 1929. In 1938, Lady Densham, who was president of the club, donated a silver Challenge Cup to the club to be played for every year. The final always took place on Whit Monday. The club stopped playing during the war years but resumed successfully after the war.

In 1952 the Club put up a trophy consisting of a casket containing the ashes of old cricket bats which was called the Withys. The trophy was played for each year on August Bank Holiday Monday between the club and, usually, the

Harewood End pavilion derelict in 2006, prior to its demolition

Harewood End
Left: Dave Sharland, captain, with trusty sheepdog

Above: Frank Davies

Hoarwithy, Lady Densham Cup 1960
Back row: Brian Hehir, Bill Reynolds, Bill Harris, Les Dallow,
Ron England, Stan Brookes (chairman)
Front row: Frank Edmonds, Sid Harris, Stan Partington, Ray Davies,
Tony Hehir, Norman Owen

Hoarwithy branch of the British Legion. In 1960 the team beat Woolhope for the cup (left).

The ground was in the centre of the village behind the New Harp public house, and the club fixtures were nailed to a tree outside the pub. Before the pavilion was built tea was served in the village Reading Room. The pavilion is shown in the background of the photograph when Bill Harris won the Player of the Year award in the 1960s (below). In July 1971 the club entertained a Gibson-Watt XI which turned up with a side including Captain J.M. Gibson-Watt who was president of Llandrindod Wells Cricket Club in 1913; his son David Gibson-Watt, one time M.P. for Hereford who later became Lord Gibson-Watt; and David's son, Robin. Hoarwithy batted first and scored 131 runs for 8 wickets. The highest scorer was Keith Bishop with 28. The Gibson-Watts took four of the Hoarwithy wickets. The tea interval maintained the quality of the occasion when appropriate socialising took place. In the

The cartoonist, Grier, links up Mr. Gibson-
Watt's recent cricket playing activities with some
of the difficulties he faced as Hereford's M.P.

Hoarwithy pavilion is in the background of this
photograph of Bill Harris receiving the
Player of the Year Trophy

10539

J. B. & O. TOPPING

Grocery, Provisions and Newsagents

THE STORES
HOARWITHY, HEREFORD

M   Hoarwithy Cricket Club 26-8-1967

1	*by Serviettes 2/6 Dish Cloth 1/-*	3	7
2	*Sr. Vinegar 1/2* ___ *HRO 8/8/67*	1	2
3	*Afternoon Cake " Serviettes 1/- NRO 14/8/67*	1	10
4			
5	*2 Sugar*	1	6
6	*1/4 Tea*	1	6
7	*1/2 cheese*	1	11
8	*Tn Salmon*	3	1
9	*2 Tomatoes*	1	4
10	*1 onion*		4
11	*eggs*	1	11
12	*1 fruit cake 2/6 1 angel cake*	4	10
13	*1 Madeira cake*	2	2
14	*2 Pints Milk*	1	8
15	*1 Tn Milk*	1	5
16	*11/3 Magic Magazine*	2	5
17		£1	10 9

Hoarwithy bill for teas supplied in 1967

second innings the Gibson-Watt XI were all out for 118 runs, David Gibson-Watt scoring 18 of the team's total. Hoarwithy bowlers Les Dallow and Bill Harris took seven wickets between them. All had a wonderful day.

When the Hon. Gentleman was batting it is rumoured that village humour took over when he was hit in the box and, whilst adjusting himself, a close fielder commented that it must have been the quickest recount of his Parliamentary career!

The cost of providing the ingredients for the teas for both teams in 1967 was the grand sum of £1 10s. 9d. The feast included salmon, cheese and tomato sandwiches, and three different types of cake.

A Basset hound belonging to the jockey Michael Scudamore was a frequent unwanted visitor on match days because he refused to leave the field of play! Michael received regular telephone calls to ask him to remove his dog. The club ceased playing in 1973 and the pavilion was transferred to Holme Lacy; the ground is now used as a camping site. Even so, the foundations of the pavilion can still be seen and the roller was still on the site of the old ground in February 2006.

Garway / Skenfrith

At the beginning of the 20th century the villagers acquired 23 acres of land behind the Garway Moon Inn and turned it into a sports ground, including a cricket pitch. They are recorded as playing until 1910 when they won the Goodrich Cup. No further records have been found until they re-formed in 1971 as the Merry Millers.

Merry Millers

The team was formed in 1971, mainly made up of local farmers. In the first season they played in jeans and trainers. The team had no pitch of their own, and it was exceedingly generous of Wormelow to allow them to play on their ground in the first season. The biggest decision at the first A.G.M., held at the Hereford United Social Club, was to play in whites. The team did not play in any leagues, and only played friendlies, but they believe that they were one of the first teams to encourage limited-over cricket to ensure that, weather permitting, a result could be achieved. The team moved to Garway Common in 1972 and created a pitch from scratch. There was no changing room so they changed in the local garage or pub. Because they played on common ground they could not have a pavilion. Many members said, 'We cannot have a permanent erection on Garway Common!' The team also boasted that, whilst they might be beaten on the field of play, they would not be beaten in the bar after the match!

One of the highlights of the year was the annual dinner, held initially at Park Hall Ballroom, then at the S.A.S. camp at Bradbury Lines, and finally at the Three Counties Hotel in Hereford. The club invited well-known sporting celebrities to speak at the dinners, including Tommy Docherty and Dickie Bird. There was a hard-core team, the remainder

Above: Richard Illingworth Worcestershire Testimonial Match 1997
Above: Merry Millers Team: Back row: M Evans, A. Nicholls, J. Roberts, A. Watkins,
C. Heath, J. Foley, V. Hope, B. Gilg
Front row: A. Heath, I. Pugh, S. Perks, S. Dix (captain), N. Evans, F. Lane, I. Evans.

Right: Merry Millers 1997. (Richard Illingworth benefit match)

being guest players from other clubs. They played between 20 and 23 games per season. In the 1990s the club won the Golden Valley Knockout Shield.

In 1997 the club hosted a benefit match for England and Worcestershire player Richard Illingworth at Brockhampton, raising about £1000 for Richard and also boosting the Millers' club funds. The Howells family from Brockhampton featured prominently in the game supplying two umpires, Gerald and Bert, and the scorer, Jean, Gerald's wife. In 1980 the club could boast a world champion in their team – club member Vivian Samuel won the world ploughing championship in New Zealand. The year 2000 saw the outbreak of foot and mouth disease in Herefordshire, and because one of the worst affected areas was that around Garway, no cricket was allowed. The younger players went elsewhere to play and sadly the team folded.

Strollers' Cricket Club
Strollers' Cricket Club was formed in 1964 when a group of young Christian men got together at the Barton Hall in Hereford following a youth rally. The club draws members from churches of all denominations county-wide. The ethos of the club was, and still is, to enjoy cricket, to play fair, to play to win but not at all costs. The first match was played on 16 May 1964 against Hunderton Youth Club at Red Hill. Captained by Vic Newman, who is now president of the club, the Strollers made 139 runs for 7 wickets with James A.D. Roberts making 52. Hunderton was bowled out for 49. Home matches were played on King George's Playing Field. In the early years the Strollers' bowling was dominated by Phil Keene and Peter Metcalfe, but it was boosted when Michael Bentley-Taylor returned from university. James Roberts, Vic Newman and Peter Metcalfe scored most of the runs.

The team moved their home games to Widemarsh Common in 1972 before returning to King George's briefly. In 1983 home matches were relocated to the Grammar School ground behind the Fire Station at Ross-on-Wye. In 1987 they moved to the bouncy artificial wicket at John Kyrle school in Ross and remained there until 2005, when they moved to their present location at Ledbury Rugby Club.

It took 21 years before a Stroller scored a century, but in 1985 Neil Hartley scored 100 against Ewyas Harold. It did not prove enough though as Robin Michael scored a century for the

Strollers versus Presidents 1983

Back row: James.S. Roberts, Andrew Watkins or Chris Powell's son, Chris Powell,
Martin Skirrow, David Davies, Jonathan Stephens, David Stephens, Rhoda Roberts,
Steve Timbrell, Betty Barnfield, John Rudge, Rob Powell, Aubrey Barnfield,
Stewart Wigney, Frank Ware, Dave Morgan, Peter Metcalfe
Front row: Paul Wilson, Steve Rudge, James A.D. Roberts (president),
Dave Roberts (captain), Dave Price

opposition and Strollers lost the match. In 1989 Neil Hartley, Dave Roberts and Rob Powell all scored centuries. The longest serving captain was Martin Skirrow who was in charge from 1988 to 2005 apart from a couple of years working away. The longest playing member is Rob Powell who first played for Strollers in 1968 against Hoarwithy. He was still keeping wicket in 2006.

In 2005 the team won every league match culminating in victory at Hay-on-Wye. Strollers continue to go from strength to strength and in 2006 they started a second team for the first time to encourage younger people to play and develop. They also embarked on their first tour, travelling to the Bournemouth area in September 2006.

Holme Lacy

There were two grounds at Holme Lacy. The original ground, which was by Pound Farm opposite the Holme Lacy Agricultural College, is now used by the college as a sports field. According to Francis

Strollers' 2005

Back row: Doug Roberts, Keith Bushell, Richard Lerego, Simon Albright, Peter Skirrow
Front row: Rob Powell, Mark Powell, Martin Skirrow (captain),
Rob Bentley-Taylor, James Powell

Strollers' three centurions 1989
Neil Hartley, Dave Roberts, Rob Powell

No. 12   Sch 20 1939

Received of Mr. G. Lewis

the Sum of _____ Pounds

Two Shillings and six Pence

subscription for 1939

£ : 2/6.

Holme Lacy

Above: Receipt for subscription for 1939

Right: Fixture list 1960

HOLME LACY CRICKET CLUB

CRICKET FIXTURES
SEASON - 1960

President—Mr. F. F. Poole

Vice-Presidents—
Mr. G. C. Pryse-Rice, Mr. J. Mathews,
Mr. Williams, Mr. P. Perkins

Captain—Mr. A. G. Bishop

Vice-Captain—Mr. C. Basford

Hon. Secretary—Mr. A. Bishop,
2, Wyelands, Holme Lacy

Charge of 2/- each for Teas Home Matches

Perkins the club was formed in the 1920s by Percy and Monty Perkins. Francis, of Moreton and Lyde Cricket Club, was Percy's grandson.

The second ground was opened sometime after 1935 and is behind the village hall. There is a football changing room there now, but originally the teams used to change in the village hall. One of the best known players was the late Bert Bishop who, in addition to playing cricket for Holme Lacy, also played football for Hereford City.

In 1921 the club at their A.G.M. agreed that for that year they would only play friendly matches. The club stopped for the war years and reformed after the war.

The club's last full year was 1960 when they unfortunately folded even though they had a full list of fixtures. The pavilion, which is now used as football changing rooms, was moved to Holme Lacy from Hoarwithy when that team ceased playing.

Little Dewchurch

There is evidence of a cricket ground at Little Dewchurch during the Second World War because in June 1944 a piece of ground called Croft Cricket Little Dewchurch was sold. It was described in the sale particulars as 2.460 acres of pasture, orchard, house and buildings.

The club ground was on Court farmland behind the bakery and they played there until 1965. Noel Lewis, the local headmaster, founded the team in 1954 and ran the team during the late 1950s and early '60s. He also coached the boys in his school including Ken Hook, one of the authors of this book. Ken recalls being asked to play when the team were short when he was only 12 years old.

Holme Lacy pavilion 2006

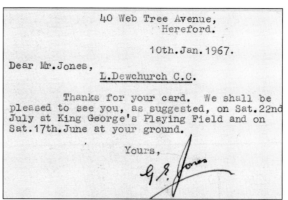

Little Dewchurch

Left: The score card for a match against Painters' Second XI in 1958

Above: A 1967 note confirming future matches with the Burley Gate team

There is a story about one of the stalwarts of the club who always insisted on playing immaculately dressed. He wore a fancy cap, had a tie round his waist, and wore creams instead of whites. On one occasion when he came in to bat, he noticed that a buckle was broken on his pads and trooped off the pitch. He insisted on changing both pads and when he returned he complained that the sun was in his eyes so he went off again to get a cap. When he returned about 9 minutes later, the bowler who had been kept waiting at the end of his run was none too pleased. His off stump disappeared first ball.

The offside boundary at Little Dewchurch created an interesting problem for the batsman because the ground dropped about four feet and he could only see the head and shoulders of a fielder at cover point. The ball would disappear down the slope, which made running an interesting proposition.

The team left their ground at Little Dewchurch in 1967 and Derrick Jones recalled that they then played on the King George Playing Fields in Hereford from 1968 until finally ceasing a few years later. The original ground at Little Dewchurch is now a housing estate called Court Close.

Blanches

Blanches cricket ground was at Green Crize and was a private club run by Cyril Blanche. The team was an invitation XI and, in addition to friendly matches, they played in the Leominster and Ross knockout competitions. Cyril Blanche was a baker, and Maurice Joseph, one of his regular players, recalled that on one occasion some of the team travelled to an away match in the back of one of Blanche's works vans and that by the time they had completed the journey they had polished off a whole tray of éclairs that had been left in the van.

Before the housing estate was built at Newton Farm, Angela Powell, now wife of Danny Wright, a former Hereford cricketer, was living in the original farmhouse and remembered sitting in the bedroom with her sister Joyce and hearing a loud bang caused by a bomb exploding about two miles away. At the same time a member of the cricket team was cycling home along Holme Lacy Road after a match when he felt the tremendous blast from the exploding bomb and nearly fell off his bike!

Blanches won the Evening League Division Two in 1953 and Division Three in 1959. They also won the six-a-side competition in 1963. In about 1962 Blanches boasted that play was suspended for a most unusual reason, namely play was stopped because a flock of low flying swallows flew over the pitch catching insects. Terry Court, a former player, remembered playing in the last ever game at Blanches after which Peter Hutchinson's socks were ceremoniously hung up in the pavilion. There is a rumour that they were still there many years later. The club ceased to play in the late 1960s or early 1970s.

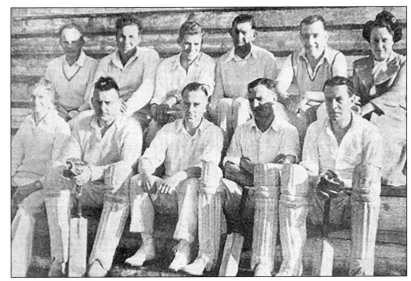

Boundary XI

The team was formed by Danny Wright and Colin Morgan and played during the 1950s on ground owned by Colin Morgan at Grafton Lane. The team consisted of a group of friends and family who did not play regular cricket. It included the late Ted Jones, who ran a well known agricultural parts business in Hereford cattle market. Their opponents included Hereford Taxis, Credenhill and Stretton Sugwas, Madley R.A.F.A, Ambulance Station,

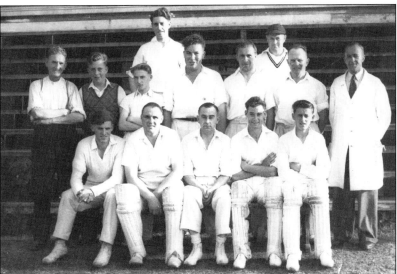

Blanches

Top left: 1952 team in the Hereford Evening League Division Two

Centre left: Hereford Evening League Division Three Champions 1959
Back row: W. White (grounds man), B. State (scorer), J. Palamountain, D. Preece, B. White, W. Williams, E. Hill, Cyril Blanche, L. Savory (umpire)
Front row: M. Joseph, W. Jones, J. Armitage (captain), D Sockett, B. Savory

Blanches pavilion, derelict in 2006

B.T.H. v BOUNDARY	
Played at Rotherwas on Sunday.	
B.T.H.	
M. Roebuck b Wright	4
K. Roebuck b Wright	36
J. Peterson b Jones	2
N. Yarwood c Wright b Jones	53
J. Hall b Wright	14
J. Crump b Wright	0
J. Chawner b Wright	20
R. Elton not out	10
L. Gore not out	0
Extras 8 (7 dec.) —	144
Jones 2-58, Wright 5-49.	
Boundary	
A. Morris c Jones b Roebuck	2
N. Davidson b Roebuck	13
D. Wright b Roebuck	0
T. Curtis c Jones b Roebuck	2
R. Heath run out	2
W. Bishop c Chawner b Roebuck	0
E. Jones c Jones b Peterson	1
F. Tilby b Peterson	0
C. Moreton b Peterson	0
B. Leonard not out	6
F. Powell c Chawner b Peterson	1
Extras 1 —	28
Roebuck 5-10, Peterson 4-5	

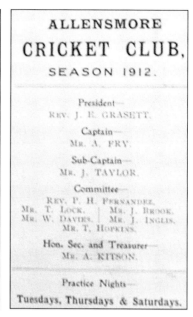

BOUNDARY CRICKET CLUB 1958

Chairman—Mr. K. POWELL

Vice-Chairman—Mr. C. MORGAN

Hon. Secretary—Mr. D. POWELL
(Hereford 3366)

Hon. Treasurer—Mr. E. JONES

Hon. Match Secretary—Mr. D. WRIGHT
(Hereford—Business 3057 ; Home 5346)

Captain—Mr. D. WRIGHT

Vice-Captain—Mr. A. MORRIS

ALLENSMORE CRICKET CLUB,

SEASON 1912.

President—
REV. J. E. GRASETT.

Captain—
MR. A. FRY.

Sub-Captain—
MR. J. TAYLOR.

Committee—
REV. P. H. FERNANDEZ,
MR. T. LOCK. | MR. J. BROOK,
MR. W. DAVIES. | MR. J. INGLIS,
MR. T. HOPKINS.

Hon. Sec. and Treasurer—
MR. A. KITSON.

Practice Nights—
Tuesdays, Thursdays & Saturdays.

Left: Boundary XI score card in 1958.   Centre: Boundary XI Fixture list cover 1958
Right: Allensmore Fixture list cover 1912

Herefordians, Vincent Greenhouse Social Club, Eardisland, Moreton and Lyde, and Shop Assistants. Danny Wright also played for the Shop Assistants in the Evening League.

Allensmore

The ground was behind the school. According to *Edwyn Anthony 1903* they were formed as early as 1859. They played on a regular basis in the years leading up to the First World War. In the 1950s they played on land by the Post Office, owned by the Pateshall family, and are recorded in the *Hereford Times* as playing in 1952. Gwynne Jones, current chairman of the Herefordshire Minor Counties team, recalled that he went to Allensmore as a young man in the 1950s with Mardy Cricket Club and remembered playing on the ground near the school.

Pontrilas and Ewyas Harold

Pontrilas and Ewyas Harold are geographically close and are dealt with jointly as they have been closely associated throughout the last century.

Pontrilas Cricket Club was formed in 1905. In the early part of the century the club put up a cup to be played for annually. There are no

Allensmore 1950s team
Back row: Lew Rees, Alan Morgan, Wat Hall, Aubrey Lawrence, Frank Davies
Front row: Derek Graham, [fire officer], Ernie Preece, Con Edwards,
Keith Edwards, Ivor Jones

known records and the cup has since been lost. Kentchurch, who are reported under their own name in the *Hereford Times* in 1904, amalgamated with Pontrilas in 1909. On 27 March 1909 a report in the *Hereford Journal* notes that, because of the pending departure from the area of Rev. A.J. Bannister and several prominent members of the Kentchurch and Grosmont Cricket Club, operations by both Ewyas Harold and Kentchurch were to be suspended. All the equipment belonging to these clubs was handed over to the members of Pontrilas Cricket Club. The new club was fortunate that Mr. W. Morgan from Pontrilas Court promised them the use of a suitable meadow at Elm Crossing.

Father Ignacio, a priest in the remote monastic order of Capel-y-finn, generously left a cricket ground to the village. He apparently used to walk round the village in his monastic habit frightening the local children.

Reg Michael, who was also associated with Ewyas Harold for many years, was secretary of Pontrilas in 1930 and advertised for fixtures in the *Hereford Times*. He was still playing for the club in 1952. Elmer Sayce was president of the club during the 1950s. Pontrilas won the Perrystone Cup in 1930. Pontrilas were playing under their own name in 1952, having started playing at the Recreation Ground in about 1950.

Players who should be mentioned are Bill Beekes, who played after the war and was apparently an enormous hitter of a cricket ball and who scored many runs for the club; Tom Morgan, from the garage at Ewyas Harold, who remembered

Pontrilas 1940s
Back row: [-], [-], Billy Johnson
Centre back row: Billy Beekes, H.R. Highnam, Chris Evans, [-], [-],
B.A. Williams, [-], Cecil Smith (umpire)
Centre front row: Emily Kennard (tea lady), Alf Smith, Reg Michael, [-],
Sid Cole, [-], Sissie Cole (tea lady)
Front row: W. Morgan, [-], Dorothea Bowkett (scorer), Humphrey Haynes, [-]

Ewyas Harold 1954 Runners up H.G. Stone Cup
Back row: V. Evans, R. Brisland, T. Brisland, T. Morgan, W. Davies,
H. Jenkins, F. Didcote (umpire)
Front row: H. Bishop, D. Cole, A. Smith, S. Hurle, W. Morgan

Ewyas Harold 1982
Back row: Ian Wigglesworth, Tommy Yaylor, Phil Brookes, Geoff Yapp, Keith Manning, Martin Wright,
Nick Osborne, Les Dallow, Robin Michael, John Middle, Bob Davies, Hugh Jenkins, Derek Manning
Front row: Billy Beavan, John Wigglesworth, [friend of president], Dr. Richardson, Harry Prosser, Tom
Morgan, Elmer Sayce (president), Reg Michael, Peter Davie, Derek Smith, David Smith

playing at Pigeon Meadow after the Second World War; and Jim Cole, the landlord of the Red Lion who owned the ground and allowed the team to leave the club kit in a spare room and who provided the teas in the tea interval.

Ewyas Harold cricket team, playing jointly with the football club, were runners up in the H.G. Stone Cup in 1954 when they were playing at the Recreation Ground. They played friendly matches for many years until they joined the Hereford and District League and thereafter the Marches League where they still play. Reg Michael, who was closely associated with both clubs both on and off the field of play, is in the above photograph together with many other stalwarts of the club when they celebrated the opening of their new pavilion. Ewyas Harold are a traditional local village club who still enjoy their cricket and no doubt will continue to do so.

CHAPTER IX

The Golden Valley, Kington, Presteigne & West Herefordshire

Hay-on-Wye

Hay-on-Wye is about 21 miles from Hereford and seven from Brecon and in recent years has become famous as the town of books. There is evidence that the local team played every year from the turn of the 20th century until the outbreak of the First World War, and resumed after the war was over. The club played on the playing field in Brecon Road.

Dr. Tom Hincks is seated centrally at the far end of the table on the playing field in the early 1900s. In the 1920s Dr. Hincks was treating the wife of Henry Rowse Armstrong the infamous Hay solicitor and also Oswald Martin, a solicitor in a rival practice. Dr. Hincks suspected that both Mrs. Armstrong and Mr. Martin were suffering from arsenic poisoning; the authorities were informed and as a result Armstrong was successfully prosecuted and hanged for the murder of his wife

The club ran a knockout competition in the 1920s and at that time the ground was on the English side of the Welsh border in Cusop. The next ground was at Cooper's Hall in the Clifford area, again just over the border. The 1950s saw a major change thanks to the efforts of Cliff Carr, Eric Gittoes and Sid Wilding, who revamped the ailing club with new players.

The new regime took on the task of reshaping and resurfacing the Playing Fields pitch, where the current side still plays. Members could often be seen carrying buckets of stones off the outfield at weekends. The club originally only played friendly matches but joined the Hereford League in 1974. They climbed the league and eventually settled in Division 2. A second team was formed to cater for the younger members. Their biggest achievement was when the under-13s reached the semi-final of the Welsh Cup in 1993. Regrettably the second team folded in 2000 because of a lack of young players coming through.

Hay can boast one of the most unusual reasons for a match being held up. A Hay bookshop owner, Greg Coombes, landed his helicopter on the pitch whilst play was taking place.

Golden Valley

Guy Goring, Owen Davies and his brother, Nigel, formed the team in 1948. The first president was the Rev. G.H. Powell in 1949. The first match was in April of that year against Presteigne. Several touring sides visited Dorstone over the years including a London Police side and the Falcon's touring team.

Owen Davies, one of the founder members, had a trial for Worcestershire before the Second World War and both Owen and Nigel played for the club for many years. Nigel was an opening batsman who bowled occasionally; Owen was a fine bowler. He applied for a trial with Glamorgan, but was turned down because he was not born in Wales. However, he went to Worcestershire before the War and played in the Nursery XI in 1936. In the *Worcestershire Year Book* the following year it was reported that: 'Davies has made good strides and now that he has developed a much smoother run and follow through, we are hopeful that he may prove his worth shortly in first class cricket.' He was offered a contract at 48 shillings per week, but could not afford to accept it, so he returned to farming and the Golden Valley in 1939. In 1940 he went for a trial with Gloucestershire, but decided to return to Dorstone and he spent the rest of his life playing local cricket. He continued actively with the game and played until he was 72 years old, just a year before his death.

Golden Valley team 1950
Back row: Glyn Williams, Bert Welsby, Jack Johnson, Guy Goring,
Frank Shufflebotham, Cecil Williams, Ken Carter,
Mr. Shufflebotham (umpire), Dave Oxenham
Front row: Don Thomas, Eddie Phillips, Owen Davies, Mrs. B. Welsby (scorer),
Elwyn Jones, Jack Davies, John Deville

Nigel Davies, at the age of 92, was delighted to recount his family history for inclusion in this book. The pitch at Dorstone was on loan from local farmers, the Gorings, who lived at Dorstone Court. The rent was £25 per annum and did not increase throughout the life of the club. Cricket was in the Davies' blood; Nigel and Owen's father, John, was a cricketer and was a student at Clyde House School at the turn of the century together with the county's most famous all-round sportsman, Jack Sharp (Chapter I). The team also ran a ladies' side in the late 1950s and the team included Miss Cobb – an England player.

The pavilion stands empty today and its concrete pitch is idle – the matting pad gathers dust on the tea table. The club drew stumps in

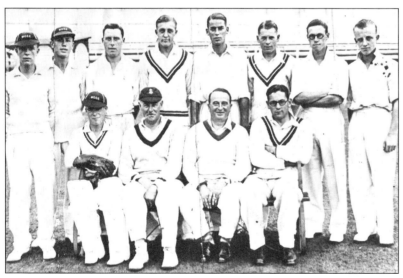

Worcestershire Nursery Team 1936
Back row: [-], Roly Jenkins, Owen Davies, Eddie Cooper, Joe Horton, Leonard Oakley, Charles Palmer, Vernon Grimshaw
Front row: Hugo Yarnold, George Platt (coach ex Surrey), Albert Lane, Phil King

2005, mainly because of lack of support, and its gates closed for the final time.

Support of a different kind helped some of the club's youngest members in one of those stories that seem to follow village cricket around. Several years ago, at the start of the season, the boys arrived early to set up the pitch. The coconut matting that used to cover the concrete pitch was still where it had been left at the end of the previous season, rolled up on the pavilion table out of the way of the mice. As the team lifted the mat to carry it out to the square someone cried 'Stop!' and the mat was replaced. An enterprising pair of wagtails had built their nest in the centre of the matting roll and there, sat impassively on the nest, was one of the pair, blinking back at the bemused cricketers. Compassion prevailed and one bright spark had an idea. After the bird had been allowed to fly off (out through the broken pane in the home side's changing room window where it had got in) the nest (containing four shiny eggs) was carefully slid out onto a piece of board. The shell-bound occupants and their nest were placed up on the rafters of the pavilion in the hope that the sentry would return. It was all down to hope. All through the game anxious eyes watched the pavilion to see if the bird returned. The tea interval was met with an even madder dash than usual to the pavilion, as the team was keen to see if their ploy had worked. To their delight, there, peeping over the edge of the nest, was the stoic wagtail, seemingly unconcerned by the clinking of

tea cups and general babble below, or by the fact that its nest had been moved to a more lofty location. At the end of the match the rolled mat was returned to the table and, out of respect for its original choice of nesting site, the nest and its four eggs were returned to the centre of the mat and the door closed gently behind them.

This wildlife-friendly ritual was repeated at subsequent home games until the day came when the nest was retrieved from its hiding place within the mat to be greeted by four hatchlings. With the nest safe in the pavilion rafters, the game got under way and, to the delight of the home side, the two diligent parents could be seen ferrying copious quantities of food to their brood. Neither wagtail parent ever seemed to worry about why their usually stationary nest could be in one of two places – home and away the team called it. The moral that a disturbed nest is abandoned was happily not true for the Golden Valley Cricket Club wagtails as the four newcomers grew steadily until the nest threatened to burst open. The day came all too quickly when the team arrived to find an empty nest and the youngsters grown and flown. If wagtail parents could talk to their offspring, the team would be happy to know that there are four new wagtail parents out there in Dorstone somewhere telling their partners that a cricket pavilion is not a bad place to rear a family!

Dorstone

The club was formed in 1974 and grew from a local desire to play cricket when the Golden Valley Cricket Club had too many players. The club played originally on the Golden Valley pitch when the Golden Valley was playing away, but

The disused Golden Valley pavilion in 2006

Dorstone pavilion

now play on Dorstone sports ground, which is owned by the church. They have gone from strength to strength since they were founded, playing regular cricket on weekends. Dorstone enjoyed a memorable season in 1998 when they won the Gateway Building Society Cup, which is now the Burgoyne Shield. The club issued a booklet in 1999 to celebrate the first 25 years, and the chairman, Chris Barker, wrote:

2000 might see developments like an enlarged pitch or astro-turf but the essence of the club will remain the same: enjoyable cricket played in the right spirit.

Bert Morgan was the groundsman in the 1970s and '80s and contributed greatly to the club. Their first recorded game, against the Harold Bishop XI, is recorded in a scruffy book kept under Philip Parrington's bed! Early members, keen to form the club, were Ross McIntyre, Chris Barker, Ken Dillon, Ian Beaton and Owen Davies. Owen continued in later life and was an inspiration to the team. A regular guest player is Antonio Mayers, who played for the West Indies A. He is a regular player in Barbados and has fielded as substitute in a test match.

Moccas

The modern Moccas club was formed in 1975 by Joe Brown, David Brown, Colin Hinksman and Laurie Whittal, although there is documentary evidence in the *Hereford Times* confirming that there was a club playing in 1909 and 1910 and again from 1963 until 1969. The team play in the grounds of Moccas Court which is owned by Mr. and Mrs.

Dorstone 2001 team
Back row: Tim Corner, William Barker, Tyson De Souza, Chesterfield Walcott, Miles De Souza, Dave Parker
Front row: Antonio Mayers, Barry Swain, Nick Osborne, Chris Barker, Ian Beaton.
On floor: Rob Garrad

Moccas pavilion in 2006

Chester-Master. The new pavilion was built by Arthur Howells, his son Russell, and Joe Brown. After the 1990 season Moccas won the Gateway Building Society's Hay-on-Wye Shield. Members of the team recalled an unusual incident when Bill Bowen took 9 wickets in a game against Dymock, one of the wickets falling in unusual circumstances. The batsman was Les Darker and when he hit the ball it struck Bob Bowen on the head. All was not lost, for Bill Bowen caught it on the rebound to get his 9th wicket.

Tyberton

An early Tyberton cricket team played at Stoney Field, Madley and on 28 August 1937 they played an invitation XI. The team was very much influenced by the Lee-Warners from Tyberton Court. One of the umpires was Major C.B. Lee-Warner, and J. Lee-Warner, whose address was given as 'London', played in the match. For the record, Tyberton scored 80 and the visitors 61. This must have been good for morale, for the opposition included players from Whitbourne, Hay, Preston and Blakemere. As with many teams cricket ceased at the outbreak of the Second World War. Frank Hancorn, who lives locally, confirmed that sometime during the 1950s there was an attempt to re-start a cricket club in Tyberton. They played a few friendlies for one season but the club then folded, and instead the members changed their interests and formed a rifle club, which still exists.

Madley and Eaton Bishop

Sam Lilley and the Rev. Heywood, who was vicar of Eaton Bishop, started Madley and Eaton Bishop Cricket Club in about 1953 and they played until 1961. Their ground was at Church Farm, Madley, and then at Hays Meadow, Blenheim Farm. Rev. Heywood was elected

Moccas 1980s team
Back row: Oscar Pligh, Robin Davies, Bill Bowen, Colin Hinksman, Joe Brown, Dave Morgan
Front row: Ian Bannerman, Keith Williams, David Brown, Peter Saunders, Paul Williams

MADLEY CRICKET CLUB

SEASON — 1959

President : A. Thomas, Esq.

Vice-Presidents :

Mrs. S. Jones	Mrs. E. Hickman
Messrs O. Hillyer	S. Jones
C. Green	E. Hickman
W. Bullock	W. Bayley
F. Powell	H. Gibbons
J. Edwards	C. Watkins
W. Matthews	S. Lane
T. Guy	W. C. Farndon
S. S. Jones	J. Davies
G. S. Lea	T. Hobey
S. Lilley	

Committee :

Chairman : Mr. N. Lovesy

Hon. Secretary : Mr. J. R. Chawner, Thunder Castle, Bridge Sollers.

Hon. Treasurers : Mr. C. Price, Mr. D. Gilbert and Mr. J. Morgan

Club Captain : Mr. J. R. Chawner.

Vice-Captain : Mr. N. Lovesy.

Madley Fixture Card cover 1959

president, Sam Lilley was the first captain, the treasurer was Bill Matthews, and the secretary was Philip Skyrme. Philip's future wife, Joan, was involved in the catering side of the club, which was known for the quality of its teas. Their son is Richard Skyrme, the Herefordshire coach and former player. The club regrettably closed in 1966 through lack of support.

Trout Inn Cricket Team

In 1982 David James, the landlord of the Trout Inn at Dulas, formed a cricket club at the Trout. They played on a small pitch next door to the pub by the river. The ground was extremely small and on one occasion the umpire had to give an unusual signal to the scorers – six leg byes – when the ball hit the batsman's pad and flew straight over the boundary. He caused great amusement by raising both arms in the air and at the same time hopping up and down on one leg to signal both the six and the leg byes. Chris Barker, the headmaster of Peterchurch School, was playing for the club and recalls the incident. The club did not last long and folded in 1986; the pub closed shortly afterwards.

Kington cricket team, 1910

The Kington pavilion built in the 1960s

Peterchurch

Peterchurch had a team in the early part of the century, but a report in the *Hereford Times* in April 1913 stated that the club had disbanded. There was another team in the late 1940s and early '50s that played on the ground that is now the showfield. The team was originally run by Brigadier Lyon; he was followed by a Mr. West; and then Mr. Griffiths, the headmaster of the local primary school. Stalwarts of the team included Ronnie Hancorn, Brian Williams and Percy Wilde. They folded in the late 1950s when many of the players moved on to play for the Golden Valley team.

Kington

Kington is north-west of Hereford on the Aberystwyth road and in the Welsh Marches. The club was formed in 1844 and in that year they played Presteigne on that club's ground at Broadheath. Because this was a new experience for the people of Kington, the game attracted a large crowd. After the match which, for the record, was won by Kington the participants retired to the Old Oak Inn in Broad Street for dinner.

The club's first home ground was at the King's Head field, then they moved to Park Avenue, and then Mill Street, finally settling at the Recreation Ground where they still play. The ground is in a lovely setting surrounded by trees, but still in the middle of the town.

The club had some organisational problems according to the *Hereford Journal* of 25 April 1908:

> At the Kington Cricket Club annual meeting, chaired by the President Rev. Preb. Craigie, Cecil Price the Secretary explained that owing to the score book being lost he was unable to give account of matches played during the season, but he did recall that Presteigne in one match were dismissed for a total of 10.

Cricket was played in Kington throughout the last century, apart from 1934, when there were no fixtures, and during the two World Wars, apart from fixtures against British Army Units based at Hergest Camp before the arrival of the U.S. Army during the Second World War.

KINGTON CRICKET CLUB.

Hon Secs. :
Mr. T. A. DEYKES,
and
Rev. R. S. PELLY, B.A.

Season 1919.
PRESIDENT:
THE REV. H. E. H. PROBYN, M.A.

Playing Field :
The Recreation Ground.

Above: The Kington team card heading, 1919

Kington 1960 team
Back row: [-], Rob Andrews, David Appelby, Nigel Griffiths, Ted Nicholls, J. Prieby
Front row: Rodney Bowdler, Peter Smith, Roger Pye (captain),
Tony Collins, George Phillips

In 1937, Sydney Barnes of Lancashire and England, who was then 62, guested for Kington against Pembridge. He showed his class by taking 8 wickets for 37 runs and scoring 17 runs in his innings. In 1951 they achieved success winning the Presteigne Knockout cup beating Byton Nondescripts in the final.

The club's present pavilion was built in the 1960s and was officially opened by the Worcestershire and England cricketer Basil D'Oliviera. There then followed a match between Kington and a Worcestershire XI for D'Oliviera's benefit year.

In 1966 the club had a fixture against Worcester Old Elizabethans,

The victorious Kington team at Lords
Back row: David Hall (president), Mike Cronin, Dave Morgan, Rob Goodwin, Rob Johnson, Clive Scott, Nigel Scott,
Jim Lewis, Dave Phillips (scorer), Carl Yeomans (secretary)
Front row: Kevin Gwynne, Rodney Bowdler, Alan Stansbury-Stokes, Edward Price (captain), Martin Powell, Mark Porteous

who are the old boys of Worcester Royal Grammar School. The side included Imran Khan, the future captain of Pakistan and one of the greatest all-rounders of all time. He made 146 runs and took several wickets.

In the 1960s Robbie Richardson's father-in-law, Percy Biggs, presented a cup to the club. It was called the Kington Knockout Cup and was played for annually. On one occasion during a match in the competition, Dr. Phil Cleland was batting for Kington and facing Tony Maine who was playing for Builth Wells. Just as Tony was about to bowl, the doctor stepped back because he noticed that his sheepdog, Nelly, who was not fussy about nipping backsides, was encroaching onto the ground. Naturally concerned, he shouted 'Would someone please put Nelly in my car.' He then took up his stance again. Tony Maine walked back to his mark mumbling to himself and obviously not very happy. He steamed in, bowled, and the doctor looked back to see his stumps flying in all directions. Tony ran up to him, placed his hand on Phil's shoulders, and said to him 'You can put Nelly in the **** car yourself now!'

The Kington Club entered the Herefordshire Cricket League in 1975 and won the championship at their first attempt. Between 1975 and 1990 the club won the championship 11 times out of a possible 16.

In 1993 the Kington club enjoyed the greatest moment in their history when they travelled to Lords and won the national Whitbread Village Championship. They played Frocester in a match that will never be forgotten by players and spectators alike. Kington batted first and scored 191 runs for 8 wickets off their 40 overs. In reply Frocester were all out for 189, the final wicket falling off the last ball of their innings. The victory was one of the finest achievements ever managed by any Herefordshire Cricket Club and the club is proud to have a photograph of the successful side taken at Lords – the home of cricket (page 121, bottom).

In 2006 the side won the Crusader Worcester County League Division I. They will be playing in the Birmingham League in 2007 under the captaincy of Duncan Morgan.

Mention must be made of one of Kington's most well-known personalities – the late Robbie Richardson. Robbie joined the club at an early age and served them in every capacity throughout his life. He gave tremendous service as a player, and when his playing days were over, he coached the youngsters at the club and at the local school where he was a teacher. He was also just as happy sitting on the mower or roller and helping the groundsman. A clock was put on the new pavilion in his memory and a plaque placed on the wall of the building.

Almeley

Almeley had a cricket team as early as 1859 (Anthony 1903), but they must have disbanded at some later date because the present club was only formed in 1952. The new club played originally on a field at Bridge Farm before moving to Spearmarsh Common in 1973. The first pavilion was an old gypsy caravan which was eventually replaced by an old chicken shed from Kingsland Cricket Club. The first ever game when the club was reformed was against Titley and, perhaps rather inevitably, the club suffered a heavy defeat.

A family scene at Almeley pavilion in 1997

Fortunes improved when John and Peter Mokler erected a building on the edge of the Common that has been used by the club as a pavilion for the majority of the time since 1973.

Until 1974, apart from playing in some knockout competitions the club only played friendly matches, but in 1975 they became a founder member of the Hereford District League and remained in the league until it folded in 2003.

Robert Hudson did a feature on Almeley in 1976 on the radio programme *The Countryside in Summer* when it was appreciated that Almeley was one of the few teams that still played on the traditional village green. Robert Hudson returned to the ground with two Worcestershire and England cricketers – Basil D'Oliveira and Norman Gifford – to speak at the club's 50th Anniversary celebrations in 2002.

In 1973 the club played against the Hereford United F.A. Cup 'giant killling' side on the common to celebrate their 21st anniversary, and played another match against Hereford United in 2002 to celebrate the club's Golden Jubilee. The team is still very active and now plays in the Marches Leagues.

Almeley on Tour 2003
Back row: C. Reid, D. Duggan, R. Hughes, N. Raybould, C. Baker, A. Duggan, M. Ingram, B. Bedford, P. Lewis, S. McGowan
Front row: R. Williams, K. Duggan, A. Ball, D. Hughes, S. Jones, J. Duggan

Lyonshall

The club played on a ground called Bryncurl in Lyonshall village. There is reference to them in the *Hereford Times* in 1914 and also in the 1930s. Three Burgoynes, Pryce, Bob and Fred, are shown in the 1936 photograph (bottom left) in front of the pavilion that was sold later to Titley Cricket Club. In 1938 the team won the Kingsland and Presteigne knockout competition.

The 1936 Lyonshall team – Winners of the Presteigne Cup
Back row: R.H. Bromley, Rev. C. Lighton, A. Bromley, F. Burgoyne, P. Burgoyne, R. Burgoyne, G. Munslow, Col. C.T. Hudson
Front row: W. Jones, H. James, F. Bromley (captain), J. James, T. Davies, W. Price

Burgoyne XI

The team was based at Lyonshall and not many families can boast that they can raise their own team. However, it was a fact that in 1963 the entire team of 11 players was made up of members of the Burgoyne family (left). They played a friendly match against C.O. Price's XI in September 1963 and the scorecard (below) confirms that all eleven members of the team were Burgoynes.

The team also put a select XI together to compete in the Ted Rees XI and other major clubs in the Kington Knockout cup. They had an annual match against local auctioneers, Russell, Baldwin and Bright. The fixture was started by Pryce Burgoyne and Bill

The Burgoyne family XI of September 1963
David, Michael, John, Reg, Andrew, Philip, Fred, Lionel, Roger, Pryce and Peter

C. O. PRICE'S XI	
Littleworth b J. Burgoyne ...	2
E. Jones lbw b J. Burgoyne ...	17
Hern b R. Burgoyne	47
Scott b J. Burgoyne	9
Philpotts b J. Burgoyne	1
Hamer lbw b J. Burgoyne	7
Pye b P. Burgoyne	22
Thomas c P. Burgoyne b P. Burgoyne	2
Wart c P. Burgoyne b F. Burgoyne	2
D. Jones not out	0
Price c M. Burgoyne b P. Burgoyne	0
Extras	10
Total	**119**

Bowling: F. Burgoune 1-19, J. Burgoyne 5-37, P. Burgoyne 1-19, R. Burgoyne 1-11, P. Burgoyne 2-3.

F. BURGOYNE'S XI	
P. Burgoyne c Pye b Littleworth	7
J. Burgoyne b D. Jones	30
R. Burgoyne c E. Jones b D Jones	14
P. Burgoyne b D. Jones	0
R. Burgoyne b D. Jones	0
F. Burgoyne c Pye b Price ...	9
M. Burgoyne c Hern b Price	6
P. Burgoyne run out	2
A. Burgoyne not out	1
L. Burgoyne c Hamer b Price	2
D. Burgoyne b Price	0
Extras	1
Total	**72**

Bowling: Price 4-38, Littleworth 1-17 D. Jones 4-15.

A family tradition – eleven members of the Burgoyne family in 1963 – but they lost!

Gallimore and the game is still played annually more than 50 years later. Even now, the Burgoyne team still fields four members of the family – James, Matthew, Mark and Stephen.

Terry Court and Peter Burgoyne ran the team for over 30 years and Mark Burgoyne and Richard Binnersley run the current sides.

Titley

They are referred to as playing as early as 1859 (Anthony 1903). The team played regularly until the outbreak of the First World War. Two brothers named Gwyther, who were later killed in the Second World War, restarted the team in 1929. The team was re-formed yet again in 1952 and played at Dinehill on the Eyewood Estate, part of the Titley Court Estate. When Kinsham folded in 1951 Titley purchased their pavilion, which was an old shepherd's wagon, for £100, which was paid by Walter Greenly, who also made a substantial contribution to the club by supplying all the equipment that was needed for the coming season. The main umpire for the club was a local man, Frank Mills, who stood for many years.

Major General Walter H. Greenly played for Harrow against Eton and made a great contribution to the club both on and off the field of play. A post-war founder member of the side was Roger Pye, who played for them until 1960 when he went to Kington where he was made captain; however he eventually finished his cricketing career back at Titley. When Titley folded as a team in 1977 they amalgamated with Kington and became Kington Seconds.

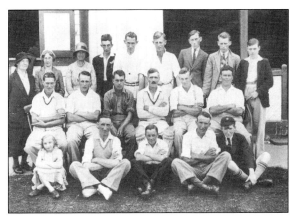

Titley 1930. Taken in front of Kington Pavilion
Back row: Mrs. Brinkley, Florrie Brinkley, Mrs. Lloyd, Bill Turner, Bob Burgoyne, Fred Burgoyne, Ronnie Diggery, Cyril Lord, Jack Burton
Middle row: Tom Davies, Harry James, Charlie Lloyd, Jim Ruff, Jack James, Henry Mills
Front row: [-], Ernie Lloyd, Wesley Jones, Frank Mills, Jack Christopher

Weobley 1977 team
Back row: L. Jones (umpire) R.Wydenbach, R Griffiths, R. Canning, S. Dyer, J. Lewis, G. Tomkins, B.Baugh
Front row: L. Amos, S.Vivian, K. Hill (captain) K. Jones, D. Griffith

Weobley

A cricket team is mentioned at Weobley in the *Hereford Times* in 1850, but little is known until they are recorded playing from 1900 until the outbreak of the First World War. Weobley did not have a very good season in 1908 when, according to the *Hereford Journal* of 19 August, they played 11 matches – won 2, drew 2 and lost 7. According to the report the chairman hoped for better things the following season. It

Weobley pavilion 2006

does not appear to have been so, for on 21 March 1921 there was a meeting at the Red Lion Hotel in Weobley when it was resolved that the village would once again run a cricket team. They played from then on until the 1930s and then from 1951 to the present. From 1989 the cricket pitch was by the village hall and next to the school.

Weobley played in division three of the Hereford and District league in 1977. In June 1979 the team included a father and son partnership – Robin and David Griffiths – in a division three match against Brockhampton Seconds. Together they put on 82 for the first wicket. David was only 15 at the time and went on to play for the Herefordshire Minor Counties XI. The Griffiths family was well-known in Herefordshire sporting circles; Robin's brother, Roger, was Hereford United's full back who broke a leg but continued to play in the game against Newcastle United in the epic giant-killing victory in 1971.

Staunton-on-Arrow

The team was formed pre-war and ceased to play in 1951, but many of the players went on to play for Corton Cricket Club which played on the Corton Estate. One of their best matches was when Bailey and Ash Bullock had an opening partnership of 247 to beat Barnards Green from Malvern by 10 wickets in a Worcester League game.

Burton Court

The club was founded in about 1864. In a 19th-century score book the batsmen were referred to as strikers. The Clowes family

Staunton-on-Arrow
Back Row: Fred Thomas and Richard Edwards
Middle row: [-], [-], John Edwards jnr, David Griffiths, [-]
Front row: Richard Edwards Jnr., David Sayers, [-],
Ken Griffiths

owned the Court at the beginning of the twentieth century. They were great benefactors to the village of Eardisland and supporters of the cricket team. Colonel Clowes played for Hereford Club and Ground in 1904. The Burton team played in the grounds of the Court. Colonel Clowes presided over the annual general meeting in May 1923, which was held in the reading room in Eardisland. He reported that the accounts showed a deficit of a little over £2. He announced that there would be 20 games in the following season and that the first match would be against Kinsham. Mrs. Clowes agreed to provide the teas for the following season. Colonel P.L. Clowes was captain of the cricket team until his death in February 1925. They continued to play until the

Burton Court versus the Hereford Militia in June 1902

outbreak of the Second World War. Tom Wood, headmaster at Eardisland school for 40 years, lived at the school house and captained the Burton Court team. The club was disbanded in 1939 when the cricket field was required for growing crops throughout the Second World War.

The Burton Court club re-formed as Eardisland Cricket Club in the late 1940s and played on several pitches.

Eardisland

The Eardisland team is first recorded as playing between 1921 and 1930. They stopped playing prior to the Second World War. An article in the *Ludlow Standard* in August 1948 confirmed that the club had just reformed with members of the old Burton Court club. Many of their players had been playing for Pembridge in the early part of the 1948 season. They are recorded playing from 1948 until 1966 and then 1998 to date. There was a pavilion in the old cricket meadow which was removed in the 1930s. Subsequent pavilions included railway carriages, tents, gazebos, and the present porta-cabin. The club members have always provided teas although the original Burton Court Cricket Club used the Cross Inn. The current team has used the Swan since 1998.

In January 2006 the *Hereford Times* reported that the cricket ground was being lost because Edward Thomas, the owner of the field, had to plough it up due to European Union regulations.

Eardisley

The team played in the years leading up to the outbreak of the First World War and they are recorded in the *Hereford Times* as playing between 1927 and 1931.

The club's annual dinner was reported in the paper in October 1912, and on 2 November an old player, C.J.L. Abbot, in response to the report, wrote to the *Hereford Times* from his new home in Hove.

He reminisced about his time with the club before the First World War. He joined Eardisley in 1906 and in his letter he wrote:

> Old Sam Davies was the life and soul of the club. He and Mr. Guest gave enormous service to the club before the First World War. The team was recognized as a powerful side with snorting pitches.

He went on to reminisce about the delightful teas that were provided on the ground that had been placed at the disposal of the team by Mr. Griffiths. He advised that the old stagers in the club had a 'Merry Time'. The team members before the war were S.C. Davies (captain). E.M. Douglas (vice-captain), G.L. and L. Gwyther, C. Philpotts, Dr. Darling, J. Downing, B. Ross, H. Mills, H.T. Jay, and T. Jones.

Burghill St. Mary's (Burghill Hospital)

The team is recorded playing in 1904 and in 1913-14. In 1920, after the war, they were first known as Burghill Hospital Cricket Club. They were re-formed in 1952 and played Talgarth Mental Hospital that year. They started playing as

St. Mary's team in the late 1970s
Back row: Molly Jones (scorer), Bill Lambert, Val Treagus, Roger Lane, Ian Ferguson, Brian Taylor, John Wade, Melvyn Lee
Front row: Colin Rogers, Dr. Julian Wheeler, Trevor Jones (captain), Robin Matthews, Rob Godsall

entertainment for the patients – the players being the doctors and staff.

The cricket ground was made from soil excavated from the Henry Wiggin's factory site in Hereford and was a well-maintained and snugly-placed ground adjacent to the hospital. In the beginning they played friendly matches, usually against other hospitals and doctors XIs. One of the players, David Wragg, was a patient at the hospital and played for many years, usually opening the batting. Dr. Julian Wheeler, a Hereford doctor, was a regular in the team and he also supported them in an administrative capacity.

They joined the Hereford and District League in 1976 and quickly went through the Divisions to Division One. Robin Matthews had an exceptional season in 1979. He bowled 140 overs taking 33 wickets for 197 runs at an average of 5.96.

Because of redevelopment at St. Mary's, the club had to relocate and were rescued by Sir. John Cotterell from Garnons. The club reformed as Garnons Cricket Club and cricket returned to the Garnons Estate with Sir John being elected President. In 1989 Trevor Jones received a plaque from Sir John in recognition of his 25 years service to the club.

Garnons original pavilion is now a private house

Garnons (Byford)

A match was played at the Garnons Estate as early as 1880 (Anthony 1903). The original ground, which was on the opposite side of the road to the present one, was described in the *Hereford Times* of 28 May 1904 as follows:

> The Garnons is a pretty castellated mansion, finely situated on the south western acclivity of Bishopstone Hill, and offering views of some of Herefordshire's most delightful scenery. The Cricket Ground is admirably placed between the Hereford and Hay road and the house.

The pavilion for the original ground was a black and white building which was extended to become a house, planning permission being granted providing that the original structure became part of the house.

The original Garnons team who were playing at the beginning of the 20th century held an annual fixture between Hereford Club and Ground and the E.C.s (The name 'E.C'. comprised the initials of the reigning ladies of the houses of Holme Lacy and Garnons – namely Lady Enid Chesterfield and Lady Evelyn Cotterell).

In one match at Garnons a young Sir John Cotterell pulled into the ground on a combine harvester, jumped off, batted, and when he was eventually out, returned to his harvesting. The club started up again in 1947 after the war and played throughout the 1950s. under Sir Richard Cotterell.

The present club was formed in the late 1980s, when St. Mary's cricket club lost its

Garnons cricket team c.1935-6

ground. They were offered a pitch on the Garnons Estate which they gratefully accepted. Sir John provided a new pavilion, nets and a short-term artificial pitch until a suitable grass square could be established.

The new club has a modern pavilion and is in the delightful grounds of the Garnons Estate on the house side of the A438 Brecon road.

The St. Mary's Hospital side had won the Brockhampton Cup three times in the early 1980s

Hereford Club and Ground versus Lady Elizabeth Cotterell's XI,
an annual fixture in the early 20th century

The present pavilion at Garnons (St. Mary's)

and, after moving to Garnons, won it again in 1989 and 1992 under its new name. The team went on to achieve success in the Marches League winning Division One in 1995, 1999 and 2000. They also won the League Cup in the 1994, 1999 and 2000 seasons.

One of the most successful social occasions each year is the match organized by Sir John Cotterell between the Chairman's XI and the Presidents XI.

Burghill and Tillington

A Hereford policeman, Len Sparrow, and the Rev. Peter Lind-Jackson, the local vicar, formed Burghill and Tillington Cricket Club in 1972, the first game being played the following year. On August 8 1975 they became the first side to be pronounced champions of the newly formed Hereford and District Cricket League.

Burghill and Tillington 1978
Back row: Bill Bishop, Derek Coles, Chris Johnson, Kevin Baylis, Dave Griffiths,
Len Sparrow, Howard Meredith
Middle row: Derek Budgen, Peter Lind-Jackson, Ian Fletcher, John Downes,
Rodney Lodge, David Wilkes, Stan Nicholls
Front row: Paul and Duncan Sparrow

The ground is a lovely one, set in open country-side. The team was lucky that two cricket enthusiasts, Mason and Desiree Helme of Brick House Farm, gave them the Brick House Field – ideally placed adjacent to the road and close to the Bell Inn at Tillington.

The ground is also close to the church and the vicar, Peter Lind-Jackson, was known to carry out christenings whilst wearing his cricket whites under his cassock so that he lost no time in getting to the ground for the start of play!

The original pavilion was bought in 1973 from

Burghill and Tillington 1980
Back row: Dave Jackson, Paul Quested, Ronnie Burbeck, Kevin Arrowsmith, Jeff Kramer,
Kevin Baylis, Howard Meredith
Front row: Paul Sparrow, Stewart Kramer, Derek Budgen, Len Sparrow (captain) John
Downes, Ian Macklin, Rodney Lodge   In front: Duncan Sparrow

Docklow cricket club at a cost of £12.50. The new pavilion, which was ordered in about 1990, was the first one built by Taylor Lane, a local company then in its infancy, at a cost of £1,200. Many club members helped in the construction, especially John Downes who still continues to maintain it.

The team was a force to be reckoned with in the 1980s and '90s and won many competitions including the Marches Division One Championship on two occasions. They also won the Senior Cup, the League and Cup double, the Wormelow and Kington invitation Knockout Cups, the Eastnor and Colwall six-a-side knockouts, the Brockhampton six-a-side, and the Hereford six-a-side under the name of the Cockspur Cops. In addition, they were regional finalists in the Norsk Hydro National Village Knockout competition. The club was also successful at indoor cricket, winning the League and Cup on numerous occasions; they were also runners-up in the National Indoor Cup losing to Weymouth in the West of England final.

One afternoon in the early 1980s, whilst on police duty at the Three Counties Show at Malvern, Len Sparrow began chatting to a car full of farmers who were from Kent and visiting the area for a few days. He directed them to a suitable parking area and they all soon realized they had something in common – namely cricket. The visitors showed interest in bringing their side, Castle Hill Cricket Club, to Herefordshire for an extended weekend cricket tour. They duly came the following year and played Burghill and Tillington, and Canon Frome. The cricket was played very competitively and the tour was such a success that Burghill and

Tillington decided to tour Kent the following year. This was the start of some wonderful cricket and friendships over a period of 15 years.

During the years many well-known guest cricketers joined the tour and enhanced the cricket. They were also lucky enough to play against Brian Luckhurst and Alan Dixon, both ex-England and Kent players. On one of the tours the team enjoyed a trip round the Grey Nichols factory on the kind invitation of the managing director, Jock Livingston, formerly of Northamptonshire and Australia. After an interesting

Burghill and Tillington pavilion 2006

Burghill and Tillington June 1986
Back row: Adrian Price, Kevin Baylis, Ian Macklin, Simon Wilton, Paul Quested, Jeremy Symonds, Brian Symonds, J. Downes
Front row: Len Sparrow, Dave Mockler, Ken Hook, Paul Sparrow

trip the club invited Jock for lunch. This turned out to be a fascinating experience as Jock was a personal friend of Don Bradman. He was most enjoyable to listen to, the climax being when he produced a letter that he had recently received from Don Bradman commenting on a recent test match.

The club stopped playing league cricket in 1996, either because players retired or because they had moved on to play Worcester League Cricket. However, in 2000, with the help of the late Jack Roberts (County Youth Co-coordinator) a refreshing youth culture helped the club to regain its position and it was accepted back into Division Two of the Marches League. In 2002 they were promoted into Division One and in 2003 a second XI was formed and the club's future was secured.

The Burghill club tour members are planning a reunion with a view to revisiting the Maidstone area for a few days and playing a remembrance match.

Credenhill and Stretton Sugwas

The club was formed in 1946 following several meetings. Initially they only played friendly matches, usually on opponent's grounds, and they only played on Saturdays in the 1950s. Practice sessions were held on land belonging to Frank Price of Magna Castra Farm, which was immediately behind the present Community Hall, but it was not considered suitable for matches. Many members of the team were formerly members of the pre-war Garnons team.

The club moved to a ground situated a few hundred yards past the turning to Burghill for the 1947 season and remained there until they folded. The pitch was above average and the outfield well prepared which gave the batsman a fair chance as well as the bowlers. The pavilion was a large wooden building with a central section for preparing teas. The club also had a practice net. The very first match on the ground was between the Captain's XI and the Vice-Captain's XI. The president of the club was the rector of Credenhill – the Rev. William Henry Willoughby Goddard-

CREDENHILL
and
STRETTON SUGWAS
CRICKET CLUB

President—
REV. W. H. GODDARD-FENWICK

**FIXTURE LIST
1948**

Captain—   E. BIRCH.
Vice Captain—   E. G MEREDITH.

Hon. Secretary & Treasurer—
MRS. H. A. FAULKNER, "Sundown",
Stretton Sugwas, Hereford.
PHONE NO. BURGHILL 80.

The Credenhill fixture list for 1948

Fenwick. The honorary secretary and treasurer was Hilda Faulkner and the captain was Ted Birch. The club went from strength to strength and very soon fielded a youth team as well as the senior side. Regrettably the youth side broke up largely because eligible young men were called up for National Service. The senior team won the Brockhampton cup in 1957 and continued playing until 1960.

Maurice Joseph, who played for Credenhill and for Blanches, recalled a match played at Credenhill when a batsman struck a mighty six. The ball landed in a truck on a passing train. The station master, who was watching the match from the station platform, telephoned the station master at Moorhampton, the next stop and several miles down the line, and told him that there was a cricket ball in one of the trucks. Maurice's girl-

Credenhill team c.1954
Top row: Tom Watkins, Mike Stallard, Bill Bishop. Albert Kitchen, Eddie Jones, Maurice Joseph, Alan Holiday, Fred Faulkner
Bottom row: Arthur Portman, Albert Williams, Frank Stallard, Percy Meredith, Ernie Allsop

The Canon Pyon team about 1920

The 1938 Canon Pyon team
Team members: Harold Edwards, Charles Powell, Tom Preece, Peter Yeomans, Herbert Yeomans, Tom Bird, Cyril Powell, Rev. Roberts, Reg Byard, Henry Southall, Bill Barber, [-], Ruth Powell (scorer)

friend and later wife, Terri, who was scorer for many seasons, supported him during his time with the club.

Canon Pyon.
An article in the *Hereford Times* of 27 September 1913 stated that the club had been founded that year and had been reasonably successful, having played 12 matches and won six of them. The team played in 1914 up to the outbreak of the First World War and was revived in 1920 following a meeting that took place on the 21 February that year. They played their first league match against the Y.M.C.A. in May 1921.

The team was active and quite successful during the 1920s and in 1928 won six of eleven matches played. Throughout this period two of the most successful bowlers were Charles Powell and J. Pritchard. Powell also became quite a useful batsman and on one occasion, voicing his opinion, said 'We do not play with a straight bat, but this has to be remedied!'

A notice in the *Hereford Journal* dated 28 Feb 1931 stated that Canon Pyon would not be running a cricket team in 1931. However, it had been re-formed by 1937 with the assistance of local schoolmaster Frank Cook and L.T. Evans, who supplied the playing field. In 1938 they played on ground owned by a Mr. Yeomans and used an old railway carriage as a pavilion. Stalwarts of the team during its revival were Harold Edwards, Charles Powell, Tom Preece, Peter Yeomans, Herbert Yeomans, Tom Bird, Cyril Powell, Rev. Roberts, Reg Byard, Henry Southall and Bill Barber.

Sadly, the outbreak of the Second World War saw the cessation of cricket not only in Canon Pyon but also throughout the country.

Kingsland / Luctonians
The Kingsland club was formed about 1910 and played until the outbreak of the First World War, recommencing immediately afterwards. The club

ground was on glebe land next to the old rectory. In the early days one of the leading lights was the local vicar, the Rev. George Jobling, who made sure that wonderful teas were served at the rectory. The club had a small wooden pavilion, which had a small area fenced in front where only players and officials were allowed.

In 1920 the chairman, R.H. George, confirmed at the A.G.M. that the club had a credit balance of £3 3s. 11d. and he stated that the membership fee for the year would be two shillings. Not much cricket was played during the Second World War with many of the older players retiring and the younger ones being away in the forces. However, cricket resumed to a full programme immediately after the war, but it did not last for long as the club folded in 1952 because of a shortage of players. This was the end of cricket at the recreation ground.

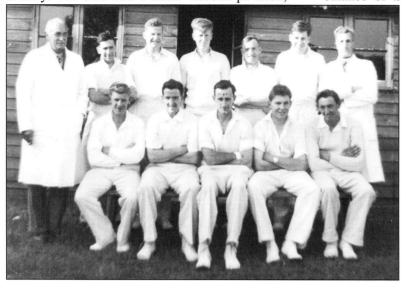

Kingsland team about 1961
Back row: Captain Wickham, Hugh Lyke, George Wall, Fred Davies, Bob Whittall, Percy Pudge, Cliff Davis
Front row: Arthur Sankey, Lynne Jones, Ray Jones, Robin East, John Williams

There was no cricket at Kingsland for eight years, but in 1960 a few of the players who had joined other clubs got together and decided to re-form the club. A committee was formed and Dr. Vaughan was elected president; Ray Jones, captain; and Cliff Davis, secretary. The biggest problem was to find a suitable ground. The Luctonians Rugby Club agreed to the side having a square at the side of the rugby field and so the club was reformed. A small wooden sectional building was purchased and the first game was held on their home pitch against Bromfield.

The club introduced their own knockout competition in 1960. They won it themselves in that year and in the following year won the Weobley Cup. In 1962 they were successful in the Ludlow Trophy. They won the Ludlow Cup six-a-side tourna-ment in spectacular fashion using

Luctonians c.1975
Back row: Bill Jackson, Jim Apperley, Richard Davies, Robert Thomas, Tim Whitbread
Front row: Glyn Norman, John Amos, Cliff Davis, Dave Price, Adrian Hope

only two batsmen, Ray Jones and Boyd Davies. They batted throughout the competition to claim the trophy without losing a wicket.

In 1968 the club followed the Luctonians Rugby Club to their new premises at Mortimer Park. The sectional building was dismantled and re-erected at the new venue and was in use until a new clubhouse was built. Kingsland Club continued until 1973 when a decision was taken to amalgamate with Luctonians and to name the team Luctonians Cricket Club. The vice presidents of the two sections were merged, and one unified club emerged to serve the local community for both rugby and cricket. For the first two years friendly cricket was played, including entry to the Haig National Village Competition. In 1980 the club embarked on their first overseas tour – the Taverners tour of the Isle of Man – a tour that has since been repeated on many occasions.

In 1983, Mortimer Park – the home of Luctonians – staged floodlit cricket matches during which there were visits by eminent cricketers such as David Gower (when he was England captain), Glenn Turner (then New Zealand's captain), Derek Randall, Norman Gifford (the Worcestershire captain and England spinner), and the entire Worcestershire first XI squad.

In 1993 the first team won the Marches League Premier Division, the third team was promoted to Division One, and the fourth team promoted to Division Three.

The club produced its first international player, Stephen Price, who played for England under 14s against Wales. It also staged its first ever Minor Counties match – a one-day fixture, but unfortunately it poured with rain all day.

They joined the new Worcestershire Cricket League, part of the Birmingham and District Premier Pyramid, in 1999 and were placed in Division Two. Luctonians Cricket Club continues to thrive both in improving numbers and standards. This development is expected to continue under the enthusiastic directorship of Mike Radnor and his team. Members and friends are ensured of a warm welcome during the summer months. Many have given dedicated service to the club as players and officials over the past 47 years, including Ray Jones, Malcolm Morgan, John Brown, Duncan Platford, Jim Apperley, and Adrian Hope.

In 2005 the club was awarded the prestigious Clubmark accreditation. This is a kite mark for cricket clubs who have achieved certain high standards in all aspects of cricket and club management. It is testimony to the groundwork laid by members in the early days.

Shobdon
There was a cricket team at Shobdon as early as 1921 and the team is recorded as playing from then until 1970, excepting the war years. The ground was at Shobdon Court and it was known then as now as 'The Hayes', and clubrooms were in buildings adjacent to Shobdon Court stable block. One of the most memorable matches was in 1931 when they played Leintwardine and the latter team was all out for 2 runs.

The club was granted a formal lease at Shobdon Court in 1952, for which they paid the princely sum of £1 10s. per annum. In the early 1960s they were almost unbeatable, winning the Ludlow, Kington, Leominster, Weobley and Kingsland knockouts – some more than once. They also won several six-a-side competitions and in one season they dismissed four teams for under 10 runs. In August 1967 they won the Orleton League and Cup, beating Eyton in the cup final. They were so renowned that there was a write-up in the *Daily Mail* under the heading 'Shobdon Skittlers'.

Continuity must have been a good thing for Shobdon. The captain of the club for approximately 23 years was Archdeacon Simpson, who did not give up the captaincy until he was 75. Jon Ammonds succeeded him and was captain for 21 years until the club finally disbanded in 1970 and the ground was returned to farmland.

In 1984 the club was re-formed and played at the Torvale work's sports ground. They joined Division 6 of the Hereford Times League and in the first year finished runners-up and were promoted to Division 5. Between 1992 and 1994

Shobdon League Cup winners. 1990s
Back row: Pat Teale (scorer), Terry Teale, Chris Hammond, Steven Jacques,
Richard Ball, Mark Morris, Derek Teale
Front row: Matthew Teale, Richard Lancett, Mervyn Dean, Tom Ammond,
Ian Jones, Andrew Teale

Worcestershire's wicket-keeper Steve Rhodes' benefit.

Stalwarts of the team have been the Teales who can claim that four generations of the family have played. Pearl Teale, who has carried out off-field duties, has consistently supported them. The Evans family have also been involved for many years.

The club has had some fine cricketers over the years including Ken (Toby) Evans, Mike Evans and Terry Teale. In the 1950s, Ernie Smith, a fine left-arm bowler, came down from the Lancashire league. Ernie was a local headmaster of slight build, a quiet man who took the area by storm with some amazing figures season after season. He skittled sides out week after week and ended up winning the club bowling averages. The team now plays in Division 2 of the Flint and Cook Marches League.

they played on council-owned ground at the Grange, Leominster. They eventually had to leave the Grange and the wheel turned a full circle for the club returned to The Hayes.

The club received a lottery grant and was able to build their own pavilion, which was officially opened in April 1996 with a match against a Worcestershire XI in aid of

Staunton-on-Wye

They are mentioned in Edwyn Anthony's book, indicating that they had a team in 1859 (Anthony 1903). Bert Barnfield, who lives in Staunton,

The 1996 Steve Rhodes' benefit match – the first match on the new Shobdon ground

The Shobdon Teale Trio
Terry, Matthew (father) and Andrew

Shobdon new pavilion lottery presentation to
Colonel Corbett (president)

recalls an old pavilion in the 1930s. Mr. Pearson Gregory, who owns the ground on which the team played, started the cricket club again in the late 1950s or early 1960s. When the cricket club finally ceased the ground was taken over by Staunton-on-Wye Football Club.

Presteigne

Although Presteigne is not in Herefordshire, the cricket ground at Broadheath, where the team once played, was in Herefordshire. The site of the ground is confirmed by an old building that was once a public house called the Cricketers Arms. It is understood to have been built in 1851 to look after the town's great interest in cricket. A report in the *Hereford Journal* in 1851 notes that:

> Cricket – Liberally supported by the gentlemen of the town and neighbourhood and under the patronage of Mr. F. Evelyn. (Landowner), J.G. Cooper and J.R. Ince esq. Twice weekly practices are being held on the Broadheath preparatory to the grand match, which is to come off on Friday. The Ground has been levelled, recently turfed and is equal to any in the kingdom. A new tent will be purchased by the members and a commodious inn is about to be erected near the cricket ground.

Anthony (1903) refers to a match at Broadheath in 1844 when Presteigne met Kington and, for the record, Kington won the match by four wickets. Presteigne seems to have enjoyed mixed fortunes during the 19th century. However, things changed when the club moved from the Broadheath site and made use of Grove Meadow from 1880 to 1914. This was when three members of the Green-Price family, and three of the Evelyn family, all played. During the 1890s they boasted having the Australian test cricketer, Trumble, playing for them on his visits to the area. They were very successful in the years leading up to the First World War and in 1914 employed a professional. After a break during the First World War the team started up again and were active between 1927 and 1930.

The team entered the Hereford Times League on its formation and they enjoyed a successful period in the 1970s. However, the club's fortunes dipped in the 1980s and at one stage it nearly went out of existence. A few diehards kept the club alive and the team re-entered the Hereford Times League in the bottom division. They were successful and climbed rapidly through the divisions, winning the third division title in August 1997. The club joined the Flint and Cook Marches League and currently plays in division three.

Godfrey Brown moved to Presteigne from Ludlow and has been an integral part of the club. He was a Leominster Grammar School boy and has been involved in administration and youth

coaching. His family are also committed to the club – his sons James and John travel home from Oxford and London every week to play for the club.

Another stalwart is Steve Chilman who has served and played for the club for many years. The team now plays at the John Beddoes School and its future is looking brighter than it has for some time.

Presteigne 1951 team
Back row: J. Green (chairman), D. Jones, K. Bishop, G. Thomas (umpire),
C.F. Lambert, J. Millichamp, E. Restall (scorer)
Front row: D.D. Perkins, J. Jones, G. Collett, L.H. Lister (captain),
E. Hughes (vice captain), N. Hartley, D. Lancett

Presteigne 1963 team
Back row: A.J. Pettifor (vice chairman), A. Bradley, M. Herrits, E. Traylor, R. Dayas, M. Davies, R. Sparey,
C. Sellars (Hon. secretary), R. Gummer (scorer)
Front row: R. Neville, J. Jones, G. Collett (captain), Major R. Freer-Ash T.D. (president), L..H. Lister (vice captain),
R. Barton, T. Morgan

CHAPTER X

Leominster & North Herefordshire

Leominster Cricket Club

Leominster Cricket Club was formed in 1837 and until the end of the 1974 season the Club's headquarters were at the Grange in Leominster. The rent in 1837 was 1s. per annum. The ground was in parkland and one disadvantage was a public footpath cutting across the outfield. There are many reports of matches being played at the Grange watched by hundreds of spectators.

Leominster pavilion pre-1906

There is documentary evidence confirming that the club shared their original ground at the Grange with the Grange cricket team.

In 1897 the club employed an outside professional bowler whose pay was £1 a week for play and 8s. for work on the ground. The original pavilion was erected in 1901.

At the A.G.M. on 27 March 1909 J.S. Arkwright from Hampton Court was re-elected as president of the club. The club's expenditure for the year unfortunately exceeded the income by over £23. W. Bradford offered to arrange a smoking concert to help pay for the deficit and his offer was accepted with enthusiasm by the committee. A similar fundraising event would be unlikely to be received with similar enthusiasm today!

The club has created a special trophy in memory of one of their oldest vice-presidents – Cecil Hankinson – who died in 2004 aged 107. The trophy will be played for annually between a Chairman's XI and a President's XI in an end-of-season challenge match. Cecil was first connected with the club in 1912, after he had left school, and in his reminiscences said that his best year was in 1919 when he scored 131 not out against Ledbury. In 1921 there was an unusual fixture at the Grange when the club made arrangements for the Australian touring side to play an invitation XI at Leominster. The Leominster side included H.K. Foster, the former England and Worcestershire player, who lived at

This 1912 photograph shows Cecil Hankinson seated with the boatered gentleman on the bench fourth from the left. The schoolboy nearest the scoreboard is Brian Taylor who went on to become a club captain. This particular match was Leominster versus the Fitz-Herbert Wright XI

Tarrington and was an England selector at the time. In October of the same year R. Preece was presented with an inscribed plaque to commemorate his achievement against Tenbury in June when he scored 151 and took 7 wickets for 38 runs.

It was agreed at the A.G.M. in March 1925 that the club would employ a groundsman who would work in conjunction with the local tennis club.

The club set up a knockout competition for local teams in 1927 which proved to be very successful. On more than one occasion in the post-Second World War years, 2,000 spectators turned up at the Grange to see local teams competing. One of the finals, between Stoke Prior and Nondescripts, ended in a tie – each side scoring 126. The match was replayed the

following week and once again over 2,000 people turned up to watch this needle match.

The club had serious problems with the local council in 1929. On 7 September a report in the *Hereford Times* informed its readers that the club had written a protest letter to the council about a proposal to make tennis courts and a bowling green on the western side of the ground at the Grange. The club advised that if the council went ahead with the scheme the boundary would be reduced by 20 yards. Thankfully for the club the proposal was defeated at the committee stage.

In 1951 the club entered into an agreement with Leominster Council enabling them to build a new pavilion at the Grange. The agreement, which is dated 28 Feb 1952, stipulated that the building was to be a wooden construction with a brick foundation. It was a condition of the lease

Leominster Club waiting to catch the coach for the Blackpool trip on 31 May 1950
John Beaman, Dick Burke, Dennis Parker, Mas Noden, Jim Merrett, Jack Williams, Gordon (Pokey) Powell,
Stan Harvey, D.A. Davies, Uncle Bill Hall, Dennis Arrowsmith

that the club would pay a licence fee of 2s. 6d. per annum payable on 25 December. Either side could give 12 months notice to terminate the licence.

It is rather unfortunate that one of the most memorable games played at the Grange was to be one of the last played there. In an exhilarating game, the home side bowled out a visiting Worcester Nomads side for just 5 runs.

The Leominster Club joined the new Herefordshire and District League in 1975 and entered two teams. They also joined and were successful in the Indoor League.

Leominster in the Hereford League, taken at the Sports Club 1990
Back row: Don Cahill, Dave Hodges, Richard Sparey, Steve Hodges, Jeremy Finney,
Dave Barrington, Richard Marsh, Mark Morris, Dennis Parker,
Front row: Anthony King, Russell Palmer, Richard Finney, Noel Withers, Adrian Gore

Alec Haines – former Mayor of Leominster and club centurion

In the 1980s the Leominster Sunday 3rd XI played a match at a local village club. Water had to be taken to the ground to make the tea and, after tea had been taken, the home side was not pleased to find that one of the Leominster players had washed his feet in the washing-up bowl. It is not recorded whether the team were invited back or not.

The club have had several long-standing loyal servants over the years including Norman Davis, a former Mayor of Leominster, who was club secretary for over 50 years; Reginald Cross, who was associated with the club for 46 years; E.E. (Jimmie) Hall, who served the club for over 50 years as a player and official; Alec Haines, who also became Mayor of Leominster and was associated with the club for many years. In 1955 Alec scored 100 out of a total of 157 against Bulmers including one six and 16 fours. In his long Leominster career he scored 4 centuries for the team. Age did not dim the enthusiasm of some members – the late Dennis Parker scored a 50 for the Sunday 3rd XI against the Grange Cricket Club on his 70th birthday.

In 1974 the club vacated the Grange and moved to the Leominster Sports Centre. They still owned the pavilion at the Grange and eventually sold it to the Council in 1979 for £500. It has now been turned into a café.

Richard Sparey has in recent years been both chairman and president. When the club celebrated their 150th anniversary Basil D'Oliviera, the former England and Worcestershire batsman, was the guest of honour. John Beaman played for the club for many years until finally moving on to umpiring. He has put much back into the game by means of his tremendous fund raising exploits for numerous clubs including Herefordshire Minor Counties. Many people will recall his many wonderful sportsmen's evenings at the Rankin Club.

Grange 1982. Promoted from Division 4 in R.B. and B. League
Back row: Ian Beaton, Peter Clarke, David Boughroyd, Lyndon Brown, Eddie Philips, Martin Ward
Front row: Steve Beaton, Adrian Davies, John Richards, Mike Jarvis, David Owen

Leominster Thursday XI 1947/8

Back row: Alec Haines, Billy Harris, Bill Gurney, Danny Wright, Cyril Moss,
Mervyn Bufton
Front row: Fred Hicks, Harry Scholfield, Russell Cooper, Gordon Davies, Mike Seagar
Far right: Andy Robinson (umpire and groundsman)

Leominster Thursdays

The team consisted of a group of local businessmen and associates who kept Thursday afternoons free for their cricket as the day coincided with traditional half-day closing.

There is evidence of the team playing as early as 1904. The team photograph (above) was taken in front of the pavilion at the Grange in either 1947 or '48.

Leominster Nondescripts

The team played during the 1950s. One of the main players was Dai Davies who still lives in Leominster.

Hampton Court Cricket Club

Cricket in the 19th century and during the early part of the 20th was primarily an amateur game. The social difference between the amateurs and the professionals continued until well after the Second World War when the players could still be seen coming out of separate dressing rooms. Until fairly recently it was the done thing for the captain of the side to be an amateur. The matches between the amateurs and professionals continued until the 1950s.

The home of the amateur game was usually the 'Big House' where the Lord of the Manor often had his own cricket team. He had both the ground and the money, and cricket was then much more of a social event between the upper classes than a serious sporting occasion. The Arkwrights of Hampton Court were no exception.

The first recorded match at Hampton Court was in July 1844 when the opposition was called 'The Break of Day of Leominster'. Games were played every July, August and September. In one match in 1851 51 byes were recorded in one single innings. It was recorded that the umpires and scorers would all have free lunches at each game and receive a gift of £1 at the end of each season.

By 1867 the club had printed rules, but there was no modern scorebook until 1868 when officers of the club were elected, the club having 16 members. There was a vast improvement by 1872 when there were 52 members. In 1909 the playing members' subscriptions were 5s. and 2s. 6d.; boys

Hampton Court

paid a shilling. Not suprisingly, J.S. Arkwright of the Court was the president. At the A.G.M. for that year the secretary informed the members that he had arranged the usual number of fixtures. It was left to the committee to arrange the teas and the purchase of materials for the season. They were still playing in 1910 but cricket ceased at Hampton Court when the Arkwright family moved to Kinsham.

Dales cricket ground and pavilion

Kinsham

The Arkwrights, formerly of Hampton Court, came to Kinsham Court in 1910 and the team are recorded as playing from 1913 until 1930 and then from 1946 until 1953.

Dales

Frank Dale formed the team in 1947. He had formed a company making farm buildings and was able to share his enthusiasm for cricket by developing his own company ground on the outskirts of Leominster where the team still play. Dales won the Kingsland cup in 1964.

Dales 1980 team – Orleton Cup Winners
Back row Danny Morgan, Keith Hodnett, Mel Rooke, Phil Smith,
Graham Rooke, Russell Clewer
Front row: Chris Beddoes, Noel Withers, Cecil Jones,
Jack Lewis (captain), George Moseley

Kimbolton

The team was formed in April 1949 by the local vicar – the Rev H.S.G. Thomas – who was the chairman; Billy Mills, a local headmaster, Keith Hodnett and Geoff Morris.

The ground was on the Tenbury Road. The groundsman was Charlie Wright and the umpire was Jim Smith. At the A.G.M. in 1951 the club was in profit in the sum of £37 18s. 8d. Subscriptions were 2s. 6d. per annum and the pavilion was insured for £150. The club had a successful side throughout their existence winning the Orleton League on five occasions,

runners-up twice and they also won the Knockout Cup in 1964. In 1951 they had an outstanding season winning 19 out of 22 matches in the Orleton League. On 13 April 1956, at a meeting of the club, the groundsman asked for his wages to be increased from 8s. to 10s. per week, but no decision was made at the meeting. However, on 17 September 1957, at a further meeting, Roger Jones was appointed groundsman because Charlie Wright did not accept the terms offered.

Raymond (Tufty) Davies and Jack Lewis took over 200 wickets between them in 1957.

Davies bowled 265 overs for 105 wickets and Lewis 296 overs for 109 wickets. Keith Hodnett was one of their most consistent players and he won the Orleton League wicket-keeping trophy three years running between 1959 and 1961. The photograph (below) shows this small village side on tour to Porthcawl in 1955, and the receipt for fare and hotel reservation is a memento of their Devon tour in 1952. The club folded in 1964 and two of the founder members, Keith Hodnett and Geoff Morris, meet at a local pub on a weekly basis to reminisce about the past.

Docklow

The club was started in 1951 and had a memorable beginning for in their first match against Bodenham they were all out for 9. In January 1967 the club's secretary wrote to the secretary for Burley Gate and advised that, following the sale of Docklow Manor, access to their ground would be by the gate opposite on the Leominster side of the King's Head public house. The club ceased playing in 1972 when they sold their pavilion to Burghill and Tillington.

Ivington

In April 1920 a meeting took place at the Social Club in Ivington, presided over by the Rev. George Walter, when it was agreed that the village should run a cricket team. A committee was appointed and it was agreed that the captain would be W.D. Edwards of Brierley Court. Mr. J. Harris of Dishley Court offered a meadow and it

Kimbolton 1950

Back Row: Chris Bird, Terence Jones, Geoff Morris, Trevor Hodnett
Middle row: Fred Morris, Harold Nottingham, Johnny Jones, Jim Smith
Front row: Harley Jones, Philip Morris, Jim Bird, Keith Hodnett, Morris Lloyd
On floor: Roger Jones, Ken Davies

Kimbolton on the Porthcawl trip 1955

Back row: Keith Hodnett, Geoff Morris, Dennis Parker, Jim Smith (umpire),
Terence Jones, Jim Bird, Maurice Lloyd
Front row: Philip Morris, Johnny Jones, Jack Lewis (captain),
Dennis Bird, Chris Bird

The cost of the tour to Devon in 1952

was agreed that the new club would apply for admission to the new Hereford League.

The club did have some problems in its first year. On 28 August they were due to play Great Brampton in a League Match, but could not raise a team because it was harvest time so the match was awarded to Great Brampton. They had the same problem the following week when they were due to play Wye Valley.

Pembridge

Pembridge is recorded as playing in 1913 prior to the outbreak of the First World War and there is a record of them playing Kinsham in 1921. There are no records after 1939 until 1946 when they are recorded playing until 1975. The ground was on the side of the road leading towards Shobdon.

Orleton

The team was formed to play in the Orleton League. They played on a field near Portway Farm by kind permission of Mr. J.M. Sparey. In 1947 they had a corrugated iron pavilion that was transported on a lorry from Wolverhampton and then erected by Cyril Sparrow. They amalgamated with Brimfield to play in the Orleton League for a while. They also hosted the final of the Orleton League Knockout Cup every year.

Orleton versus Eyeton in the Orleton K.O. Cup 1956
Back row: Michael Sparey, Mick Cadwallader, John Evans, Desmond Fortey, Michael Ball, Dick Tipton
Front row: Alan Wall, Roy Gittings, Jim Collings, George Morgan, John Lewis

Sutton

Sidney Andrews, a local farmer, and a local publican, Len Jancey, formed Sutton in 1947. The ground was owned by Mr. Andrews. Before the club had their own pavilion they changed in

Sutton cricket club in the 1950s
Team members: Les Jancey, Pip James, John Griffiths, Ken Cottam, Bill Andrews, Harvey Millichap, Sidney Andrews, Bill Rawlings, Percy Barber, John Badham

Sutton pavilion, now derelict,is used as a shelter for sheep

a large tent. The original ground was on the left-hand side of the Hereford to Sutton Road, just past Wergins Bridge; the pavilion came from Bodenham cricket club when they folded and, now Sutton has also folded; it is now used as a sheep shed by Sidney Andrews' son Richard. Hereford man Richard Thomas, confirms that his father, Rev. William Thomas, was the vicar of Marden and he played for the Sutton team in the 1950s. One of the stalwarts of the club and a successful bowler for them was John Griffiths. The local hostelry after the day's play was the Golden Cross and many a happy hour was spent discussing the events of the day. The club ceased to play in 1968.

Bodenham

The early history is unknown but the club started afresh in 1890 and was active at the beginning of the 20th century. The cricket ground was in an old hop yard on Bodenham Court farm. Mr. J.S. Arkwright of Hampton Court was a member of the team at the end of the 19th entury.

They played until about 1909 prior to the outbreak of the First World War and after the war they started up again in 1920. On 12 November 1929 at the A.G.M. it was reported that they had made a profit from a fund-raising dance of £16 8s. 8d. Thus all the season's debts were cleared and the current balance was in credit by £6 19s. 8d. The club rented a field from Mr. G. Knott for £5 per annum. In 1930 membership fees were 5s. per annum. So successful were they that in the same year the committee discussed the provision of a latrine. They must have come down to earth,

for in 1932 the minutes record that a spade was purchased for the groundsman for 5s. In the same year a match was arranged against Hereford Cathedral School.

The Bodenham team of 1890 included J.S. Arkwright of Hampton Court

BODENHAM CRICKET CLUB.

Balance Sheet. Season 1929.

DATE		RECEIPTS.	£.	s.	d.	DATE	EXPENSES	£.	s.	d.
		Member's Subscriptions	6	12	6.	March	As details in Exs Book.	6	12	4½
		Voluntary Subscriptions.	10	11	6	April	--do-- --do--	3	9	8
Feb.	12.	Net Proceeds of Dance	10	19	10½	May	--do-- --do--	9	1	5½
April	11.	--do-- --do--	10	--	6½	June	--do-- --do--	3	15	2½
April	30.	--do-- --do--	5	10	6½	July	--do-- --do--	16	-	10½
May	23rd	--do-- --do--	2	10	6	Aug.	--do-- --do--	1	17	1½
						Sept)				
		Sale of Tea &c.,				Oct)	--do-- --do--	25	5	4½
		during Home matches.	1	12	-					
Oct.	17	Gross Receipts of Dance	25	3	4.					
							BALANCE IN HAND	6	19	8½
		Total.	£ 73	--	9½		TOTAL.	£ 73	-	9½

Certified correct.

J. P. Cook Chairman.
Joseph Linton . Treasurer.
Secretary.

The Bodenham Club accounts for 1929

In 1934 the rent of the ground was reduced to £4 per annum with the agreement that the owner would have the ground properly grazed. On 17 November 1935 the name was changed to Bodenham and District Cricket Club. The club was doing well at the beginning of the war and on 25 April 1940 the manager of Lloyds Bank wrote to the secretary asking if he was aware that the club had had a credit balance of 5s. 9d. since January 1939. Trevor Barrer, the wicket-keeper and local blacksmith, built the mobile pavilion in 1951. It was eventually sold to Withington when the club ceased to play in 1963.

Raj Hoon and Keith James of Bowley Court reformed the club in 1979. Raj Hoon is a member of a cricketing family – his brother Bill played for an Indian club side against the M.C.C. and scored 150 before lunch, and Raj recalled a team of 11 Hoons playing in India. The ground was at Bowley Court, but the club regrettably started to run down in 1984 and finally ceased in 1989 – their pavilion went to Sutton.

Marden

On 30 August 1983 a meeting was held at the Volunteer Inn, Marden, with the intention of forming a cricket club. The prime movers were Trevor Ford, the landlord; Lionel Price, formerly of Bodenham C.C., and Mike Bryan, a local cricketer. A committee was appointed and a local man, Bev Hinkley, was appointed chairman; the other enthusiastic inaugural helpers being Eric Sperring, John Green, Robert Vaughan, David Lloyd and the Rev. David Hewlett.

The potential ground was an overgrown patch of land to the rear of the Volunteer Inn which was supplied by the brewery. The team members turned it into a proper cricket ground, mainly thanks to the hard work of Robert Vaughan, who was appointed groundsman. Friendly fixtures commenced the same year.

In the early stages the teams changed in the skittle alley in the pub, but prior to that they had to change in a tent. In 1986 a pavilion was built.

Most teams have a family connection – Marden was no exception. Selwyn Williams joined the club in 1986 and was a stalwart of the club until his tragic early death in 2005. He was a fine bowler who on one occasion took 8 wickets for 8 runs. The family tradition continues with Mike, his son, who has carried on in his father's footsteps. Other stalwarts of the club are Lionel Price, who has been chairman for many years, John Green, who has been a long-serving treasurer, and

Marden 1994. The 10th anniversary photograph
Back row: S. Marshall, S Hunt, M. Bryon, N. Nenadich, K. Gilbert, S. Marshall, J. Green, A Sykes, D Sawkins, E Haslam, R. Vaughan, R. Lilly, M. Barnard, P. Leeuwangh, J. Bryan, S. William, R Haslam, L Steele, T Dounes, A Lacy, A Hewlatt
Seated: Mike Williams, L Price, P Milliken, E Sperring, A Keith, F Keating, A Bryan, M. Thomas

Jonathan Blackman, the current club secretary and Marches League representative.

The team has made good progress in its twenty year existence, having joined Division VII of the Hereford and District League. Friendly matches were still played on Sundays, and latterly the club competed in the Evening League and Bromyard Indoor League.

In 1995 Mike Williams was batsman of the year of the Hereford and District League with an average of 68.5. In 1997 the club, as a result of successful youth coaching, won the Under-15 XI County Championship, Mike followed on from his late father's successes and in 1986 was Hereford and District bowler of the year, having taken 50 wickets at an average of 3.76.

Lottery money was obtained and the ground was further developed with practice nets, showers and toilet facilities. A move to the Marches League followed. In 2001 the side was promoted to Division 11 and enjoyed a successful season with a league cup final appearance. In 2002 a qualified scorer, Phillip Mellish, joined the club – he also works for Worcestershire as an analyst. In

Marden Cup finalists 2001
Back row: Nick Robinson, James Bryan, Scott Garrett, Paul Leeuwangh, Rupert Lawrence, Adam Hewlett
Front row: Rod Haslam, Ed Wells, Jonathan Blackman, Matt Wells, Delvon Cunningham

2003 the side merged with Wyesiders Cricket Club and is now hoping to go from strength to strength.

Moreton and Lyde

The club was formed in 1953 and ceased in 1974, which was the year that they ran a single wicket competition.

The team first played on a pitch under an oak tree at Harry Pask's farm and played there for two years. They then moved to land owned by Crawford Perkins where the pitch had a concrete wicket and coconut matting. Francis Perkins, now sadly deceased, recalled the Queen and the Duke of Edinburgh's visit to the county. On their way from Leominster to Hereford the Duke noticed a lovely quaint cricket pitch on the right-hand side of the road and admired the spot, remarking what a lovely little cricket ground it was. Later that day the Perkins family were showing prize county Ryeland sheep at Hereford Market to the Queen. The sheep were standing on turf cut from the pitch when the concrete strip was laid. The Duke was informed that the turf originally came from a cricket pitch and he

Marden's original pavilion was a tent

Moreton pavilion in 2006 covered in ivy. It is now a games' room at a caravan site

MORETON AND LYDE CRICKET CLUB
FIXTURES FOR 1974

President——P. J. Meredith, Esq.
Chairman——H. Perkins, Esq.
Vice-Chairman——B. Lambert, Esq.
Captain of Club——V. Jones, Esq.
Tel. : Hereford 2253
Vice-Captain of Club——John Griffiths, Esq.

Vice-Presidents

C. Blanch, Esq.	B. Moore, Esq.
C. D. Davies, Esq.	E. Moreton, Esq.
J. Davies, Esq.	C. Perkins, Esq.
C. Foden, Esq.	H. Perkins, Esq.
L. Hoddell, Esq.	A. A. Price, Esq.
C. Knipe, Esq.	R. Pomeroy, Esq.
B. G. Lambert, Esq.	R. Probert, Esq.
J. M. Langford, Esq.	E. J. Rees, Esq.
H. Lyke, Esq.	J. Rees, Esq.
W. Makin, Esq.	G. Rosser, Esq.
R. C. Manning, Esq.	G. O. Sainsbury, Esq.
P. J. Meredith, Esq.	D. R. Bishop, Esq.

General Secretary——C. H. Foden, Esq.
Chaveron, Moreton-on-Lugg
Tel. : Burghill 287
Hon. Treasurer——F. Perkins, Esq.
Upper House, Moreton. Tel. : Burghill 245
Fixture Secretary——W. J. Jackson, Esq.
3, Broad Street, Leominster. Tel. 3401

Moreton and Lyde fixture list cover, 1974

observed that he had seen a lovely ground close to the A49 on his way from Leominster. When told that the turf came from that particular ground the Duke then made one of his typical comments, saying that he hoped that the turf would be returned after the show was over! The Moreton and Lyde team played an annual game Presidents XI versus South Hereford Hunt Jockeys. They won the Brockhampton cup in 1958 and the Goodrich cup in 1963.

Bishop's Frome

Bishop's Frome had a cricket team as early as 1869. The club played an anniversary match against Upper Sapey to celebrate their centenary in 1969.

The most recent team was formed about 1938 by Bertie Davies and Jack Fowler. The first ground had a concrete wicket with a coconut mat, and the team changed in the village hall. Cricket ceased during the war but the team restarted in 1949 playing friendly games. In 1981 there was a picture of Mrs. Christine House, the wife of the wicket-keeper, David, sweeping the pitch with a

Moreton and Lyde 1950s

Back row: Percy Perkins, Charlie Foden, [-], Howard Perkins, Gittins Jones, Ken Edwards, Ernie Moreton, [-], Tom Weale, Jimmy Smith, [-], [-], Mike Hughes, Mrs Preece (teas)

Middle row: Crawford Perkins jnr, Randy Langford, [Frank ?], Ron Manning (president) Marcus Manning, Trevor Vaughan,

Front row: [-], Derek Powell, Jimmy Smith's son, Godfrey Edwards, Laura Edwards (teas), Brian Edwards

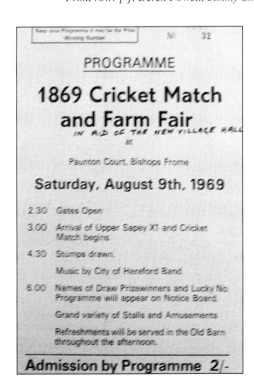

Above: Upper Sapey arriving at the Bishop's Frome centenary match 1969

Left: Bishop's Frome programme 1969

151

Bishop's Frome 1969 Team

Clive Crowther, Phil Lewis, Bertie Davies, John Hadley, John Gummery, Mick Tomkins, Geoff Godsall, Donald Ree,
Norman Fowles, John Hotchkiss, Jack Fowler, Lionel Ford

dustpan and brush as the wicket had been concreted and green Wilton carpet substituted for grass. The club moved to a new ground and received a grant and a new pavilion and a proper grass pitch was the outcome. About 1977/8 they joined Division VII of the Hereford and District League and eventually reached Division III. One of the contributors to their success in 1977/8 was Chris Graham, who won the batting averages in both years and was player of the year in 1978. Bertie Davies has been involved with the club for 65 years and Alan Flaxman for over 30. Bishop's Frome continues to have a thriving village Cricket Club.

Canon Frome Club in 1990 with founder members in foreground.
Foreground: Don Robinson, Ivor Hunt, Charles Davies, Stan Barnes
Seated: Elliott Davies

Canon Frome

The club is reported in the *Hereford Times* as playing between 1910 and 1930, but the inaugural meeting of the new club was held at the Hopton Arms in 1938 and was chaired by Henry Hayward. It was agreed that they would play at Mainstone Court by kind permission of Rev. Toynbee. In 1939 the club moved to Nupend

Canon Frome 1948
Back row: Joey Guest, Charles Davies, Jack Pitt, Puggy Powell, Reg Corns, Rev. Joplin
Front row: Sam Pedlingham, Elliott Davies, Ted Wargent (captain), Ivor Hunt, Les Footman
In front: Susan Corns, Tony Wargent

Canon Frome 1970s. Presentation Evening with Hereford Div I, Fox K.O.,
Brockhampton Challenge and Canon Frome Six-a-side trophies.
Back row: Bob Thirkle, Brian Caffelle, Ivor Hunt, John Evans, Chris Smith, Charlie Eversham
Front row: Phil Stock, Brian Goode, [-], B. Pearce, T. Belcher, George Whittaker

thanks to Nobby Clarke. Cricket ceased during the war apart from a few friendly matches against Withington but directly after the war, on 21 January 1946, a new start was made on a site at Canon Frome Court, with tea being taken at the Hopton Arms. The venue was made available by the generosity of Mr. N.E. Clarke.

Ted Wargent replaced Charlie Woolf as captain and Ivy Woolf became the first lady scorer for the club in the 1950s. The club prospered in the same era and profitable fund raising enabled the team to purchase club caps – the

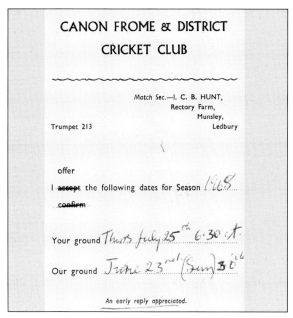

CANON FROME & DISTRICT
CRICKET CLUB

~~~~~~~~~~~~~~~~~~~~~~~~~~~~~~

Match Sec.—I. C. B. HUNT,
Rectory Farm,
Munsley,
Trumpet 213   Ledbury

offer
I ~~accept~~ the following dates for Season *1968*
~~confirm~~

Your ground *Thurs July 25ᵗʰ 6.30 o't.*

Our ground *June 23ʳᵈ (Sun) 3 o'c*

An early reply appreciated.

*A 1968 note from Canon Frome to Burley Gate
regarding the arrangement of fixtures*

colours being those of the Hopton family as a gesture to mark their generosity to the club.

In 1965 a new ground was needed and Canon Frome moved to their current pitch at Wassington and Brian Goode was appointed captain. The pavilion was built on raised ground on the spoil heap left behind from the construction of the Hereford and Gloucester canal in the 1840s. In the following years, under Brian's and his successor John Evans' captaincy, the club were highly successful in winning many trophies including the Hoarwithy, Lady Densham and Goodrich Cups, and the Brockhampton and Woolhope six-a-side competitions. They were also the indoor cricket league championship in 1974/5, the Hereford Cricket Association league champions in 1979, and they reached the area finals of the national village knockout competition of 1984. John Evans, who was captain in the 1970s, sadly died at a relatively young age.

Canon Frome c.1980
Back row: [-], Brian Caffelle, Mike Sterry, John Evans, [-], Phil Stock.
Front row: Maurice Embrey, Chris Smith, Brian Goode, George Whittaker, [-]

One of the stalwarts of the club, Ivor Hunt, who first played for Canon Frome at the age of 12 in 1938, has served the club in various different capacities ever since. His father was a founder member and Ivor became secretary in 1951 and remained in the post until 1988, the only breaks being brief periods when he organized the fixture list and when he took on the post of chairman.

Canon Frome have experienced many memorable matches including one in 1974 when Rachel Heyhoe-Flint, the England Ladies' captain, brought an England Women's XI to the ground; and in 1980 when Canon Frome recorded the remarkable score of 419 runs for 7 wickets in 40 overs against Much Marcle and then dismissed their opponents for 47.

Ivor Hunt recalled that in the early days there were only two car owners in the village so the team had to travel to away matches on the back of a lorry. He also recalled an incident when a fielder in the deep raced round the boundary, took a brilliant catch, slipped, and sat straight down on a large cow pat! The unlucky fielder's comments and those of his team mates cannot be printed!

In recent years they won the Brockhampton Cup from 1969 to 1974 inclusive, and again in 1977, and the Hereford and District Senior Cup in 2003.

Lugwardine

The earliest record found of the team is in 1892 when they played a match at Widemarsh. The *Hereford Times* of 21 May 1894 reported a match involving Withington and another at Barton on 2 July 1902. The team is also recorded in the *Hereford Times* as playing between 1904 and 1910 and then in 1930. In the following year they were reformed, according to a report in the *Hereford Journal* in May 1931.

Lugwardine played under their own name until the outbreak of the First World War. Shortly after the First World War, according to the late Francis Perkins, his great uncle Crawford Perkins reformed the club when he moved to Lugwardine Court. The rival match of the season involved the Perkins family when Holme Lacy played Lugwardine.

Bartestree & Lugwardine inaugural match 1998

Back row: Les Tippins, Graham Monteath, Sean Powell, Nigel Shore, Paul Davies, Ron William, Ian Smith, Arthur Morris (president), Chris Cooke, Andrew Rogers, Chris William, John Davies, Paul Liddell, John King-Salter, Chris Smith, Giles King-Salter
Front row: Mark Townsend, Nick Freeman, Richard Fisher (captain), Graham Jones (chairman), Ian Fletcher, Paul Sockett, Richard Hughes

The Evans twins prior to being in opposition

Bartestree and Lugwardine

The founding meeting of this new club took place on 19 September 1997, and was chaired by Nigel Shore. About 26 people expressed an interest in playing. Graham Jones was elected chairman with Arthur Morris as president and a full set of officers.

The opening match was an internal 'Chairman's XI versus President's XI' on 17 May 1998. This fixture has now become an annual event. During the first season of 1998 the club fielded one team, captained by Richard Fisher, in the Hereford Times League, and played occasional Sunday friendly matches. Informal youth games were held in the evenings.

The club has since gone from strength to strength, gaining a Second XI, then a Third XI, plus an ever-increasing involvement of youth with now three youth teams and qualified coaching sessions on several weekday evenings. The successive team captains have all contributed hugely to the club's success and should be mentioned – First XI captains, Richard

Bartestree and Lugwardine First XI 2005
Back row: Richard Fisher, Martin Hobbs, Craig Beach, Paul Shannon, Ron Treagus
Front row: Steve Beach, Dean Smith, Peter Hinckley, Dave Robinson, Scott Tipping, J. Williams

Fisher, Colin Rees and Peter Hinkley; Second XI captains, Ron Williams, Terry Nixon and Graham Jones; and now Third XI captain Ron Williams, who has also worked very hard on coaching and youth development. Derrick Jones was secretary of the Evening League, treasurer of the Hereford and District League, and secretary of the Marches League. He has a long history of service to various clubs in the county and has now made the Bartestree and Lugwardine Club his home, contributing enormously both as player and administrator. The following must also be mentioned because of their contributions to the development of the club – the three Jones brothers (Graham, Geoff and Kevin), Ron and Chris Williams, Richard Fisher, Steve Beach, Paul Liddell, John Davies, Paul Sockett, Ian Carr, Stuart Evans, Greg Jones, and Nigel Shore.

In August 2003 Bartestree and Lugwardine were in the news because they were able to produce Herefordshire's answer to the Bedser Twins; Stuart Evans was playing for Bartestree and his identical twin, Steve, was playing for Ledbury. To celebrate the occasion the two clubs agreed that the twins should go out to the centre to toss up before the match. The occasion was photographed and sent to the *Hereford Times* who duly published it and a copy was eventually included in the 2004 edition of *Wisden*.

Wellington Evening League side 2001.
Back row: Ross Sample, Mike Haugh, Steve Faithfull, Adam Chalkley, Jamie Williams, Paul Follis, Chris Stokes
Front row: Chris Fry, Phil Chalkley, Matt Williams, Alan Lacey

Bartestree and Lugwardine is close to securing grants to construct a new pavilion which will become a real home for the club and greatly enhance the changing, spectating and catering facilities.

Wellington

Records confirm that the village had a team between 1904 and 1909. There was then a team in 1914 and again in 1920. There were clearly difficulties in raising and maintaining a team because there was a meeting in 1921 when it was agreed to put the club in abeyance for 12 months. It was agreed that the clubs assets of £8 12s. be put into a bank account for the 12 month period.

The club was reformed in the early 1990s and was successful in raising money from the National Lottery to build a sports centre in the village. They played Evening League cricket and joined the Marches League. Sadly, one of the founder members, Paul Follis, died of a heart attack aged 46 on 9 Jan 2005. The club now stages an annual match between the football and cricket teams in his memory.

CHAPTER XI

Bromyard, Ledbury & East Herefordshire

Bromyard

Bromyard is a small market town about 14 miles from Hereford and close to the border with Worcestershire. The team did not play continuously throughout the 20th century and they also had a somewhat nomadic existence, playing on more than one ground. However, the club was in existence during the first part of the century – a

Bromyard Team 1905
Back row: J. Addyman (umpire), E.F.H. Evans, Preb. Hewitt, G.Rouse,
J.D. Boards, F. Turner
Middle row: Rev. Kenwood, J.E. Cuff, Dr. P.K. Lewis (captain), W.E.A. Hartson
In front: W.H. Shuttleworth, J.C. Custance

photograph (below) taken of the team in 1905 is believed to be the earliest one known. An article in the *Hereford Times* dated 26 April 1913 stated that because there was no interest in cricket in Bromyard for the season ahead, the club would be wound up. There was a further article in May 1914 confirming that the club had failed to be revived for the year and that, despite the fact that there was a good ground available, there was no support. Nothing happened during the First World War, but on 12 May 1920 there was a meeting at the Hop Pole in Bromyard to consider the possibility of re-starting the cricket club. T.E. Mitchell was elected as the chairman and it was agreed that the new team would be called Bromyard Cricket Club. A committee was appointed and the subscription for playing members was fixed at 5s. per annum. A deputation was appointed to ascertain the assets of the old club and to arrange the provision of a suitable cricket field. It was agreed that the club would apply for membership of the newly-formed Hereford Cricket League. The team clearly did not last long, because in 1930 there was another article in the *Hereford Times*

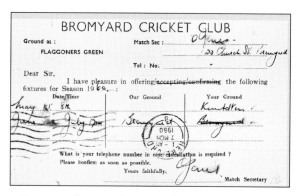

Bromyard printed postcard of 1960 seeking a game against Kimbolton

stating that the team was to be revived and that they would play at Berryfield.

In 1947 they did not have their own ground, so the secretary wrote to the Headmaster of Bromyard Grammar School on 7 January requesting permission for the revitalised club to play on the school ground for the coming season. He confirmed that the club had had a successful season in 1946 winning the Leominster Knockout Cup – the first time that the club had achieved that distinction. He said in the letter:

Upper: Bromyard old club house 1980
Lower: The new club house 1981

As I outlined in my letters last season our greatest handicap is the lack of a ground for practice and the playing of matches.

Despite the fact that they did not have their own ground, they won the cup again in 1947 and 1948. In 1948 John Smale's widow presented the John Smale Challenge Cup.

In 1949/50 George Warley from Hereford was playing against Bromyard for the Hereford City Sports Club Second XI. He recalled that he took all ten wickets and was promised the match ball by the Bromyard Club – he is still waiting for it!

The club was re-formed once again in 1953. The present ground is alongside the A44 Worcester to Leominster road, on the outskirts of Bromyard. In 1954 they bought two damson orchards at Flaggoners Green for £400 as a potential site for their new cricket

Bromyard c.1980
Back row:, Bobby Mckewan, Mick Holsten, Jeff Bayliss, Paul Westmacott, Kenny Burston, Terry Rogers, Andrew Lamb, Keith Young
Front row: Sam Griffiths, Ivor Lloyd, John Evans, Roger Penson

ground. Between 1954 and 1958 all games were played away whilst the members prepared their new ground. In 1958 a prefabricated bungalow was bought for £60 and erected and renovated by the members. In July 1958 Sir Archer Baldwin M.C., M.P for the Leominster Constituency, officially opened it. At the event the deeds of the ground were officially handed over to the Rev. W.G. Walton, a trustee of the club. Derek Hince remembers the first match on the ground very fondly as he kept wicket to Reg Perks, the Worcestershire and England fast bowler, in one of his final matches.

Pencombe 1995
Back row:. Alan Davies, Bob Townsend, Matthew Davies, Andrew Rogers,
Stuart Barrett, Tony Davies, Stuart Graham, James Brown
Front row: Chris Elliott, Brent Thomas, Brian Pilliner, Chris Graham,
Owen Thomas, Steve Townsend

Because Bromyard is close to Worcester, several Worcestershire county players have played testimonial matches on the ground during their benefit year. These included Don Kenyon, the Worcestershire captain and England opening batsman in 1964; Brian Brain in 1981; and Ted Hemsley in 1982.

The new clubhouse was completed in 1981 and was officially opened by Mike Procter, the South African all-rounder, who was playing for Gloucestershire at the time. The club started to play league cricket in the 1970s. They won the Fox six-a-side competition in 1977 and the Eastnor six-a-side cup three years running in 1987/8/9. They also won the Goodrich Cup in 1992. The club continues to prosper.

Pencombe

Pencombe is a small village close to Bromyard which is recorded as playing cricket in the early part of the 20th century. However, an article in the *Hereford Times* dated 26 April 1913 stated that there was little prospect of cricket for the coming season.

There is no further evidence of the team playing until 1953, but sometime thereafter they folded again, only to be re-formed in 1979.

They could only play away fixtures for the first three years because they did not have a ground of their own. In 1982 they managed to rent a ground at Broadbridge, in Bromyard, where they played for two seasons. They then played at Queen Elizabeth School in Bromyard for the next few seasons, finally moving back to Pencombe in 1989 where they still play. The ground is set on a piece of high ground on the edge of the village with the benefit of wonderful panoramic views. The team shares the ground with the local senior and junior football teams.

In January 2006, 16-year-old Matthew Davies was bowling in the indoor league and had only bowled one over when he stopped playing as he felt unwell. The doctor diagnosed leukemia and, sadly, Matthew died in March just three months later.

Pencombe is a small family club and attracts several playing members from the same family. In the current team are brothers Bob and Steve Townsend and father and son Chris and Stuart Graham. In 2007 the modern club is celebrating 25 years of being able to play at home.

Whitbourne Cricket Club 1923
Back row:, L.Matthews Snr. (umpire), R. Jones, C. Smith, C. Williams, J. Vernall, J. Mitchell,
J. Grub (umpire), F. Green (scoper)
Front row: J. Tomkins, W. Matthews, C. Robinson, W. Mitchell (captain), E.F.H. Evans,
W. Griffiths, E.H. Griffiths

Whitbourne

Whitbourne is a small village close to Bromyard which was playing at the beginning of the 20th century – the 1903 fixture card confirming that the president was E.F.H. Evans. His grandson, Chris Evans, is in the 1995 team photograph (opposite page) which illustrates the family's long association with the club. An article in the *Hereford Times* dated 26 April 1913 was pessimistic in stating that there was little prospect of cricket in the club for the coming season, presumably because of the imminent prospect of war.

The ceremonial burning of the Whitbourne pavilion at the end of play in 2001

Whitbourne 1995
Back row: Roger Davies, Rick Freeman, David Congrave, R. Grove,
Andrew Lamb (president)
Front row: Chris Evans, Andy Turner, Ben Owen, Derek Madment

However, the team was playing again by 1923 and is shown on the photograph (opposite page) of the team that year. They played on the Whitbourne Hall Estate owned by Captain E.F.H. Evans who is in the 1923 photograph.

The club ceased playing sometime later and was re-formed in 1974, thanks to the efforts of the late Dick Moore. The first wicket was a coconut mat on concrete. Ian Botham, of England fame, lived in Whitbourne when he was playing for Worcestershire and was president of the club in 1990. However, his cricket commitments prohibited him from taking an active part in the team. In 1991 a new pitch was made on the Beaufield adjacent to Whitbourne Court. One disadvantage was that balls often landed in the moat which surrounded the Court. The Club sadly ceased playing in 2001 – the photograph shows the ceremonial burning of the pavilion (opposite page).

Rowden Abbey Cricket Club

Rowden Abbey is on the Tenbury road, about 2 miles from Bromyard. The club is known to have played in the 1920s and '30s; this is evidenced by the letter to a Bromyard solicitor in 1926 and by the photograph (above right) of the captain, Preb. Lushington, taken in the 1930s. Little else is known.

*Rowden: Preb. Lushington at tea
time complete with cigarette*

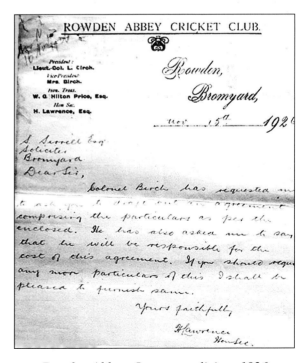

Rowden Abbey: Letter to solicitor, 1926

Bringsty cricket ground

Bringsty

The club is geographically close to Bromyard and in 1930s they played on common ground nearby having no pavilion of their own.

The latest club was re-formed in 1947 after the war. The founder members were F.C.L. (Les) Essenhigh (who was elected chairman), Eric Hawkins (secretary) and E.Y. Robinson (president). Les Essenhigh was the headmaster of Brockhampton School and organized many school matches in the early 1940s. His son, David, who played occasionally for the team, went on to play Minor Counties cricket for Wiltshire.

Originally the members had to change under a convenient thick holly tree, but they then progressed to a garage-type hut, which miraculously grew up overnight! They won the Leominster Knockout cup in 1957, beating Old Luctonians in the final. In 1965 the club had a new pavilion, which was a prefabricated concrete building with two cedar wood entrance doors. It was officially opened by the president, E.Y Robinson, in October 1965.

Alan Roberts took over the job as secretary from Eric Hawkins and remained in the post until the club folded in 1998; he was also the Club Umpire. At the final event he was presented with a gold watch for 25 years

Bringsty 1992 winning Andrew Morris Cup
Back row: Mick Thomkins, James Hine, Ian Oliver, Paul Barrett, Barry Hine, Tim Weaver
Front row: Brian Pillinger, Ted Thomas, Ian Barnes, Mike Harding (vice captain), Kevin Griffiths
Inset: Steve Thompkins (captain)

service to the club. Ironically, the club's most successful period was in the few years before they folded. In 1991 they won the League and the Andrew Morris Knockout Cup, which they also won the following year and again in 1995. They were beaten in the final of the cup in 1993 and 1996. Bringsty was a typical club that was kept afloat by a dedicated few but, regrettably, had the same fate as many others which folded in the 1990s.

Burley Gate 1955-6
Back row: Mr. Waldron (umpire), R. Bullivant, D. Hince, R. Hince, R. Pomfrey, S. Morris, N. Eastwood, Nellie Eastwood (scorer)
Front row: ? Howells, G. Price, E. Bayliss, J. Bowler, R.Jones, C. Amos

Burley Gate

Burley Gate is a small village on the main road between Hereford and Bromyard. The first team was formed as a youth club team in the late 1940s becoming a senior side in 1952.

In the first year they played friendly matches on Thursdays, Saturdays and Sundays. The original ground was a field at Monckton owned by Tom Gummer. They then moved to Castleton on land owned by their member Sonny Morris, and from there to Preston Wynne, by the village hall on farm land owned by one of the members, Dave Westoby. In October 1953 they purchased a sectional building from Wynnes, a firm in the Station Yard at Hereford, for use as a pavilion. The pavilion was in use for the first time in the 1954 season and during that year the club agreed to continue to use their grass wicket. All these efforts were in vain and the club eventually closed down in about 1967 because of lack of support.

Withington

Withington is about five miles from Hereford on the Bromyard road. Cricket was played at Withington from the turn of the 20th century. One of the regular players in the early days was H.J. Dent who in 1904 also played for Hereford Club and Ground

against a Worcestershire 2nd XI. He was described in his obituary years later as: 'A typical farmer at the crease who did not hang around and slogging was his speciality'.

The photograph (below) was taken in 1907 at a match played on the old ground at Thinghill Court. Mr. and Mrs. Abbot owned the property and they encouraged cricket to be played in their grounds. Sadly Mr. and Mrs. Abbot's two sons were killed in the First World War and, partly due to that, they sold up and moved away from the area.

In 1913 the *Hereford Times* reported that the club was playing their home matches at Whitestone. They won the Brockhampton Cup that year.

Withington 7 September 1907. Match between married and singles

There was another report in the *Hereford Times* on 5 May 1914 stating that at the A.G.M. the secretary, who resided at Nunnington Court, confirmed that he hoped that the club would have another successful year. There is no evidence of cricket during the First World War but the *Hereford Times* noted that the team was playing at Withington Court in 1921.

In June 1935 the newspaper reported that they played a match against the Post Office, which they won thanks to some fine bowling of 8 wickets for 20 runs by Groves.

Regular cricket was played between the wars, but stopped again at the outbreak of the Second World War. Play commenced again in 1946 and continued until 1956 when there was a break until Ray Norton moved into the area in 1962. He had moved to Withington from Birmingham and was advised by the locals that no cricket team had been in existence for some years. Ray was a cricket lover and resolved to rectify the situation. One day he went to a fête in the village and was asked by some teenagers if he knew the test match score. This opened up a conversation and he discussed the lack of a cricket team with the teenagers who were keen to play and asked him if a club was going to start up again.

The last known ground was behind a garage belonging to Eric Williams near the Cross Keys Inn. The square was still protected by a barbed wire surround and Ray noticed that, whilst the outfield was covered in molehills, the square was completely clear. Some time later he found out that before the war a trench 6ft. deep had been dug all round the square, filled with broken glass and topped with soil. Not surprisingly, this had stopped the moles altogether! Eric Williams still had some kit and a Savings Bank account containing £16 4s. 2d., which was duly handed to Ray.

There was a meeting to put the revived club on a proper footing. John Hawkins was elected president and the local vicar, Jack Williams, was elected chairman. The field belonged to John Hawkins and, at the time, the grass was let to a local farmer but the hay was not taken off until the end of June. Therefore, if the team was to start

immediately, all early season matches would have to be played away from home. The team had no money apart from the old savings account so the villagers held a jumble sale which raised £25. An old British Rail brake van was purchased for use as a changing room. At the time the team was made up of local youngsters only. In 1992 the club moved from Withington to Preston Wynne and was re-named Cross Keys.

Ledbury

Ledbury is in the east of the county close to the Malvern Hills and Worcestershire. The cricket club was formed in 1837 and has always played on the same ground behind the Full Pitcher inn in New Street. The pub has been there since well before the cricket club was founded – the Biddulph family originally owned the ground and the pub was once called the Biddulph Arms. The club has always been closely connected to the pub, hence the current sign which shows a full pitcher (as a glass) on the one side and a cricketer bowling on the other (opposite page). When a photograph of the team was taken in 1913 (below), Mr. C.B. Masefield is reputed to have said to a young Mr. Bill Clarke, 'Come and sit in front of my big feet!' Before the Second World War the club leased the ground to the Girls' Grammar School twice a week.

Ledbury 1913 team
Back row: L.P. Hoult, A.W. Brown, Walter Williams, H.J. Smith, Archie Chadd, W.G. Davies (club professional and groundsman), H. Corbett
Middle row: Tom Rogers, R.E. Harding, C.B. Masefield, Guy H. Smith, J.C. Smith (captain)
Sitting: G.R. Birks, W.P. Clarke

The Full Pitcher inn sign

The Ledbury Colts team was re-formed in the summer of 1945 after the war was over, with a team comprising: J. Barnes, R. Newman, P. Pitt, M. Leach, B. Messam, M. Paul, G. Yapp, S. Bramley, B. Masters, G. Symonds, and I. Collett.

Jim Smith, who played for the club for many years, also played first-class cricket for Worcestershire.

Brian Messam was one of the most successful bowlers for post-war Ledbury. He was a fast bowler and played for the club for 30 years. In a late 1950s match against Hereford he took 6 wickets for 14 runs. His figures for that season were 58 wickets for 552 runs in 236 overs, 57 of which were maidens.

Wilf Lawrence was another successful team member who played for 40 years in the first team from 1928. He scored 26 centuries and took over 1,000 wickets. Peter Jackson, the former Worcestershire player, played for Ledbury after 1950 when his first-class days were over. Other players who have served the club with distinction are Frank James, Bill Clarke, Bill and John Wetson, Bob Badham, Joe Nuttridge, Bridger Champion, Fred Wally and David Juckes.

One of the most well-known players of recent years was Steve Emery, who played for the club in the 1980s and '90s. He was also a successful professional footballer and played for Hereford United and Derby County.

However, the best known family name in Ledbury, in cricket, poetry and legal circles, is Masefield, and members of the family have served the cricket club in various capacities for over 100 years.

When Ledbury celebrated their 150th anniversary, Brian Johnston spoke at the celebration dinner. The club continues to prosper.

The 1920s Ledbury team

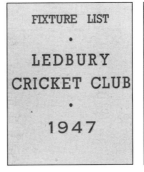

Above left: Ledbury's first fixture card after the Second World War

Above right: The Ledbury Logo taken from the tie made to celebrate the club's 150 years

Bosbury

The club has been in existence since before the First World War and even had a ladies' section as early as 1909. The team is reported in the *Hereford Times* from 1920 until 1929. After the Second World War, the club re-formed in 1946 and in 1955 played an anniversary match, which was well reported in the *Hereford Times*.

Bosbury folded in 1969 when the new primary school was built, but the club was reformed in 1981 thanks to the efforts of Ron Franklin. Since 1982 they have competed in Division Four of the Hereford and District League. The team plays in the grounds of the local primary school.

Top: Bosbury Gentlemen versus the Ladies', 1909
Bottom: The 1955 anniversary celebrations

Colwall

Colwall had a cricket team as early as 1859 (Anthony 1903) but in the early years they only played friendly cricket matches. They play on land owned by the Lloyd family of the Barton Court Estate. The ground is called Stow Lane and is situated in the centre of the village and is one of the most picturesque grounds in Herefordshire.

In 1923 Colwall played the strong Colwall Ladies' XI. The ladies batted first and scored 213 – Miss Hughes scored 87 and Mrs. Molly Scott Bowden scored 50. In reply, the men's team could only score 156 all out. Mrs. Scott Bowden was responsible for arranging the Colwall Ladies' Cricket Festival, which ultimately led to the formation of the National Ladies Cricket Association.

The men's club has fielded some fine players including, in 1946, the three Horton brothers. Bill Horton was captain and his brothers Henry and Joe also played. Henry was the most successful – he went on to play first-class cricket for Worcestershire and Hampshire and was also a successful footballer playing for Southampton and Hereford United. He played cricket for Colwall for a second time at the end of his first-class career and in 1969 won both the batting and bowling averages. For a short period of time he acted as a first-class umpire. Joe also played cricket for Herefordshire.

The Colwall team in August 1946, immediately after the Second World War had finished
Back row: E. Lawday, J.F.M. Singleton, E.R. Tobitt, H. Brazington, G.M. Singleton, E.J. Brown, P. Marsham
Front row: H. Horton, W. Horton (captain)
W.P. Singleton (chairman), J. Horton, W.E. Beach (secretary)

County cricket at Colwall

Other first-class players who have played for Colwall include Ricardo Ellcock, who was a student at Malvern Boys College in the early 1980s. He went on to play for the West Indies and is now an airline pilot. Damon D'Oliviera, the eldest son of Basil D'Oliviera, had a spell with the club when he was a teacher at Malvern Boys' College. Damon, like his father, had a successful first-class career with Worcestershire. Iordannais Kontarines, who is a Greek International who played in the I.C.C. World Cup, is playing for the team in 2007.

Local talent is important for the success of any club and Colwall is no exception. Whilst it is not possible to name all, some must be mentioned: Sandy Singleton, who was president for 10 years; Peter Pedlingham, who spent 50 years on the committee and did a tremendous amount of work for the club. It is believed that

he played twice for Worcestershire Club and Ground. Three members of the club – Peter Pedlingham, Roger Crump and Peter Jones – played for Worcestershire Seconds in the late 1970s. In the modern era, Gary Haines was a fine

Colwall 1966
Back row: R. Phillips (umpire), B. James, P. Hodgetts, D. Hind, G. Mead,
D. Ward, R. Crump
Front row: F. Voisey, J.G.E. Lampard, D. Turner (captain), P. Berry,
Y.P. Pedlingham (vice captain)

left arm spinner. There is a photograph in the pavilion showing him receiving the 1985 player of the year award from John Chadd, the Hereford City Sports Club chairman.

Like all successful clubs Colwall has had, and in some cases still has, its stalwarts. They include Barbara Berry and her husband, George, who was chairman, groundsman and captain of the club for many years, together with his brothers, Phil and Fred. During the 20th century three generations of Berrys have played for the club, Adrian (ex-captain), Kim (ex-captain) and Jonathan are all sons of George. There are also Damien, Matt and Philip – their grandsons. Barbara has been the main tea organizer for 56 years and her daughter-in-law, Cathy, now assists her. Another stalwart of the club is Derek Brimmell who joined the club as a 15-year-old player in 1959 and continued playing until two years ago. In 1976 he

took over the job of groundsman. In 2009 he will have completed 50 years service with the club. Former chairman, Geoff Lampard, was also chairman of Worcestershire County Cricket Club.

Colwall has hosted many famous matches; Henry Horton returned with a Hampshire XI for his benefit match in 1964 and two years later Roy Booth, the Worcestershire wicket-keeper, had a benefit match at Colwall. Other Worcestershire players to have had a benefit match are Martin Horton, Jack Flavell, and David Leatherdale. Graeme Hick and Tom Moody, the Australian test batsman, played in the David Leatherdale match.

Colwall played Sri Lanka on their tour of the UK in 1979. Aravinda De Silva, their most famous player, graced the pitch. Shortly after that match the one and only Sir Garfield Sobers officiated at an international police federation match, which included the Caribbean side.

The Colwall players in 1992. Insert: Derek Brimmell

Left: Colwall's memento of the Sri Lankan tour in 1979
Right: The 2001 Colwall team.
Back row: G. Carpenter, A. Coomer, M. Berry, L. McQueen, A. Blizzard
Front row: J. Fowler, D. Brimmell, M. Colquhoun (captain), C. Kendal, R. Lewis, J. Hornyold

During the 1980s they hosted an international cricket club trophy match. They also played Bermuda, Papua New Guinea, and Fiji in pre-tournament practice matches for the I.C.C. trophy. They also played the Falcons touring cricket club in early August for many years during their annual visits to the county.

In the early 1990s a team called the Clogs (Colwall League of Gentlemen) was formed for local people to play friendly cricket.

Speakers at the annual dinner dances over the years have included Glenn Turner, the New Zealand and Worcestershire batsman; Colin Ingleby McKenzie, the former Hampshire Captain; Ian Greig; and the late Trevor Bethell, who was well known to all Herefordshire sportsmen.

The club joined the Three Counties League in 1974 and moved on to the Gloucestershire and Wiltshire League. The Colwall six-a-side competition started in 1978 and continued for 20 years. Three Herefordshire clubs have won the competition – Hereford Nomads, Bosbury, and Burghill and Tillington.

Colwall won the Three Counties League in 1982. Andy Murtagh, the former Hampshire player, played six times for the team. One of Colwall's finest moments was when they reached the semi-final of the National Village Cricket Knockout Cup in August 1991. Unfortunately they missed the final, losing in a close game against Harome from West Yorkshire.

The club entertained a Lashings XI in 2006 featuring Lance Cairns, the New Zealand test batsman; Phillip De Freitas, the former England player; and Rohan Kanhai, of the West Indies.

Colwall currently play in the Worcester League, Division Three. They are closer to Worcester than to Hereford and this reduces travelling costs.

In 2007 the side will field 10 teams consisting of four mens' teams, several junior sides, and a ladies' team.

Eastnor

Lady Henry Somerset provided the original ground when she inherited the Eastnor Estate in 1883, and cricket began in the village in the summer of 1884. In 1912 the first village hall was built and was also used as a pavilion with cricket continuing against local sides until the outbreak of the First World

War. At the 1914 A.G.M. the chairman gave special thanks to Lady Henry Somerset for her kindness in not only providing the ground but also financing its upkeep. The treasurer confirmed that the club had a credit balance of £1 10s. 5d. The last match before the war was against Malvern College Servants on 5 September 1914.

Cricket recommenced on 5 July 1919 with a match against old rivals, Ledbury, who won by 77 runs. Cricket continued to be played between the wars on one day per weekend with a break during harvest time. There was a limited amount of cricket during the Second World War. In 1951 the headquarters was the village hall, rebuilt since the original one had been destroyed by fire in 1939. The subscriptions for 1951 were raised to 10s. per season and 1s. 3d. for tea. In 1960/61 the changing rooms had major structural work carried out including the replacement of the old thatched roof with one of slate.

Towards the end of the 1973 season the B.B.C. filmed a scene for the drama series *The Pallisers* at Eastnor. Members of the team took part in a filmed cricket match sequence in which young Lord Silverbridge was to play and star and the team was photographed with one of the other stars of the series, Susan Hampshire.

In 1974 a six-a-side competition was introduced and the club also entered the National Village Cup Competition. A new pavilion was started in 1982, just two years before the club celebrated its centenary, and was finished in the centenary year. The old tea hut was demolished in 1985. The main force behind the venture was Roy (Daisy) Mayo, who was assisted by other members of the club.

Eastnor player Charlie Taylor made the headlines in the *Hereford*

Times in May 1985. He scored his maiden century just a week before his wedding. The headline read: 'Charlie Taylor hits his century which was also his last as a bachelor century'. Eastnor won the Herefordshire Senior Cup in the 1980s.

The club has hosted many benefit matches for first-class players over the years including Bob Carter, Norman Gifford, Basil D'Oliviera, Alan Ormrod, Brian Brain (from Worcestershire) and Bob Willis (from Warwickshire), who was guest of honour at the club's annual dinner in his benefit year.

The team has gone from strength to strength, joining the Marches League in the 1990s and winning the league in 1998. By 2003 the club was

Eastnor's new pavilion

Eastnor winning the Kington cup 1980s
Back row: John Eversham, Malcolm Hughes, Jamie Drew, Ron Davies, Tony Beale, Charles Taylor, Dave Entwhistle, Roly Mayo (umpire)
Front row: Bob Hale, Daisy Mayo, Jim Sandford, John Taylor

running three sides and a second ground was made available at Eastnor for the Third XI. There is now a Colts side and three junior teams and the club has in the region of 15 coaches. Eastnor also runs a popular six-a-side competition.

The club's success is due to the enthusiasm of many members including Jim Sandford, John Taylor, Bob Hale, Mike Kidd and Mal Hughes. The club has had two umpires who have offici-

Eastnor dinner dance 1976

Back row: Richard Tandy, Cliff Hill, Tony Burton, Charles Taylor, Tilly Mayo, Norman Gifford, John Taylor, Terry Goode, Jim Sandford, Phil Hodges, Roly Mayo
Front row: Pete Adams, John Belbeck, Daisy Mayo, Dave Entwhistle, Rodney Jarrett

Eastnor in the early 1980s

Back row: Gary Rumfrey (scorer), Derek Wilkinson, Ron Franklin, Terry Goode, John Taylor, Cliff Hill, Rodney Jarrett
Front row: Pete Adams, Jim Sandford, Daisy Mayo, John Belbeck, Dave Entwhistle

ated for many years – Jim Lane in the 1960s and '70s and Roly Mayo in the '80s and '90s. In 2006 the club hosted a Herefordshire Minor County cricket match. Jim Sandford was presented with the Rob Staite Trophy in 2007.

Stoke Edith / Frome Valley
Stoke Edith cricket club was based at the Foley Estate on the Hereford to Ledbury road and was the home of the Frome Valley Club as well as Stoke Edith itself. The estate is the only local one known that could boast possessing its own fire engine; ironically, the house (page 174) was destroyed by fire in 1927.

In April 1907 Frome Valley was involved in a low scoring match with Brockhampton when they scored a total of 20 runs, but managed to dismiss their opponents for 17. The Brockhampton team included both C. and A.W. Foster, both of whom were a great influence on the team at that time. They won the Brockhampton Cup in 1903/4/5 so their poor showing at Frome Valley is somewhat of a mystery.

One of the most successful cricketers for Frome Valley was the Rev. A.E. Green Price, the Rector of Tarrington from 1902 until 1925. His cricketing career extended to nearly 50 years during which time he scored over 20,000 runs including 25 centuries. In four separate years he scored more than 1,000 runs in a season. When he was 51 years old he scored 207 not out for Radnorshire Gentlemen against Hereford Gentlemen, and he then scored 138 not out for Frome Valley. In 1925 he left Tarrington to take over the living of Norton in Radnorshire. In July 1926 he was playing cricket for Knighton.

The club also had other fine players including, in the early days,

A 19th-century print of Stoke Edith

An early photograph of the Frome Valley team in front of Stoke Edith House

was told that, on professional advice from Fisons, the square had been forked with a special tool and fertilizer, lawn sand, and weed-killer had been used, resulting in a much more vigorous growth of turf. The club had a balance in hand of £80 15s. 7d. and A.T. Foley was re-elected president.

A special general meeting was held at the Foley Arms, Tarrington, on 10 May 1963 to hear and consider the president's proposal to plough up the cricket ground and the surrounding meadow. Capt. A.T. Foley, the president, opened the meeting by explaining that economic considerations made it necessary for him to make alterations to the running of the Stoke Edith Estate, by increasing the area of arable land for which purpose he would need the cricket meadow. He regretted the necessity for this and hoped that some solution could be found. Mr. E.G. Toyne spoke as the oldest member of the club, saying that he remembered the present playing square being laid down by Mr. Paul Foley in 1902. The previous ground had been behind the Ledbury Lodge. The president brought the meeting to a close by accepting the principle that the club should retain the ground on a rental basis subject to negotiation.

At a meeting on 7 November 1963 a letter was read from Captain Foley in which he advised the club that they would have to move before the summer of 1967. By the A.G.M. in December 1963 Captain Foley had resigned as president and the future of the club was discussed. It was agreed that they had three years to obtain a new ground or become a wandering club. The choice was to share a ground or disband. By 1965 the ground was already an island in the middle of a cornfield, with an unploughed access track and room for about 7 or 8 cars under the tree. Two nearby sites for an alternative ground had been inspected but were not suitable. An unofficial approach had been made to Canon Frome, who

members of the Foley family: Tom Bradstock, Mike Tidmarsh (who played from 1952 until the club ceased in 1969), and Pat Kendle (who was also one-time captain of Gloucestershire Seconds).

Stoke Edith Ladies and Much Marcle Ladies had annual fixtures in the 1920s. After the Second World War they played from 1946 until 1969.

At the A.G.M. held on 8 Jan 1962 A.T. Foley, the then chairman, advised that Mrs. Curran the hall caretaker had been paid 7s. per home match to assist with preparing teas and washing up – a princely sum over 40 years ago. On 10 Dec 1962 the club were also having to move, and it was suggested that the two teams should amalgamate. Canon Frome had a new ground at Walsopthorne in Ashperton. The majority of the members favoured staying independent if a ground could be found.

The club struggled on in the following years living with the uncertainty, but in autumn 1967 the ground was ploughed up thus ending 60 years cricket at that spot. The club was suspended for one season and could not find anywhere else to play and, at a meeting in May 1969, it was finally wound up.

Some years later Mike Tidmarsh was on holiday in Namibia. He was sitting in a bar when he was approached by a former cricketing colleague. They had not seen each other for 25 years and spent some time reminiscing about their playing days. Mike also remembered playing in a game at Eastnor in the 1960s when bagpipes were being playing on the Castle Walls.

A regular umpire for the Stoke Edith club was the Rev. Simey, the vicar of Dormington, who always sat on a shooting stick and caused great amusement when a straight drive was hit in his direction.

Much Marcle / Weston Sports Club

Much Marcle were playing from 1920 until the outbreak of the Second World War. The team was based near the Slip Tavern. Len Weston of Weston's Cider founded Weston Sports in 1949. They played until 1968. Len had a close association with Hereford United Football Club and Worcestershire County Cricket Club and often called on players from the clubs to make up the side for certain games. Henry Horton played on more than one occasion. Charlie Thompson, who was better known for his football career with Hereford United, was a good all-round sportsman who also played cricket for the Weston's team.

One interesting match worth recording because of the well-known local players involved was in 1958 when Weston played Stroud Brewery. Stroud batted first and scored 105. Sammy Chilvers, formerly of Hereford United, took 6 wickets for 37 runs, and Alf

Marston (Stan Marston's father) took 3 for 33. Weston won the match with a snick for 4 off the last ball of the match. The Weston score was made up as follows: G. Wilson 11, B. Farley 12, R. Baker 0, S. Marston 15, S. Chilvers 25, J. Warley 20, H. Pudge not out 6, W. Alexander 6. A. Marston 1, K.Campbell 3, K. Shaw 6.

Dymock

Dymock is on the borders of Herefordshire and Gloucestershire, but the team played most of its cricket in Herefordshire, having a side in the original Hereford and District League. The club's emblem is the coat of arms of Lord Dymoke, the King's Champion. The club was founded in 1868, only stopping between the First and Second World Wars. In the original scorebook for 1868 the batsmen were 'thrown down' rather than run out and two runs was recorded for each wide.

Much Marcle / Weston's
Charlie Thompson coming out to bat

The club has had two pavilions in its history. The original was a chicken hut which was replaced in the mid-1970s by a purpose-built pavilion. The team photograph of 1910 shows a good example of the fashion of the day. The lady in the photograph is dressed immaculately, complete with hat; one of the gentlemen is wearing a top hat, another a straw hat, and there are several flat caps on show (right). Dymock won the Perrystone Court Challenge Cup in 1923. In 1930 the Dymock versus Much Marcle match was the first time village sides had a match commentary by the BBC. During the 1930s a local member of the club, Ernie Morgan, protected the pitch by removing his donkey's shoes before the donkey pulled the heavy roller over the pitch.

Dymock.
Top: 1910   *Bottom: 1980s*

During the Second World War the War Agricultural Department attempted to requisition the ground for ploughing. The local schoolmaster, Jack Hobbs, told them in no uncertain terms that the pitch was to be left alone. He effectively stopped them in their tracks and they duly departed with a flea in their ear. During the same war team member Ernie Morgan was a member of the bomb disposal unit and was decorated. Another member of the team, Alan Simpson, was a prisoner-of-war and learnt to knit his own socks. He made use of that skill after the war – if he was dismissed early in a match he was known to have taken his socks out of his kit bag to darn them during the rest of his team's innings.

Immediately after the war the club purchased their own ground for £160. The 1980 team photograph includes Frank Miles at top left, who later became chairman of Hereford United Football Club. Some of the other players are Keith Bishop, Trevor Goulding, Geoff Darley, John Gurney and Dave Bakewell.

CHAPTER XII

Youth Cricket

Many schools in the county have produced fine cricketers in the past. Some of these schools no longer exist and there is unfortunately far less cricket played at those that remain. This is a national trend, and the development of young cricketers is now left to the first class and club sides.

In this chapter the various schools and youth club sides in the county that have influenced the development of the sport in the last 100 years are described with examples where appropriate.

Clyde House School

Clyde House was a small private school in Moorfields Street, Hereford. The headmaster in 1902 was J. Lingham-Lees. The school had both boarders and day pupils and had a good cricketing pedigree mainly due to the enthusiasm of the headmaster.

The most well-known cricketing pupil was Jack Sharp (Chapter I), who attended the school along with his brother. The school is recorded as playing local teams during the latter part of the 19th century and continuing until 1910.

Hereford Cathedral School

The school has played a prominent part in Herefordshire cricket for well over 100 years and is recorded as far back as 1859, playing the local sides (Anthony 1903). They started playing organized cricket in about 1870 on Widemarsh Common. The first recorded match was against the King's School,

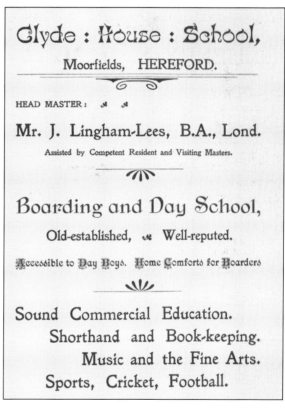

Cricket was on the menu at Clyde House School

Gloucester in 1880; they also played Llandovery College, Christ's College Brecon, Oswestry Grammar, Monmouth, and King's School Worcester in the same year. By 1883 the ground at Wyeside had been developed and the first match was played there on 16 May, a wooden pavilion having been built in time for the opening. On 26

177

Hereford Cathedral School

Top Left: Stephen Price, England Schools under-14 and under-16, 1993 and 1995

Top right: First XI 1948
Back row: M. Gray, T.C.B. Porter, Mr. R.D. Lancaster, D.J. Pill, J.P.L. Thomas
Middle row: G.T. Warley, B.A. Procter, P.E. Richardson (captain), P.K. Veale, H.C.W. Nicholls
Front row: C.L. Davies, J.W. Warley, M. Allsebrook

Above: The Cathedral School pavilion in 2006

May 1890 the great W.G. Grace brought a team of Gloucestershire cricketers to play Herefordshire. Lord Chesterfield captained the local team and the match took place at Wyeside. The pavilion that they used was to the side of the present one.

Dick Shepherd was groundsman and coach for over 40 years and was a great influence on the team. The school has produced many fine cricketers including Henry Horton and Peter and Dick Richardson. In 1948 the team captained by Peter Richardson won all of their 14 matches and Peter Richardson, who went on to play for England and Worcestershire, averaged over 50.

After the Second World War, the years 1947 and 1948 were a golden era for the school when Andy Connop was the coach. Several other players have produced fine averages during their time at the school including Edward Symonds who averaged 66.81 in 1992; Stephen Price who had batting averages of 52.61, 69.4 and 70.8 in the three years 1995-7; and Ben Stebbings who averaged 76.75 in 2006. The school has also produced some fine bowlers including D.J. Hayden, who took 62 wickets at an average of 9 runs per wicket, G.J.M. Morris, 1934-5, John Chadd, 1949-51, and Jamie Layton, 1994-7, who all took over 100 wickets for the First XI. In 1992 Richard Skyrme progressed from the school to become the first captain of the Herefordshire Minor Counties Cricket League. He also captained the Old Herefordians to victory in the 2003 National Brewers Cup Competition for old boys' sides, showing that the school continues to produce good cricketers.

Brian Goode, who served the school from 1979 until 2005 as groundsman, has recently retired, but still keeps in touch with the game by playing for the Herefordshire over 50s side. Joe Woodward, the former Nottinghamshire county player, was groundsman between 1949 and 1954.

Hereford High School

The High School opened in 1912 and the cricket team is recorded as playing from 1921 onwards. In 1927 their star player was undoubtedly Reg Perks. He had remarkable figures in May June and July of that year and in one match in May he scored 33 runs and took 6 wickets for 19 runs including a hat trick. In a house match during the same week he took 5 wickets for a

single run including another hat trick. Other figures of note were 7 wickets for 24 runs against Lucton, 6 for 23 and 74 runs against Ledbury Grammar School, 8 for 11 against

Hereford High School
Top: The 1932 cricket team
Back row: P.P. Pembridge, E.C. Watkins, Mr. Sawkins, D.Stacey, Mr. K.J. Jones, R.A. Stephens, E.W.H. Howe
Middle row: J.G. Wood, T.J. Stokes, B.W. Rogers, J.C. Jackson   Front row: D.A. Wargent, S.C. Wright

Bottom: The 1951 team
Back row: A.W.R. Morgan, D.J. Watkins, M.S. Preece, S. Catley, C. Gilbert, B. Savory.
Front row: S.W. Stephens, R.C. Marchant, M. Powell, D.A Luker (Capt), J.D. Mawson, P.J. Keyte, K.E. Pole

Hereford High School 1940
Back row: E.J. Cleary, D.A. Hawkins, Cliff. Roese,
S.S. Jones, D.G. Williams, Phil Noakes
Front row: J. Burleton, Bill Morris, P.T. Cleary,
R. Ingram, S.D. Jones.

Kentchurch, and 8 for 9 against Leominster Grammar School. By July 1927 he had taken 74 wickets for 214 runs at an average of 2.19. It is not surprising that just four years later he joined Worcestershire County Cricket Club. Reg was destined for a successful England career but, like many others of that generation, his career was interrupted by the outbreak of war. The school produced other fine cricketers who were successful at a local level including Bill (Spadger) Morris, who performed not only for the school but also High School Old Boys and

Hereford City Sports Club. He taught at the school and was most enthusiastic when coaching a new era of young players. The last record of the teams playing is in 1969.

Commercial Road Youth Club, Hereford
The team, formed by the Commercial Road Baptist Church, is recorded as playing from 1949 until 1955. The youth club met throughout the period under the church at which time their leader was Frank Hazel. He was a cricket survivor who unfortunately passed away in 2006 at the wonderful age of 106. One of the best known players of the team was the late George Hyde who was one time Mayor of Hereford and a Councillor and good friend to the city for many years. He played for many teams throughout his career and appears in several photographs in this book.

Hereford Working Boys' Home
The team from the Home is recorded as playing cricket in 1910. The Home was in Bath Street and was established in 1874. The object of the Home was to receive orphans and other voluntary cases of boys from 9 to 14 years of age, either in a state of destitution or growing up uncared for and under evil influences. In 1904 the Home had 125 boys. After more than a quarter of a century of caring for these waifs and strays, the Home closed in 1933.

The Working Boys' Home (date unknown)

Fairfield School at Peterchurch continue to play cricket as this informal photograph in 2006 shows

Fairfield High School, Peterchurch

Fairfield is one of the few local schools that still plays cricket and the photograph (above) shows them receiving the Britannic Coaching kit presentation from Nick Nenadich and Richard Skyrme.

Belmont Abbey School

The school at Belmont Abbey, to the south of Hereford, was founded in 1926 and the first recorded reference to cricket is in the first issue of the school *Magazine* in January 1937. The headmaster, Fr. Anselm Lightbound wrote:

> We have been fortunate in inheriting plenty of grounds for playing fields, and by the efforts of the Community and the grounds man, our cricket field is nearly finished and a new Rugger field is started.

In July 1937 there is a reference in the school *Magazine*:

> May 15th – The Whitsun Holiday began today. Our annual and very popular cricket fixture with Mr Coke's XI resulted in a draw, after a fine display all round.

In the *Magazine* there are two photos of the 1st and 2nd XIs, along with match details, and it would appear that a fixture list had been in operation for some years by 1937.

As the school increased in numbers during the middle part of the 20th century cricket, along with rugby and rowing, was well supported by staff and students alike. Indeed, Abbot Jerome Hodkinson, Fr. Nicholas Wetz, and Fr. Dominic Blaney still remain keen cricket fans.

Captain Tom Urquhart wrote the final chapter in the last school *Magazine* as the school prepared to close in 1994:

> The 1994 Season has, alas, been somewhat of a non-event. Again the rugby posts had gone, the summer timetable had arrived and the days were longer, and yet the school's closure, unfortunately, caused an exodus of the lower-Sixth Form, which left us with both depleted ranks and unfulfilled potential.
>
> Despite this unforeseen problem, the enthusiasm to play and appetite to win continued and the Hereford Cathedral School (2nd XI) privately became our first victims. The cricketing establishment at the Cathedral was put to shame by a Belmont 'composite' (scratch) XI,

Belmont Abbey School 1937

Back row: P. Davies, C.J. Millen, D. Donovan, A. Jackson,
M. Pelly, C.R. Millen
Front row: L. O'Sullivan, J. Kenny, C. Gore (captain),
J. Lightbound, R. Milner

thanks to some pinpoint bowling by Dave Jennings, a monumental half-century from Sean Collins, and some match winning tactical manoeuvres from Matt Samuels.

The match against B.A.C.C. became yet another victim of the British summer, which fittingly concluded an unbeaten season. This means we have now lost only once to a contemporary school XI in the last three years - not bad going for a school which has been

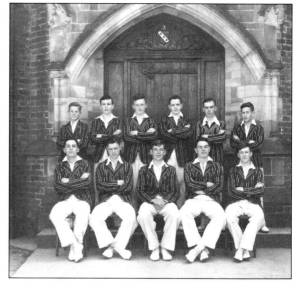

Belmont Abbey School 1942

Back row: P. Smith, C. Fahy, D. Dorling, G. Dean,
H. Oakley, C. Swan
Front row: R. Rock, A. Dorling, J. Ault (captain),
J. Woodyard, P. Ault

forced to close through lack of numbers. Rugby will always be the sport for which Belmont is remembered, but it's good that 1st XI Cricket has also left its mark, especially in the last couple of years.

Thanks to the enthusiasm of the teaching staff, the school, despite being better known for rugby, had a successful cricket team throughout its relatively short history.

Whitecross School, Hereford
Thankfully, the school is a local one that continues to run a team and encourages cricket. The photograph (left) shows the team that won the County Schools under 15s Jack Roberts Memorial Trophy in 2006. They beat Weobley by a magnificent 40 runs in the final – the success was doubly significant for it was the first anniversary of the opening of the new school buildings.

Whitecross under 15s 2006 team

Back row: Chris Evans, Matthew Tingle, James Hancock, Suttipong Kamjadphai,
Luke Chiswell, Mike Evans
Front row: Gary Griffiths, Paul Glasper, Tom Fenton, Matthew Biggs,
Mark Galpin, Daniel Marrett

Bromyard Grammar School

The school was playing cricket from the start of the 20th century and there are reports of them playing other schools and the Bromyard team right up until the Second World War. The local team at Bromyard made use of the school cricket ground when they were groundless after the war.

Lady Hawkins School, Kington

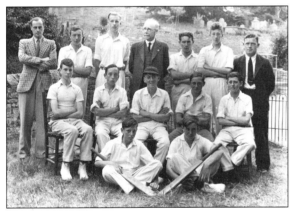

Lady Hawkins School, Kington

Top: 1926 team

Back row: Wilfred Lish, Fred Burgoyne, George Barker, Charles Powell, Alan Lund, Edward Robinson (headmaster)
Middle row: Arthur Bromley, Edward Watson, Frank Bromley, Edward Morris, George Lund
Front row: David Jarman, Clarence Diggory

Bottom: 1940-41 team

Back row: Eric Emmett, David Goodwin, Gerald Knowles, Edward Robinson, Robert Jenkins, Francis Price, Thomas Pugh
Middle row: Alfred Smith, Anthony Price, Albert Gurmin, Sydney East, John Evans
Front row: Peter Galvin, Brian Owens

The school is one of the oldest in the county, having been founded in the 17th century. Lady Margaret Hawkins left provision for it in her will and it was opened in 1632. The only evidence of cricket found in the earlier days of the school is in photographs taken in the 1920s (opposite). In recent years the school was fortunate to have the services of the former Kington stalwart and fine player, Robbie Richardson, who coached the side.

Ross Grammar School

Ross Grammar School 1940
Back row: Ivor Jones, Gordon Witts, Peter Pascoe, Edward West (teacher), Geoff Williams, David Rudge, John Evans
Front row: Jim Roberts, Roger Hicks, Rex Roff (captain), Martin Steward, Roy Pittanway

The photograph (above) shows Rex Roff in the wartime school side of 1940. Rex, like his father and grandfather before him, has played a prominent part in Ross cricket throughout his life. Gordon Witts, who became manager of the Principality Building Society and who was a leading light in the Hereford Amateur Operatic Society, is also in the photograph.

Yarkhill

Mr. John Bunn from Yarkhill produced the interesting photograph (next page). Mr. Ball, the local schoolmaster, was obviously a keen cricketer and took it upon himself to coach the pupils and organise matches for them. Unfortunately, only a few of the team members are known. Second from the left on the back

Yarkhill School 1938
Schoolmaster, Mr. Reginald Ball.
Back row: 2nd from left John Barnett, far right Ron Smith
Front row: Doug Preece, [-], Peter Carless, [-], C.O. Smith

row is Doug Preece from Shucknall Hill and second from the left on the rear row is John Barnett of Pigeon House Farm.

St. Owen's School, Hereford
A rare photograph of a small local school running a cricket side before the Second World War. One interesting player is Phil Noakes, who went on to represent the Hereford High School in 1940. On leaving school Phil joined the police force and played for the local constabulary team before finally retiring from playing and becoming a well-known and respected umpire.

St. Owen's School, Hereford, 1930
Back row: Doug Holmes, Bob Powell, Kenneth Conde, Phil Noakes, David Matthews, [-], Kenny ?, Gordon Williams, Geoff Cartwright, Geoff Henderson, Keith Worthington, Mickey ?, John Bunn, John Clements, [-] , Robert Fowkes
Front row: Ray Wooles, George Berry, John Rutty

Lucton School

As you would perhaps expect of a school well out in the countryside, Lucton produced many fine sportsmen in a variety of fields of play and some can be seen in the team photograph (right).

Ledbury Grammar School

Ledbury Cricket Club flourished throughout the 1950s and '60s mainly due to the success of the Grammar School's interest in sport in the 1940s. Many of the players shown in the photograph (below) eventually turned out to play for the town side in later years.

Lucton School First XI 1958
Back row: K. Marshall, W. Jackson, ? Watson, ? Thomas, M. Abberley, S. Edwards
Front row: G. Davies, D. Appleby, G.Farr, R.B. Williams,T.L. Williams

Ledbury Grammar School (Ash House) 1948
Back row: Ray Stockton, Phil Barnett, John Farleigh, Roly Howells, Mick Howe, Brian Law
Front row: Gordon Robinson, Norman Wetson, Roy Cotton, Tony Gittings, ? Wickham

Leominster Grammar School

The school, together with those at Ledbury and Bromyard, took part in competitive cricket in the period after the Second World War and blooded several good future senior cricketers. Several are shown in the 1947 photograph (left).

Leominster Grammar School X1 1947
Top row: Mr. Tom Howard (sportsmaster), John Griffiths, John Brandfield,
Dick Patrick, Gilly Nash, Kenny Cooper
Middle row: Kenneth Sale, Gordon Nicholas, Danny Wright,
Raymond Pugh, Michael Conod
Bottom row: Harold Clewer, Brian Eckley

Credenhill and Stretton Sugwas Cricket Club

The club ran a succesful youth section for a short period following the Second World War. The 1947 youth team photograph (below) shows many people who went on to play for the senior side. whilst others went on to play for various Hereford City teams.

Credenhill and Stretton Sugwas Youth 1947
Back row: Derek Morgan, Stan Bullock, Derry Brookes, Vivian Mifflin, Dennis Harris
Front row: Brian Davies, Maurice Joseph, Terry Strange, Trevor Watkins, Vernon Watkins

Herefordshire Youth Representative Cricket

This organisation was set up after the Second World War, and the 1958 photograph (right) of the under-18 side shows some players that went on to become very good all-round sportsmen. Worth special mention is the late Roger Griffiths, the hero of the famous Football Association Cup Tie at Edgar Street between Hereford United and Newcastle.

Ross Youth Club

In the late 1950s youth clubs were very well attended and, due to the growing membership, they produced strong cricket teams. Ross was no exception and many of the lads in the 1959 photograph (below) continued playing locally for many years.

Herefordshire under 18s 1958
Back row: Geoff Marchant (umpire) N. Ruck, Dave Hodges, John Dykes, Roger Griffiths, Tony Rosser, ? Beavan, Tex Ritter, Colin Morgan, [umpire]
Front row: Bill Lucas, Dave Marchant, Phil Grismond

Ross Youth Club 1959
Back row: P. Meek, D. Robins, M. Hill, S. Wheeler, J. Robins, M. Prosser, G. Winney, Dave Robins
Front row: L. Darker, G. Gwilliam, B. Robertshaw, T. Wenderlish, [-], D. Lewis, B. Woolf

And all the others

There were many clubs and schools that have in the past provided, and still provide, a background in the most English of games. Group photographs of long-forgotten matches abound – some are so old that the individual players are no longer known; others are treasured memories of times past.

In the future

There has been a steady decline in Youth Clubs during the last 30 years and, because of this, it is imperative that cricket is encouraged at all schools, not just the independent ones. It is noticeable that the more successful club sides in all sports, including cricket, have their own youth sections and encourage the current generation of youngsters to put their energies into sport instead of sitting in front of a television set or home computer.

CHAPTER XIII

Lady Cricketers & Ladies Associated with Cricket

"I knew it! Letting 'em play cricket at Lord's was the thin end of the wedge."

Women's Cricket Association

Herefordshire can boast that the foundations of Ladies' Cricket were born in the County. In 1926 Molly Scott Bowden formed the Ladies National Cricket Association in Colwall and since then this small village, nestling under the shadow of the Malvern Hills, has been a stronghold for Ladies' Cricket, both at local and national level, and many fine lady cricketers have played on the lovely picturesque ground. There is a report in the *Hereford Times* for

August 1929 recording that Colwall hosted the Third Ladies Cricket Festival, thus confirming that it was well established by then. When women's cricket recommenced in 1945, after the war, 66 women cricketers assembled at Colwall to play three matches a day. In 1951, 200 players turned up for the Silver Jubilee of the Colwall Ladies' cricket week. More than half a century

Ladies' cricket week at Colwall (undated)

An early photograph of Bosbury Ladies team

later Colwall is still a stronghold of ladies cricket. Rachel Heyhoe-Flint, the former England captain, has taken part in the Colwall Festival alongside other England players.

In August 1959 the *Hereford Times* reported a ladies' cricket week at Much Marcle. The local side still has a strong ladies' team and in 2007 will be entering the Midlands South West League. The Colwall Maidens have been playing for a number of years, competing in the boys under-13 League. Fiona Fortman has managed both the under-13 and the under-15 sides.

Other clubs in the county have followed Colwall's example and fielded their own ladies'

England Ladies at Canon Frome

England Ladies versus Sri Lanka at Lords (Colleen Rogers – back row, far left)

sides. These include Dymock, Ross and Hereford.

Molly Scott Bowden was clearly an inspiration both for lady cricketers born in the county and for those who came to live in Herefordshire. As a result many have achieved a high level of success, including:

Elizabeth Alexandra 'Betty' Snowball, who died on 13 December 1988 aged 82, was an all-round sportswoman who played squash and lacrosse at international level as well as cricket. But it is as one of the major figures in women's cricket for the two decades from 1930 that she is best remembered, being a fine opening bat and generally accepted as the outstanding wicket-keeper of her generation. She was born in Burnley and was coached after leaving school by Learie Constantine, the West Indian Test player. She played ten times for England and toured Australia twice recording a Test average of 40.86 and effecting 21 dismissals. Her most outstanding

innings was 189 runs in 222 minutes against New Zealand in 1935, an achievement which remained a Test record for half-a-century. She taught at the Elms School, Colwall, and continued to live in the village after her retirement. It must have been no coincidence that she chose to live in Colwall – the place described as the 'home of women's cricket'.

Sarah Potter is the daughter of the late Dennis Potter, the well-known author. She was born in London on 11 July 1961, but has lived most of her life in Herefordshire. Hereford cricketers recognised her potential because, at the age of 20, she made her debut for Hereford City Sports Club men's team in the Three Counties League. She was described as a fierce left-arm fast bowler, a sharp fielder and a batswoman to be reckoned with. Sarah played 7 test matches and 8 one-day matches for England. She started her Herefordshire cricket career playing for Ross

Ladies and played with Julie Backhouse, Colleen Rogers and Jo Greaves, to name but a few well-known lady cricketers.

Colleen Rogers is the daughter of Colin Rogers from the Woolhope Cricket Club and played for the men's team at an early age. She was the first lady to play in the Hereford and District League in 1977. She then played for Ross at the age of 17 and also played for Hereford Ladies. Thereafter she played for the West of England alongside Sarah Potter and Jo Greaves, and then gained recognition from the M.C.C. when she toured Sri Lanka in 2006 (right).

Colleen Rogers (front, second right) with M.C.C. Ladies on tour in Sri Lanka

Harriet Lowe is the daughter of Tim Lowe, the headmaster of the Hereford Cathedral Junior School, and followed in her father's footsteps in his love of cricket. Harriet was the first girl to score a half century for Hereford Cathedral School in a School Fixture and is one of the best lady cricketers that the school has produced. The photograph (opposite) shows Harriet in action for the England Development cricket team versus British Universities in May 1999. She was top scorer but was only chosen as reserve for the England under 19 tour to Ireland. She also played for the Worcestershire ladies team and represented the West Midlands at the Cambridge Festival. Harriet has not played recently, but has joined the R.A.F and hopes to resume her playing career in the forces.

Lisa Nahorniak started playing youth cricket alongside her brother, Ashley, at Brockhampton Cricket Club. She was coached by Richard

Harriet Lowe

Skyrme and played in the boys' teams at the same time as she played for the county sides. Lisa then played in and captained the Worcestershire under 15 and 17 sides and also plays for Hereford Ladies. She is a pace bowler and in 2006 was the first girl to represent the Hereford Cathedral School 1st XI. Lisa is a fine all round sportswoman who has already played rounders for England and, according to local cricketers, could represent England ladies at cricket.

Jo Greaves

Jo Greaves played Hereford League Cricket and also played for the West of England with Sarah Potter and Colleen Rogers. She won the player of the season award playing for Woolhope in 2006.

Tilly Parker played for Dorstone and Golden Valley and had one representative game for a Wales Ladies Eleven.

The non-playing ladies

One of the traditions of cricket at all levels is the social side. Without the unstinting help of the ladies who never play, but who do everything from acting as scorers to making the all important refreshments for the tea interval, cricket would not be such an important part of the community. Teas at village cricket matches are usually of a very high standard. In the early days it was not unusual for players and spectators alike to sit outside round an old farmhouse table, often with beer or cider as liquid refreshment. The traditional

Burghill and Tillington in Doctors' and Nurses' game, 1983

194

Burghill Wives in Doctors' Fancy Dress
Back row: [-], Jo Macklin, Gill Bayliss,
Judy Kramer, Marion Campbell
Front row: Pat Downes, [-], Ginn Downes, Sam Mifflin

Burghill tea ladies

Sam Mifflin, the Burghill scorer in the 1980s

fare was cheese, ham, and cucumber sandwiches followed by homemade delicacies such as fruit cake, jam sponges, welsh cakes, and treacle tart and, at the right time of the year, strawberries and cream. In addition to the alcoholic beverages an urn of tea was always available.

Scoring requires tremendous concentration and the ladies, by tradition, have carried out this onerous task with both dedication and enthusiasm. This was a tremendous help to the players because it allowed them to rest after fielding and before going in to bat. It has always been extremely difficult for a player to score and watch the tactics of the game at the same time.

Jan Herbert started scoring for Wormelow in the 1980s and was so accomplished at it that she was approached by Herefordshire Minor Counties Committee to take on the post of official scorer with them. She took on the job and was so successful at carrying out her county duties that she was approached by Cheshire and offered a position which she duly accepted.

Whilst carrying out research for this book, the authors have been given numerous names of ladies who have devoted their spare time to the smooth running of the social side of local cricket. All are well worthy of recording in this work but many must inevitably be missed – for that our apologies. The ones that have been picked out for individual mention are:

Burghill & Tillington

Special mention must be made of Sue Sparrow, for many years teas co-ordinator; Marion Campbell, the secretary for many years and teas co-ordinator; and Pat and Ginn Downes, tea ladies.

When Burghill & Tillington was formed in 1972/3 not only did a call go out for cricketers to join the club, their wives and girl friends were asked to form a team to provide the all-important tea between innings. The original tea room (or rather kitchen) was a tiny galley-like lean-to built on the side of the original tiny pavilion. To be more precise the latter was a one-room shed where both teams changed. The kitchen equipment was a double gas hob and two large, but dented, aluminium kettles together with odd items of china. Water was carried to the shed from Brick House Farm in a milk churn. There was no room inside so tea had to be taken outside come rain or shine. When the new pavilion was built, the tea ladies had all modern facilities at their disposal and the situation has vastly improved with tea being served inside the pavilion.

Colwall
Barbara Berry, like husband George, has been associated with the club for more than 50 years and throughout most of that period has been the main tea organizer. Her daughter-in-law, Cathy, is maintaining the family tradition and is following in her footsteps. Barbara also played for the ladies' team.

Lamputt's Eleven
Elaine Lamputt was scorer and match manager for G.A. Lamputt's Eleven and Hereford City Sports Club (A) in the 1940s and '50s. She also scored for Ediswan Evening League Eleven.

St. Mary's and Garnons
Molly Jones was scorer and tea lady for both these teams.

" 'E never did quite get over me being elected Captain this year — "

Ladies became involved at all levels in cricket as this Andy Capp cartoon shows

The 1950s Burley Gate wedding of
Alan Jones and Vera Davies
Guard of Honour
Front left: John Bowler   Front right: Ray Hince

Gordon and Elaine Lamputt's wedding day
26 August 1950

Wormelow

Jan Herbert was scorer for Wormelow and also scored for the Hereford and Cheshire Minor Counties. Sue Boulter was the tea co-ordinator.

Post Office

Audrey Legg was the scorer for the team for many years.

Cross Keys / Withington

Sandra Corbin was the scorer.

Richmond Club, Hereford

Anne Buchanan, Carol Rees, and Jeannette Foster were the main tea ladies. The Richmond Club is the former Labour Club in Edgar Street.

Marden

Liz Bryan, Doreen Sawkins and Angela Williams organize the club's tea rota.

Hereford United Sports and Social Club

The tea ladies included Joan Griffiths, Marion Bevan, Rosemary Everall, Phyllis Terry and Eileen Hibble.

Brockhampton

Jo Jennings and Mary and Alice Hope have been tea ladies for many years. Jean Howells was the team scorer.

Longhope

The many members of the team can thank Fay Gurney who was responsible for the teas for 25 years. Mrs. Yemm was a long-term scorer.

Eastnor

Cynthia Hughes was a long-term scorer. The players' wives took on the responsibility of preparing teas.

N.A.L.G.O.

Dorothy Johnston was scorer in the 1950s.

Kimbolton

The scorers for the team were Freda Williams (neé Lloyd) in the early 1950s and Barbara Jones (neé Bird) in the late 1950s. They were followed by Roberta Hodnett (neé Griffiths).

The tea ladies were Nelly Williams and Mrs. Harley Jones.

Above: Jock and Florence Thomson's wedding reception at Hinton Club room 1956

Right: Brockhampton modern-day wedding 2006. Groom – Nick Denny (player / coach) Bride – Tracy Jones (scorer)

Above: Shobdon tea ladies: Jenny Evans, Pearl Teale, Anne Kent-Phillips

Left: Gladys Bishop, the tea lady for the Shop Assistants' team

Burley Gate

Village life in rural Herefordshire, like many other similar communities in the countryside, has created a close-knit community and this was especially true in the 1950s after the trauma of the Second World War. Cricket brought people together and when one of their own was married the whole team would be involved. An example of this is the wedding photo at Burley Gate in the 1950s when Alan Jones married Vera Davies. Members of the team, including John Bowler and Ray Hince, provided the cricket bat guard of honour (page 196).

Canon Pyon

Ruth Powell was scorer for many years.

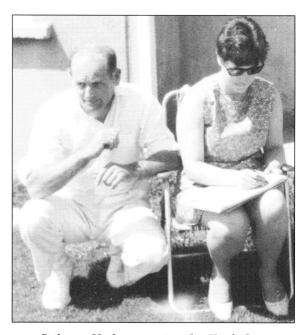

Roberta Hodnett scoring for Kimbolton

Ross

Betty Hill, Sally Clarke, and Mrs. Gammond were the main tea ladies and graced the ladies' pavilion for many years.

CHAPTER XIV

Notable Performances & Tributes

Performances

This chapter is devoted to people who have, in different ways, by their influence, keenness and enthusiasm over many years, improved the standard of cricket in the county. Many cricketers and cricketing personalities have influenced Herefordshire cricket over the years.

There have been some outstanding individual performances by local cricketers. The following statistics represent but a small selection of the material that has come to the authors' notice from various sources whilst researching this book. The individual achievements are detailed under the club that they were playing for at the time.

Bartestree and Lugwardine
D. Jones took 7 wickets for 19 runs against Leominster in 2001.

Three batsmen scored big centuries on their home ground in 2003:
G.Thompson – 187 versus Builth Wells.
D. Robinson – 183 not out versus Marden.
D. Smith – 178 not out versus Knighton.

Bishopswood
Brothers O.F. and G.A. Barnes took all 10 wickets between them against St. John's Cinderford in 1904.

Brecon
R.J. Harley won the batting averages of Division Three of the Hereford and District Cricket League in 1976 playing for Brecon. He had 13

innings with 7 'not outs'; his highest score was 126 not out. He scored 743 runs at an average of 123 including three centuries.

Brockhampton
W.F. Counsell took 10 wickets for 10 runs against Bradley Court on 23 May 1914.

Tony Hope scored 3 centuries in 3 weekends in 1973. In addition, he took 157 wickets in the same season, including 10 wickets for 27 runs against Little Dewchurch. He also took 4 wickets in 4 balls in another match. He won the prestigious R.W.P Roff Single Wicket competition in the late 1960s.

Bert Howells took 8 wickets for 3 runs against Ross Youth Club, and 8 for 18 against Ruardean in the early 1950s.

Bromyard
Tony Mills scored 140 runs in a single innings in 1974.

Bulmer / M.E.B.
Stan Marston scored 10 centuries in 1968.

Dave Marchant scored 1,400 runs in 1968 at an average of 66 runs per match.

Dave Long took 141 wickets in 1968 at an average of 7 per match. In 1969 he had two exceptional bowling performances – 9 wickets for 60 runs and 9 for 27 respectively.

Nigel Yarwood, despite being seriously injured in a motor accident in 1956 and being advised never to play cricket again, did play and at a high level. In 1964 he was in a record third

Young Dave Marchant aged 13 receiving a bat from Brian Smith, Hereford City Sports Club captain, as the most promising batsman in the 1950s watched by a youthful Eric Jenkins

Nigel Yarwood cartoon by Peter Manders

wicket partnership with Stan Marston scoring 163 in 95 minutes. His innings included 8 sixes and 23 fours. In the same season he also took 80 wickets.

Burton Court
In a match at Eardisland in 1910, between Burton Court and Kington, T. Wood took all 10 wickets for Burton Court and then G.A. Bromley reciprocated and took all the Burton Court wickets. T. Wood also took 10 wickets for 23 runs when playing against Leominster on 4 July 1914.

Burghill – St. Mary's
Trevor Jones took 10 wickets for 27 runs against Hereford City Sports Club Seconds.
Robin Matthews took over 1,000 wickets in his career.

Burghill and Tillington
Nick Phillips, a young New Zealander, smashed all records in 2005 by winning the Flint & Cook League Division One batting averages by hitting 1,010 runs in 10 completed innings at an average of 101, including a top score of 189 not out. He also bowled 120 overs taking 25 wickets. He was nominated 8 times to win the man of the match award.

Canon Frome
Ivor Hunt scored over 1,000 runs in a season on two occasions.
Brian Goode scored 12 centuries in his career.
Chris Smith scored 11 centuries in what was a relatively short career.
Maurice Embrey took 50 wickets in a season on 12 occasions.
John Evans took 50 wickets in a season 11 times.

Colwall
A.S. Dagger scored 205 runs and then took 9 wickets for 63 runs in a match against Barbourne on 21 June 1914.

Cross Keys
Simon Dent scored 131 in 2006.

Eastnor

Jim Sandford has scored 20 centuries in his career to date, including a highest score of 146 not out.

Brian Miller scored 200 runs in a 40-over friendly match in the 1990s.

Eyton

Ted Amos took 10 wickets for 12 runs against A.E.I. at the Grange, Leominster, in 1956. (Another bowler took an 11th wicket because in that game they played to a last man stand.)

Frome Valley

Rev. A.E. Green Price, whilst playing for Frome Valley, Knighton and Radnorshire Gentlemen, at the beginning of the 20th century, scored over 20,000 runs including 25 centuries and, at the age of 51, scored 207 not out for Radnorshire Gentlemen against Herefordshire Gentlemen.

Garnons

Alan Jones scored 180 runs against Weobley.

Hereford City Sports Club

Ernie Morgan scored 3 centuries in 6 days in 1973.

George Warley took all 10 wickets against Bromyard in 1949.

Keith Edwards took 109 wickets in 1964 and 101 in 1966.

Brian Smith was one of the most dynamic 20th century county bowlers in local cricket. His outstanding statistics include the time in June 1961 when, in the course of one weekend, he took 9 wickets for 27 runs on the Saturday against Knowle and Dorridge and, on the following day, took 9 for 40 against Chepstow. In 1962 he took 9 wickets for 29 runs against Blanches in an Evening League game. In the 1960s he took 8 wickets for 31 runs against Monmouthshire. In 1963 he took 134 wickets at an average of 8.5 per wicket – a club record. Between 1961 and 1969 he took over 1,000 wickets including over 100 wickets in 5 separate seasons. Brian was also a useful batsman and in a game against

Brian Smith, John Chadd and Keith Edwards in 1965

Erinoid of Stroud he scored his maiden century and, in the same game, took his 100th wicket for the season.

Peter Harrison scored 4 consecutive centuries when captain of the club in the 1950s.

John Chadd, Brian Smith and Keith Edwards all took 100 wickets in the 1965 season bowling off breaks, late in swing and leg cutters, and out swing respectively.

Eric Jenkins scored 26 centuries in his career and 6 centuries in one month in 1961.

Herefordians B

O. Alakija scored 103 not out in a 20 over Division One Evening League game against Herefordians A in 1967.

Hereford Cricket Club

H.K. Foster and J.F. McLean (page 202) put on 179 runs without loss before lunch against Gloucester in May 1920; when Foster retired at lunch on 115 McLean went on to score 138.

Herefordshire Gentlemen

H.K. Foster scored 152 runs against Oxford University Authentics on 1 August 1914.

J.F. McLean presenting the Ross Challenge Cup to John Wigmore, captain of Monmouth C.C. 1955
(R.H.W.P. Roff is overseeing from the steps)

Guy Thornycroft scored 203 runs against South Wales Hunt in the 1940s, the last 100 coming in 30 minutes. His opening partner, Noel Pritchard, scored 19.

Hereford High School

Mitchell took 10 wickets for 13 runs against Ross in May 1920.

Bill Morris still holds the best batting average, scoring 492 at an average of 42 in 1940.

Hereford High School Old Boys

Bill Morris took 9 wickets for 19 runs against N.A.L.G.O. and 9 for 9 against Wiggin in the 1950s.

Holmer

H.Thomas took 10 wickets for 19 runs against Brockhampton in May 1914.

Lads' Club

Ferdy Davies scored 159 in a one hour evening league game in the mid 1930s and received a bat from the *News of the World* to commemorate the event.

Philip Daw scored 108 runs in 20 overs in a League Division Four match against the Gas Board.

Ledbury

Jim Smith scored 193 against Worcester Cinderella in the 1930s and took 10 wickets for 27 runs against the same team in 1932.

Ball presented to Jim Smith of Ledbury in 1932 by C.O. Gallimore for his achievements

Wilf Lawrence scored 1,000 runs in one season.

Bill Wetson took 100 wickets in one season.

Brian Messam took 9 wickets for 30 runs when playing against Colwall on 31 May 1957. He also took 6 wickets for 11 runs against Hereford in the 1950s when Hereford was all out for 23.

Leominster

R. Preece scored 151 when playing against Tenbury in June 1921, and later in the same match took 7 wickets for 38 runs – a feat that included a hat trick.

Leominster Grammar School

J. Pinder took 10 wickets for 30 runs in a match against Leominster on 2 July 1921.

Longhope

J. Bradley took 10 wickets for 11 runs when playing in a match against Brockhampton.

Harold Gurney took 8 wickets for 11 runs in 1981.

Multi Signs Marches League
MONMOUTH v LUCTONIANS
played at Monmouth on Saturday 11th June 1994
Bowling Performance of Adrian Hope. Luctonians.

LUCTONIANS			MONMOUTH		
R. Davis	b. Leonard	10	S. Sambrook	b. HOPE	0
D. Platford	b. Leonard	30	R. Prewett	c. Lawrence b. HOPE	10
C. Davis	c. Davies b. Leonard	0	D. Wedel	b. HOPE	7
S. Williams	b. Leonard	6	J. Jones	b. HOPE	0
J. Davis	c. Morgan b. Moaby	68	G. Grey	b. HOPE	0
L. Lawrence	b. Leonard	27	M. Etheridge	b. HOPE	12
G. Morris	not out	2	I. Morgan	b. HOPE	0
D. Morgan			M. Moaby	lbw. b HOPE	2
G. Norman	did not bat		J. Davies	b. HOPE	3
A. Hope			R. Rees	not out	0
T. Holdcroft			I. Leonard	b. HOPE	0
	Extras b1, lb5, w1,	7		Extras b2, lb2, nb5,	9
	TOTAL - 6 wkts - 45 ov.	150		TOTAL	43

F of W 1-12, 2-15, 3-24, 4-83, 5-141

F of W. 1-0, 2-13, 3-16, 4-17, 5-27, 6-29, 7-31, 8-37, 9-43

Bowling - Monmouth - Leonard 23 - 7 - 51 - 5
Morgan 13 - 1 - 48 - 0
Rees 6 - 0 - 30 - 0
Moaby 3 - 0 - 15 - 1

Bowling - Luctonians - Hope 10.2 - 3 - 19 - 10
Holdcroft 9 - 1 - 19 - 0
Norman 1 - 0 - 1 - 0

Luctonians won by 107 runs

The first occasion that Adrian Hope had taken 10 wickets in an innings.

The 1994 scorecard, when Adrian Hope of Luctonians took 10 wickets in an innings

Luctonians

Jim Apperley hit 122 sixes during the 1981 season.

Adrian Hope took 10 wickets for 19 runs whilst playing against Monmouth on 11 June 1994 (previous page).

Lyonshall

T. Burgoyne took 10 wickets for 7 runs against Eardisley in 1937.

Much Marcle

Brian Farley scored 12 centuries during his playing career.

Ross

The Roff family.
Left to right: W.G., Reginald H.W.P., Rex

W.G. Roff scored 153 when playing against Hereford in June 1927. During his career he scored a total of 53 centuries.

Walter Moss scored 101 not out and then took 6 wickets for 11 runs against the Military X1 in 1940.

John Notley scored 150 against a touring side in 1962.

Paul Notley scored 15,000 runs in his career. His highest was 144 against Chepstow in 1975.

R.H.W.P. Roff scored 136 not out for Ross Grammar School against Ross Second XI in 1942, whilst batting with Jack Bannister – a cricketer who later played for Warwickshire. On 14 August 1975 Roff took 8 wickets for 65 runs for Ross against Swindon. When he was 60 years old he took 8 wickets for 14 runs for Hereford Veterans against Dymock in the late 1980s.

John Howells took 7 wickets for 3 runs against Chepstow in 1975.

Strollers

Mark Powell scored 166 not out in a match against Weobley on 5 June 2004.

Sutton

John Griffiths took 10 wickets for 19 runs against Midland Red, Birmingham, in the late 1950s. He took 100 wickets each season for 8 years running during the late 1950s and early '60s.

Thynnes

Ferdy Davies took 5 wickets in 5 balls against N.A.L.G.O. in May 1937 and the following weekend he took 7 wickets for 7 runs against Wormelow.

Tailpiece

Whilst there are many fine batting statistics during the last century, the majority of the exceptional ones are bowling figures. Many of these achievements are because the wickets in the early part of the century were very much in favour of the bowler, hence the extraordinary figures in the match at Eardisland.

Tributes

Dick Richardson benefit match, 1964
Left to right: John Chadd, Tom Graveney, Brian Smith, Basil D'Oliviera

Brian Johnston (left) lived at Hellens at Much Marcle (above)
between 1924 and 1928

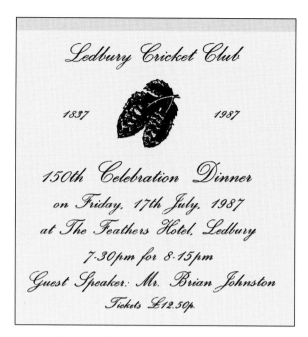

*Brian Johnston was guest speaker
at the Ledbury Cricket Club
Celebration Dinner in 1987*

Tom Graveney was a great supporter of cricket in the county and participated in many benefit matches. He also spoke at local cricket functions and at the local cricket society.

Basil D'Oliviera was also a great friend of Herefordshire cricket and played many celebrity games and made numerous dinner dance appearances. After his playing career was over he became Worcestershire's coach.

Brian Johnston, the legendary cricketing commentator, was known all over the world. He lived in Herefordshire at Hellens, a historic house near Much Marcle, for a short time between 1924 and 1928 (previous page). When giving a speech at a dinner to celebrate Ledbury's 150th anniversary in 1987 (above) he recalled buying stationery from Tilley's printers; the odd car from Hopkins; and fish from Coopers. He remembered playing the occasional game of cricket for Much Marcle when he used to take it in turn with Stafford Weston (of Weston's Cider) to keep wicket.

John Chadd, a local businessman, was born in Hereford on 27 October 1933 and attended Hereford Cathedral School. John's father, the late William Chadd, founded Chadds department store in Hereford and John has remained in the family business throughout his working life. John played his senior cricket for Hereford City Sports Club and was Captain for a period of 20 years when the Club enjoyed great success. He played for Worcestershire on two occasions in 1955 and 1956. Whilst playing for Hereford City Sports Club John, jointly with local cricketer Norman Davies, instigated and organized regular tours to Barbados, commencing in 1978 and continuing for over a decade. When John retired from playing he continued to support Herefordshire cricket in many ways. He has spoken at many cricketing functions and in 1992 he became the first President of Herefordshire Minor Counties Cricket Club. John was delighted when he was made President of the Worcestershire County Cricket Club.

Col. Guy Thornycroft was weaned on cricket by his father Lt. Col. Charles Thornycroft. His coaching took place at Hereford Racecourse during the Second World War. At this time he raised considerable amounts of money for many war related charities. He also organized cricket matches between his own eleven and local military sides to help improve the morale of troops based in the area. In 1946, after the war was over, he concentrated on building up local cricket again. To start the ball rolling he wrote strong letters to the *Hereford Times* stating that Herefordshire cricket must recommence and he urged local cricketers to start playing again. Partly because of his efforts the Hereford Evening League started up again in the summer of 1946. He also sponsored a Hereford six-a-side competition for the Thornycroft Trophy. He was influential in organizing Herefordshire Minor County Matches and a one-off match between the M.C.C. and the Combined Services.

Nick Nenadich came to Hereford from South Wales and attended Lucton School. He started to play cricket at the age of 11 for St. Mary's, Burghill, and played for them for about three years. Later in his career he also played from time to time as a guest. Nick was a fiery fast bowler playing for Burghill and Tillington, and Bromyard. He then played for Hereford City Sports Club where he enjoyed a long career. On his return from a period in the Bahamas, where he also played, he joined the Brockhampton team. In 1977 he was appointed Chairman of Herefordshire Minor Counties Cricket Club, succeeding Tracy Goodwin, and remained in the post until 2001. He was appointed President in 2005, succeeding John Chadd. He has also spent a short time on the Herefordshire Cricket Board, which is associated with the English Cricket Board.

The late Norman Davies

Rob Staite was a local man who loved his cricket. He was captain of Hereford City Sports Club and worked hard to support the club on and off the field of play. Rob sadly died of cancer at an early age. His family has donated the Rob Staite Memorial Trophy to be presented each year to the person who has contributed most to cricket in Herefordshire. Some of the recent recipients are Joe Brown from Moccas, Roy Wargen from Brockhampton, Brian Goode from Canon Frome and Wyeside, Jim Sandford (Chairman of Eastnor), and David James from the Hereford Umpires Cricket Association.

Norman Davies played cricket in the county for many years, being associated with the Leominster, Denco and Hereford teams. He was a fine fast bowler who continued to open the bowling for Hereford City Sports Club with considerable success in the Three Counties League until he was in his 50s. He became Chairman of Hereford City Sports Club and, together with John Chadd, organized many tours to Barbados. Norman sadly passed away prematurely – everyone involved in Hereford cricket will miss him greatly.

Eric Jenkins was one of the best known characters in Herefordshire cricket. In 1946 the young Eric Jenkins – he was then but 13-years-old – arrived at Hereford City Sports Club to watch a game. One of the players failed to turn up and Eric ended up as substitute. Matey, as all in Hereford cricket knew him, played his first game for the club and scored 19 runs – the first of the many thousands that he scored during his career. Eric was probably one of the most talented Hereford City Sports Club players. He played for 40 years, mostly in the First Eleven, starting in 1951. He scored 26 centuries in his career including six in one month in 1961. He was offered a chance to play for Worcestershire as an amateur but turned it down. When Herefordshire Minor Counties Cricket Club was accepted into the

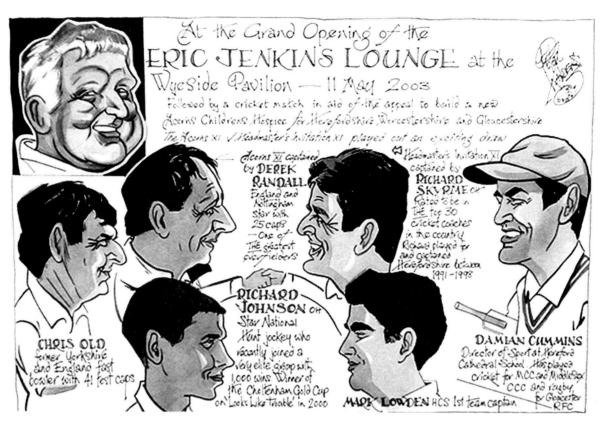

The grand opening of the Eric Jenkins lounge at Wyeside in 2003
(Peter Manders)

Tribute to Jack Roberts

Competition (when Durham became a first class side) Eric, with his usual enthusiasm, became team coach. When Eric passed away recently it was a sad loss to Hereford cricket.

Jack Roberts died in April 2004 after a lengthy battle against cancer. He came to Hereford in 1973 from Surrey to take up a new job teaching chemistry at Aylestone School. For a long time he acted as both secretary and treasurer of the Herefordshire Schools Cricket Association; he continued as treasurer until his untimely death. He started the county under-15 cricket team and was a selector for the English Schools Cricket Association Midlands under 14s for a number of years. In 1976, he founded Wyesiders – a cricket team for old boys of Aylestone School. He played for the club for many years, being a very competent all rounder. Latterly, Jack acted as Club President. After taking early retirement from Aylestone School in 1991 he introduced cricket to many children in primary schools throughout Herefordshire. More recently, he acted as the county organizer of the under-15 tournament, as well as being heavily involved in the coaching of cricket to youngsters at Burghill and Tillington Cricket Club. It is entirely fitting that the under-15 tournament has been renamed the Jack Roberts Cup in memory of this fine man.

Peter Manders and Daisy (Philip Neill)

Peter Manders was born in Shrewsbury in 1936 and at the age of 12 was commissioned to draw a caricature each week in the Shrewsbury Town Football Club programme. He started his professional career with the *Shrewsbury Chronicle* where he stayed until 1959. He moved to Hereford in 1960 as part of a team formed to launch the *Hereford Evening News* for the Berrows Newspaper Group. Peter has had a long and successful career in Hereford and is now a nationally known artist who, in addition to contributing regular sketches and drawings for the *Hereford Times*, has utilized his skills by drawing caricatures of many Herefordians including many of the the county's cricket teams, committees and individuals. He is an extremely keen cricket fan and his drawings of the top celebrities who have spoken at the Hereford Cricket Society are on display in the dining room of the Conservative Club in East Street, Hereford. Anyone who meets Peter finds him a warm friendly man who, through his work, has made many friends in Hereford.

Peter Sykes deserves a special tribute because it is rare for a County or Cricket Association to have someone who has devoted in excess of 40 years service to the sport. Peter was born in Yorkshire in 1936 and played cricket for Great Preston from the age of 14. He moved to Hereford in 1962 to work for Henry Wiggin & Company as a metallurgist and soon became secretary of the cricket team. He played cricket for the works side and was Chairman until 1992 when the team folded. He then played for two years for Wyesiders, the

Peter Sykes with Graeme Hick (Worcestershire and England)

team founded by Jack Roberts. In 1974 he became secretary of the Hereford Cricket Association which included administration work for the Hereford and District Cricket League, the Hereford Indoor League, and the Herefordshire County Representative sides. In 1997 the Association became the Herefordshire Cricket Board when the English Cricket Board took over control of local cricket.

In 1991, when the Herefordshire Minor Counties Cricket Club was formed, Peter was appointed secretary, a position that he still holds. Peter has been a tremendous stalwart of Herefordshire cricket for over 40 years. Many Herefordshire cricketers owe him a great debt of gratitude.

Sources & References

The Pubs of Hereford City. Ron Shoesmith and John Eisel, 2004
From Teddy Tail Collars to Itchy Tights. Jill Howard-Jones (A history of Hereford Cathedral and Junior School).
A who's who of Worcestershire County Cricket Club. Robert Brooke and David Goodyear.
Herefordshire Cricket. Edwyn Anthony, 1903
50 golden years of Canon Frome Cricket Club 1938-1988.
Herefordshire Cricket Year book, 1988
100 years of Brockhampton Cricket Club. 1997
150 years of Hereford Cricket 1836 - 1936
Eastnor Cricket Club Centenary 1984
Hereford Umpires Association original minute book
Kington Cricket Club – 150 not out. 1994
A Herefordshire Life. Leslie Evans, 2006
Weston-Under-Penyard. David Herrod, 2001
Pyon Years. Lynne Pugh
Eardisland, an oral history. Eardisland oral history group 1995
Herefordshire – A century in photographs. Hereford W.I.
The chequered history of Lady Hawkins' School. Alan Lloyd
Orleton in Pictures. Ann and Alf Jenkins
Bodenham in Camera. Anthea Bryan
Policing Hereford and Leominster. Gordon Forrest and Ted Hadley
Ledbury Cricket Club. 150th Anniversary book
Brockhampton Cricket Club 1897 minute book
Frome Valley Cricket Club last minute book
Goodrich Cricket Club Minute Book

Hereford Times
Hereford Journal
Hereford Bulletin
Hereford Evening News
Ross Gazette

Index of Clubs

Index of Names